TEACHING MINDFUL WRITERS

TEACHING MINDFUL WRITERS

BRIAN JACKSON

UTAH STATE UNIVERSITY PRESS
Logan

Published by Utah State University Press
An imprint of University Press of Colorado
245 Century Circle, Suite 202
Louisville, Colorado 80027

Printed in the United States of America

ASSOCIATION of UNIVERSITY PRESSES

The University Press of Colorado is a proud member of the Association of University Presses.

The University Press of Colorado is a cooperative publishing enterprise supported, in part, by Adams State University, Colorado State University, Fort Lewis College, Metropolitan State University of Denver, University of Colorado, University of Northern Colorado, University of Wyoming, Utah State University, and Western Colorado University.

∞ This paper meets the requirements of the ANSI/NISO Z39.48–1992 (Permanence of Paper).

ISBN: 978-1-60732-936-7 (paperback)
ISBN: 978-1-60732-937-4 (ebook)
DOI: https://doi.org/10.7330/9781607329374

Library of Congress Cataloging-in-Publication Data

Names: Jackson, Brian D., author.
Title: Teaching mindful writers / Brian Jackson.
Description: Logan : Utah State University Press, [2019] | Includes bibliographical references and index.
Identifiers: LCCN 2019055981 (print) | LCCN 2019055982 (ebook) | ISBN 9781607329367 (paperback) | ISBN 9781607329374 (ebook)
Subjects: LCSH: English language—Rhetoric—Study and teaching. | Mindfulness (Psychology)—Study and teaching.
Classification: LCC PE1408 .J227 2019 (print) | LCC PE1408 (ebook) | DDC 808/.042071—dc23
LC record available at https://lccn.loc.gov/2019055981
LC ebook record available at https://lccn.loc.gov/2019055982

The University Press of Colorado gratefully acknowledges the generous support of the College of Humanities at Brigham Young University toward the publication of this book.

CONTENTS

ACKNOWLEDGMENTS

A big Thank You goes to the 300+ graduate students I have taught and trained over the years. In so many gracious ways you tested and refined my pedagogy. I learned so much from you about teacher enthusiasm and goodwill. Thank you to the adjuncts I was lucky enough to work with; you've been colleagues and mentors and model teachers. Thank you to my Writing 150 students who remind me, every day, how hard it is to write well, and how cool it is when you nail it.

So many friends and colleagues looked at sketches and chapters of this work. Thank you, thank you, thank you. Here you are, in no particular order: Debbie Dean, Amy Dayton, Jon Balzotti, Jon Ostenson, Delys Snyder, Dave Stock, Jacob Rawlins, Grant Eckstein, Matt Baker, Catherine Pavia, Amy Williams, Brett McInelly, Meridith Reed, and Jonathan Garcia. These folks gave selfless, timely, and perceptive advice. Thank you, also, to my writing groups for helping me resee my work.

Thank you to the great students and colleagues at the metacognition session of the Rocky Mountain Rhetoric Symposium at the University of Utah. Thank you, BYU, for giving me a leave and assuming I'd do something with it. Thank you, BYU colleagues and students and all the friends in University Writing, for your energizing companionship. Thank you to the wonderful friends and mentors in the RCTE program at the University of Arizona.

I also want to thank Rachael Levay, Dan Pratt, Laura Furney, and Sonya Manes at University Press of Colorado and Utah State University Press for helping me through the Great Big process of writing and publishing a book. Thanks! And to the two anonymous reviewers—wow, you were fantastic!—who read a big ol' manuscript with great patience and insight. Your feedback emboldened me as much as it chastened me. The weaknesses that remain . . . well, you tried.

Finally, thank you forever to my wife Amy, the best companion and friend. And my kids: Ben, Lydia, Louisa, and Charlotte. You have no idea what I do when I leave the house for work; it's pretty boring, I know, when I explain it. That's fine with me, so long as you know I do it for you.

TEACHING MINDFUL WRITERS

INTRODUCTION

Years ago I had a student named Michael in my first-year writing class who was struggling through an awakening. He'd been a good writer all his life: always wrote with confidence bordering on snarkiness, never had to revise his first drafts much, always received praise and As from English teachers. He spent (by his own admission) very little time on our first assignment—an opinion editorial for our university's newspaper—and he'd been unpleasantly surprised at my tepid response to his draft.

In a one-on-one conference with him, I learned that Michael was beginning to think thoughts he'd never thought before about writing and about himself as a writer. His first realization went something like this: *The writing process I've been using all my life is inadequate for this class.* This was a scary admission. If a tried-and-true method of success wasn't working in a writing class, what else was broken?

His second realization was more other-directed: *I can't continue to write for my own amusement—I have to think about a reader.* On his draft, I had asked him questions about what his student audience might think about the force of his argument, his irrepressible self-confidence, his denigration of the opposing views that surely would be held by many of his readers.

At the time, I didn't have the teaching tools to explain to Michael what was happening to him. He was becoming self-aware as a writer. More deeply, he was becoming a philosopher of his own learning and thus owning his learning in a way he hadn't before. It seems not to have occurred to him—and frankly it never occurred to me when I was a first-year college student—that we can think "meta" about ourselves as writers in the middle of a writing task, almost like we're jumping out of our bodies to observe and analyze and make adjustments to the writing behavior we see in ourselves.

Teaching Mindful Writers is about how we can make sure that all our students have this "meta" experience thinking about themselves as writers in the act of writing.

* * *

DOI: 10.7330/9781607329374.c000

As a writing teacher you've chosen to help people develop skills and habits of mind that will make their lives more rewarding. In the myth of the hero's journey, you are the wise wizard distributing magic cloaks or better swords or healing potions to the brave soul who has left home seeking adventure and challenge. In your role as writing teacher, you are Galadriel, the Elf Witch.

I have been teaching college writing for seventeen years now. On the second day of my first semester teaching, on the day after the September 11, 2001, terrorist attacks on New York City and Washington, DC, the power went out in the classroom I was teaching in, rendering the only materials I'd prepared—two transparency slides—useless. Whatever I did that day as Plan B was swallowed up by collective anxiety and mourning. It was a rough start. Since then, I've taught hundreds of writing students and observed over 300 first-year writing teachers teach, and I can say with confidence that there are better and worse ways of teaching writing. In this book, I want to share what I've learned about how to teach students metacognitive habits that might stay with them after they leave your class.

This is a book for teachers of first-year writers. Specifically, this book is about how to design a major writing task so that your students become mindful, self-directed writers. While I focus on what might be called the instructional design of a single unit, I hope to share insights into other important dimensions of teaching writing, and there are many—in fact too many for my meager talents to treat. I've borrowed and remixed and repurposed from wonderful mentors over the years. Now I'm passing that mixtape to you.

I've written *Teaching Mindful Writers* with several assumptions that have influenced what I decided ultimately to include or not include. Here they are.

NEW(ISH) TEACHERS OF FIRST-YEAR WRITING (FYW)

While this book is for anyone teaching writing at any stage in a career, I've written this book with a specific kind of teacher in mind: the rookie first-year writing teacher. I assume, first, that you are relatively new to the teaching profession—perhaps a student in a graduate program. Second, I assume you are a writing teacher for first-year students—students who are likely young and/or new to college life. (In 2017, around 40 percent of college students were over twenty-five. See "Fast Facts" 2018.)

If, in fact, you are a rookie teacher, then chances are you have already been given a set of outcomes, policies, assignments, texts, a learning management software, maybe even a standard syllabus. I imagine at this moment you are building your teaching expertise by learning to teach in a specific community of practice at your institution. Because of that arrangement, I will not cover a variety of topics (like how to build a syllabus or form a plagiarism policy) covered quite well in books such as *The St. Martin's Guide to Teaching Writing* (Glenn and Goldthwaite 2014), now in its seventh edition.

THEORY, HISTORY, RESEARCH

Good teachers seek out the published wisdom of the field. Writing pedagogy has its own library of theory, history, and research, and no matter what your academic emphasis (linguistics, creative writing, literature, rhetoric), you should become familiar with it. In every chapter that follows, I synthesize some of the voluminous research on teaching writing. However, since many of you will be taking, or will have already taken, a required graduate course in rhetoric and writing studies, I'm not trying to be comprehensive. Excellent sources already exist for that kind of reading, for example Oxford's *Guide to Composition Pedagogies* (Tate et al. 2014) or the huge *Norton Book of Composition Studies* (Miller 2009), or *Exploring Composition Studies* (Ritter and Matsuda 2012), or *Concepts in Composition* (Clark 2012), or *Cross-Talk in Comp Theory* (Villanueva and Arola 2011) or *A Rhetoric for Writing Teachers* (Lindemann 2001). You will have to cut back on sleeping, eating, and going to the bathroom if you want to get all this reading done, but hey, no sacrifice too great for the writers of tomorrow. These books establish the theoretical paradigm for teaching writing of which this book will give you just a taste.

PRACTICE, PRACTICE, PRACTICE

Any teaching practice is informed by theoretical assumptions, whether self-consciously applied or not. While I will be sharing research and theory with you, I also assume that what's more appealing to you as a teacher is a list of teaching ideas that will help you immediately. Therefore, I've tried to keep the chapters short and full of ideas for the kind of "just in time" teaching FYW teachers need to master. These ideas come from a variety of places: my own experience as a teacher, the stuff I've ripped off from other amazing teachers, rigorous research, conventional wisdom, professional training or publications, my observations of other teachers, and so on. Many of these principles will work well for you; some won't and should be discarded or revised based on your experience and the philosophies you develop as an educator.

On that last point, I admit at the start that I tend to be an *overdetermined* writing teacher, meaning that often I want to control the learning experience more than I should. More experienced teachers—more intuitive and expressive and open and decentered teachers—may find some of what I propose in this work, if taken as an explicit recipe for teaching, to be stifling, and I'm sympathetic to that view. So, when it comes to the learning model I propose, decorate your teaching bower with what strikes your fancy. Aristotle talks about rhetoric not as persuasion but as "discovering the available means" of persuasion. Think of this book as a storehouse of ideas for discovering the available means of teaching mindfulness to student writers.

APPROACHES TO FYW

I assume that what I share with you can work for a variety of contents, students, and teaching situations. Like the "teaching for transfer" (TFT) model presented by Kathleen Blake Yancey, Liane Robertson, and Kara Taczak in the now indispensable *Writing across Contexts* (2014), I hope that what I'm sharing in this book will fit any of the approaches to FYW you might be teaching, and there are dozens: academic writing, personal writing, public argument, genre analysis, critical cultural studies, online classes, developmental or second language writing, advanced or disciplinary writing, writing about writing, writing about literature, first-year seminars, and so forth.

While this model is generic enough to fit a variety of writing courses, I do advocate for specific content knowledge that I think should be part of every writing course. I've been convinced by recent research on content in FYW (like the Writing about Writing movement, e.g., or genre studies) that there are some things students need to understand to be effective writers in any setting. This content provides what Kenneth Burke called "equipment for living" (1973, 293)—useful paradigms for living wisely. The content of writing is writing (see chapter 2). Surely you will develop your own content base as you continue to teach, and that content base likely will be informed by whatever branch of language studies you've chosen to specialize in. However, I argue that if you teach FYW, you should think of yourself as a teacher of rhetoric and writing knowledge and teach that knowledge to your students, no matter what reading or writing you assign.

YOUR STUDENTS

This book, which I hope might be helpful to any instructor teaching anywhere, reflects my own limitations as a writer, scholar, and teacher. While half of all postsecondary writing students are in two-year colleges (Toth, Sullivan, and Calhoon-Dillahunt 2019, 86), I have taught only at four-year institutions. In graduate school I taught at a university in the Southwest at which people of color made up a little over 40 percent of the student population. Since then, I've taught at a highly selective religious institution whose student population hovers at around 80 percent white, as I am. I am still learning the extent to which my perspective constrains my approach to teaching writing.

Considering my limitations, then, I expect moments when my passionate declarations about "best" teaching practices may seem to many of you misguided—heck, even irrelevant—considering the students you teach and your own identity as a teacher. Those moments are important for you, and for me. Therefore, I strongly encourage you to participate in professional conversations that consider diverse student populations' interests. For example, if you teach mostly students who are learning English as a second, foreign, or additional language, you will want to complement what you get here with a book such as Dana Ferris and John Hedgcock's *Teaching L2 Composition*, now in its third edition (2014), or the NCTE publication *Second-Language Writing in the Composition Classroom* (Matsuda et al. 2010). Our professional society, the Conference on College Composition and Communication, has issued a statement urging writing teachers and programs to develop instructional practices and teacher training programs in "second-language writing theory, research, and instruction" ("CCCC Statement" 2011, 11). If you're teaching, or plan to teach, at a two-year college, I suggest you balance what might be considered my "four-year-centric" approach (Toth, Sullivan, and Calhoon-Dillahunt 2019, 93) with scholarship like the "TYCA Guidelines for Preparing Teachers of English in the Two-Year College" (2016).

TECHNOLOGY

About technology, I am mostly mum. We are in an age of acceleration, an age in which Moore's law about computing power tells us that all we can predict about the future of media is that it will be unpredictable and exponentially dynamic (see Friedman 2017). To some degree I am assuming that the research-based teaching practices I promote in this book are tech-invariant. The website No Significant Difference, edited by Thomas Russell, is a gravesite of studies showing that different technologies have little effect on learning. That said, we cannot plunge into teaching writing without addressing the technologies we use to write, since "technologies influence the situation, form, and production of texts" (Bazerman 2016, 12). Considering the wide range of options and approaches, I've opted to say little specifically about digital writing, multimodality, online courses (even though I have designed one—admittedly not a *great* one), mobile composing, social media, design, or online collaboration. The teaching principles I share here can be applied in classes with a variety of tech commitments, but it is wise for us to prepare to adjust our approaches as new technologies create new literacy practices. If you feel like this tech evasion is, well, an evasion, please seek out some of the excellent literature on teaching and technology.

SCOPE

Finally, and most important, I believe that what FYW can offer the world is paradoxically more modest and more profound than has been assumed. Administrators and parents and members of the public expect FYW to be everything to everyone: to teach voice, correct sentences, research writing for all disciplines, a coherent argument, citation, paragraphing—"the full catastrophe," as Zorba the Greek would say. In *The Chronicle of Higher Education*, Doug Hesse, a writing program administrator at the University of Denver (UD), wrote about hearing from several faculty members across campus that UD students "can't even write a decent sentence." Hesse ended up coding 500,000 words of student writing just to demonstrate, in a cheeky way, that more than 90 percent of the sentences were actually "clear and error-free"—not a bad definition of *decent* (Hesse 2017). When I started running our writing program, I was asked by a senior colleague whether we were teaching our FYW students the difference between *infer* and *imply*. Another, from a different college on campus, asked me why we don't teach students how to analyze visual data. It is a wonder we are not criticized for neglecting first aid or auto repair.

Let's put aside this all-too familiar criticism. We know we can't teach everything about writing to our students, and we shouldn't tell people we can. But perhaps we can teach them practices that will help them *inhabit mindfully* any important writing task they encounter. What I'm trying to do here is focus on one aspect of teaching that I believe has become even more important in the last few years as we have studied how people learn to write and how they take what they've learned into new settings. The big picture that emerges from this scholarship is this: *What we ask students to think and write about before, during, and after they complete a major writing task is just as important as that final product they turn in for grading.* In other words, what students produce is not more important than *the kind of writer* the process produces. And I will make the case in this book that effective writers are effective metacogs, that is, mindful writers. We can offer the world this much, and maybe not much more.

I believe we can be better at teaching our students to approach every writing task with a mindful and deliberate disposition. Specifically, we can teach them how to set their own goals, practice writing strategies, make self-directed adjustments, and then reflect on their new skills. The model for self-directed writers I am proposing involves those four practices: planning, practicing, revising, and reflecting. This process is at the heart of a well-organized curriculum for a major writing task. We will discuss each dimension in separate parts. While this may sound like the old writing process model—prewrite, draft, revise—it is a significant overhaul, in this sense: While the old model concentrated on how students complete a writing task, this new model focuses on the habits of mind effective writers adopt through the whole process, whether they follow these activities in a linear or more creative, recursive way. The new model teaches students to be philosophers of their own learning.

* * *

I hope teaching writing will be as intellectually and personally rewarding for you as it has been for me. I know some of you are just passing through, teaching FYW while you complete a dissertation on digital humanities or African American literature. No matter the reason, you're one of ours now—Team FYW Forever. If your graduate program is like most others in the United States, no matter the discipline, you will not spend much time in your coursework—maybe not *any* time—studying how to teach or receiving feedback on teaching in your discipline. However, most writing programs require their teachers to take a summer training seminar, a course, and/or some in-service training on teaching writing. I hope I can help in this effort to launch you into your teaching.

In part I, I want to establish some of the groundwork on metacognition, course design, and the content of writing. Our goal as writing teachers is not merely to teach students how to write decent sentences; in fact, it would be more exciting, and perhaps more useful, to teach them to write indecent ones. Rather, we want students to develop a kind of wisdom about their communication practices. We want them to understand the principles underlying effective writing and know how and when to apply them. In the words of John Dewey, whose work has informed mine since graduate school, this kind of understanding "enables us to direct our activities with foresight and to plan according to ends-in-view" (Dewey 1986, 125; see also Wiggins and McTighe 2005, 39). Such "deliberate and intentional" use of knowledge constitutes what I call *mindful writing*, which is a form of metacognition meant to help students monitor and control their writing process for social ends.

To develop mindful writing as a habit of action enduring beyond our classes, students need to practice a variety of mini-interventions into their processes—stepping away from the process, taking their heads off and peering inside into their learning, tapping their wiser, more "meta" selves. In parts II–V, I describe the four dimensions of mindful writing identified as planning, practicing, revising, and reflecting. This model does not represent a linear, lockstep sequence but a set of necessary interventions that will help students develop the habits of mind we want them to have. Nor is this model original with me—its components have been around since early research on cognitive development and writing. I want to share this pedagogical content knowledge with teachers like you to help you design writing tasks that transform students into active learners. In part III, I will divert somewhat from the mindfulness track to talk about specific teaching practices (e.g., leading class discussion) that can refine the way we teach our novice writers.

In part VI, "The Mindful Teacher," I share a few thoughts about what it means (to me) to be a teacher and how we can get better at our work. I admit here that I have so much to learn myself. When you run a writing program, you risk hypocrisy every time you dispense teacherly wisdom. For example, I'm fond of encouraging grad student instructors to keep class discussions brief and focused on a specific writing-related goal (see chapter 15). But I'm also fond of the entirely unpredictable, emotionally gratifying, free-ranging, time-killing full-class discussions that often result from a particularly good reading or student question. You're in the presence of a flawed—but I hope not unreliable—narrator.

I believe, strongly, that, like writing itself, teaching writing is not perfectable (Wardle and Downs 2017, 15). Even so, having read more than my fair share of research on it, and having observed hundreds of hours of it and analyzed hundreds of student-generated writing and ratings, I can tell you that some teaching methods empower students and others do not. Teaching is an intellectual activity informed by an interdisciplinary, mixed-method inquiry into its craft and consequence. (In that *Chronicle* article I mentioned above, Hesse points out that "we know what works" in teaching writing because we have decades of good research on it.) We are not babysitters or stand-up comedians or book-club leaders. We are teachers. What we do influences the lives of other people and contributes to their well-being-in-the-world. In spite of the funeral dirges we often hear for the written word (e.g., Manjoo 2018), reading and writing text empowers us, delights us, helps us connect and convince. That is the work we have chosen to do.

Let's get to work.

PART I

Designing Tasks for Mindful Writers

1

WHAT DOES IT MEAN TO TEACH WRITING?

Where to begin? At the beginning, before we're neck deep in a writing task with students.

The chapters in part I will help you understand, and then plan, writing assignments for mindful writers. We begin with First Principles—specifically, how we have come to see FYW as the site for teaching students to understand writing as a social act (rhetoric) and an iterative activity (writing process) best performed mindfully (metacognition) (chapters 1–3). We'll talk about a learning cycle (chapter 4) you can use to plan each unit of writing instruction for a major writing task. To engage with the learning cycle, students will need a meaningful writing task (chapter 5) organized with ends in mind (chapter 6) and laced with minor writing interventions that will build metacognitive skills (chapter 7). First, let's take a brief look at how people learn to write.

WRITING FROM THE START

It is remarkable that almost all children, in any culture on earth, with the ability to send and receive sounds, can learn to speak a sophisticated language structure with hardly any formal training—by just babbling to the people they live with. Whether this is an instinct (Pinker 1994) or a faculty (Yule 1996) or some other ability, children pick up complex morphological, syntactic, and semantic principles in speech without us forcing them to use flash cards or complete drills. Even their so-called mistakes are brilliant. We learn to speak in social environments—some more language-rich than others—that fuel our need to understand, connect to, and influence the world around us. This is a sociocognitive theory of language.

While we routinely point out that writing, unlike speech, is an unnatural act (see Dryer 2015), we know from research that little children participate in prealphabetic writing—that is, scribbles lined up like prose—for the same reasons they participate in speech: out of a desire to

DOI: 10.7330/9781607329374.c001

communicate, to "take part in literacy activities with adults and to form friendships" (Rowe 2008, 403). Our earliest forms of full writing—sets of symbols representing phonetic values and abstract ideas—emerged ostensibly from a desperate need to interact with others, specifically to interact economically (Robinson 2009). As symbol-making animals, our first shot at written language was something like, "You owe me."

Unlike speech, writing takes a long time to master—by one account over twenty years (Kellogg 2008). While there is no absolute sequence for learning to write, children must understand that letters represent sounds, that letters combine in a particular order to form words, that one word is distinguished orthographically from other words (in speech, there are no spaces), that words muster up in particular orders called sentences, and that these sentences combine to create texts that serve a variety of social purposes. And that's just what the young writer needs to *understand*. Without also mastering the orthographic labor of writing (including handwriting and typing), children can't move to the higher-order dimension of writing as social discourse because their working memory is jammed with the challenge of just getting words on the page (James, Jao, and Beringer 2017; Tolchinsky 2016).

In short, writing is a cognitive, sociocultural, technological, and embodied activity—"a complex social participatory performance," writes Charles Bazerman, "in which the writer asserts meaning, goals, actions, affiliations, and identities within a constantly changing, contingently organized social world" (2016, 18). We write to commune.

TEACHING PEOPLE TO WRITE

Then the formal schooling kicks in. As Deborah Brandt has taught us, we all learn and use writing under the influence of *sponsors of literacy*—"any agents, local or distant, concrete or abstract, who enable, support, teach, model, as well as recruit, regulate, suppress, or withhold literacy" (Brandt 2009, 25). I see two important takeaways from Brandt's research: (1) "literacy takes its shape from the interests of its sponsors," who control the "ideological freight" and use of reading and writing (27), and (2) sponsorship takes place under "unequal conditions" of opportunities to learn and use reading and writing (29). We learn to write, as Tom Miller explains, under "prevailing ideologies and social practices" over which as children we have little control (2011, 14). While writing to commune may be a sociocultural impulse, its learning and practice are governed by sociocultural forces that don't always support equal and healthy literacy practices.

This overview of language acquisition is important to you because you are now a sponsor of literacy. You are a writing instructor with the potential to enable, support, teach, and model for a novice writer. More specifically, you are a writing teacher at the college level, and you teach a class that has been historically constructed, institutionally molded, and discursively contested for over a century.

Of course, writing instruction is way older than that. For all that Mesopotamian clay scratching to make sense, both sender and receiver had to know the conventions. Archaeologists have discovered a 4,000-year-old clay tablet upon which a student in a scribal school explains, in cuneiform, that when his headmaster reviewed his writing, the headmaster said "there is something missing," and then "caned" him as a result—an early example of how sponsors of literacy "regulate" learning (Robinson 2009, 126). In the Western tradition, writing instruction in ancient Greece was both "oral and literate," since nobody really read anything silently and most everything written was meant to be "performed aloud" (Enos 2001, 16). Greek writing students—all males, yes, like nearly everywhere else in the world for millennia—learned from a single master as apprentices, whereas the Romans instituted a system of writing education with classrooms and a common rhetorical curriculum, a system that "dominated European practice" for 2,000 years (Murphy 2001, 37).

This enduring system of writing instruction is fascinating in light of our recent turn to transferrable habits of mind (which I'll discuss in the next chapter). Quintilian had argued that the primary learning outcome for writing instruction was *facilitas*, the "habitual capacity to produce appropriate and effective language in any situation" (Murphy 2001, 36). Up until the eighteenth century—and here I'm getting necessarily breezy; see *A Short History of Writing Instruction* for the details—facilitas was practiced in the Western world almost exclusively in Greek and Latin, in exercises in imitation, literary analysis, invention, style, declamation, letter-writing, argumentation, elocution, and "themes" (written, says one Renaissance writing teacher, "with excccding paines and feare" by the schoolboys; Abbott 2001, 161). Many of these exercises were meant to prepare students to use their writing to master public speaking. The idea that you'd write in your own vernacular (English, e.g.) for a private reading audience was not widespread in writing classes in the West till the eighteenth and nineteenth centuries.

I'm compressing the story in pursuit of a higher theme: Writing instruction is a historically dynamic, culturally contingent practice that has never really been "one thing." Over the centuries, rhetoric—as classically conceived as a mode of invention and eloquence for public discourse—has waxed and waned as the theoretical base for teaching young people to write. But in some form or another, it has remained a paradigmatic constant, perhaps because it is hard to suppress language's sociocultural *telos* (though I had a few language arts teachers do their darndest). College writing instruction has been influenced by larger cultural trends (like, who goes to college, like technology) and by the sponsors of literacy at the colleges and universities that popped up in the United States between the Civil War and World War I—the era of the "Great American University" (Thelin 2004).

FORCING STUDENTS TO WRITE

But our story—yours and mine, as first-year writing teachers—takes shape from two pivotal historical moments: (1) the invention of first-year writing as a required course at the university, and (2) the construction of something called "composition studies" or "writing studies" as a profession. In 1885 Harvard University instituted if not the first then the most influential required first-year composition course, English A, with Adams Sherman Hill's *Principles of Rhetoric* as the primary text (Brereton 1995, 11). According to an early, rather grouchy report (in 1892), the course required teachers to perform "mental drudgery of the most exhausting nature" and was believed, by many Harvard intellectuals of the day, to be an "absurd" distraction from the "proper functions" of a university (75, 77). And yet English A spread across the country, becoming by 1920 the most required undergraduate course on campus (with an undergraduate student population cresting 1 million). It was also perceived as an academic backwater, an embarrassment of remediation, taught by an underappreciated cadre of overworked teachers and taught as a futile, audience-irrelevant task of correctness.

Welcome to the team!

Wait, there are alternative histories. John Brereton's collection of primary documents presents a complex intellectual struggle for the soul of first-year writing, with plenty of theoretical fuel for a more compelling model of learning to write. Even in an era obsessed with efficiency, there were progressive heroes in "comp," carrying John Dewey's banner: Scholars such as Edwin Hopkins, Fred Newton Scott, and Gertrude Buck (early writing program administrators) and various contributors to *English Journal* believed that FYW could be "student-centered, project-oriented, community-based," rhetorically sophisticated and intellectually engaging (Gallagher 2002, 21). More forward-thinking institutions serving underrepresented populations (women, African Americans, the working classes) taught writing as community service and civic engagement (Kates 2001). Institutional reformers developed writing programs that made FYW just the beginning of knowledge-making persuasion in the disciplines (i.e., students' majors), in the professions, and in public culture (Russell 2002). We have quite a legacy to draw from when we approach methods for teaching FYW and other writing courses beyond.

So, that's the first legacy: the creation of required FYW as a battleground for various ideologies and an enduring site for contingent labor (see Crowley 1998). The National Census of Writing tells me that 96 percent of the 643 institutions surveyed require FYW and that 54 percent of those require two semesters of it (National Census of Writing 2013). On the labor issue, in a 2008 study 76 percent of writing teachers at two-year colleges and 58 percent at four-year colleges were non-tenure-track faculty (Jaschik 2008). Our institutions want to teach writing badly enough to require it for incoming students, but not badly enough to offer full-time status to all those who teach it. Many of you are grad students passing through a writing program on your way to full-time careers. If you are an adjunct, I sincerely hope that the institution you work for is making efforts to apply the recommendations found in the "CCCC Statement on Working Conditions for Non-Tenure-Track Writing Faculty." I'll have more to say about professionalization at the end of this book.

The second historical trajectory has more to do with the content of the class you teach. When I interviewed to teach FYW for the first time in 2001, I was asked, "What kind of texts would you use to teach writing?" I said, "Uh . . . like . . . the *Best American Essays*, maybe?" I didn't know it at the time, but my clumsy answer reflected an unspoken theory, however half-baked, about teaching writing. In this case, my assumption seems to be that you teach writing by having students read what Alan Lightman or Cheryl Strayed believe to be the year's best magazine nonfiction. By reading Stephen King's account of being hit by a car in 1999, my students would . . . what? Well, learn what it means to write good! Lacking any pedagogical content knowledge, I had full faith that students would internalize the tricks of the masters just by reading them—kinda like you'd learn to bake a good razzleberry pie by eating one at Marie Callender's restaurant.

All teaching, whether the teacher knows it or not, proceeds from certain assumptions about the way the world works—in our case, the way we learn, the way language works in the social world, the way (and the *why*, and the *ought*) people develop literacy practices. These assumptions can come from experience—intuition about language cultivated by a lifetime of reading and writing and forming judgments about them—and they can come from a more systematic inquiry into these questions—what we would call *research*. In the early days of required FYW, it seems the leading intellectuals thought of teaching writing as an art, not necessarily a science worthy of the name "field" or "discipline." It didn't stop them from forming the first professional society concerned with teaching writing, the National Council of Teachers of English, in 1911. But it wasn't until the 1960s that a research agenda started to emerge, with graduate programs encouraging doctoral students to study student writers and the processes by which they write. As Louise Wetherbee Phelps explains, "Composition Studies" became a self-aware field in the 1960s and '70s, when three major traditions merged: a teaching tradition in higher education, a rhetorical tradition that renewed the paradigm situating writing in the classical study of eloquence, and a new research tradition studying the writing process using a variety of methodologies (including ethnography or sociolinguistics) (Phelps 1996, 124). This merging made possible a variety of theories related to teaching writing. To paraphrase the Geoffrey Chaucer character from the movie *A Knight's Tale*, we walk in the garden of this turbulence.

(A quick aside: When we talk about research in FYW, we often separate *composition studies* from *writing studies*. Writing studies is a more broad field of inquiry about writing as a human activity in any setting, for example, workplace writing or public writing. When folks in the field talk about *composition*, they're most likely talking about FYW and the research/admin apparatus of that single college course.)

THE METATHEORIES

Call them theories (Berlin 1982) or approaches (Fulkerson 2005) or pedagogies (Tate et al. 2014), we now have a host of emphases for FYW that take shape around various values and research findings from the field. The FYW course you teach will reflect one or more of these theories, as your program has embraced and packaged them in a first-year curriculum. Each program draws from these theories to make their own recipe, but the two essential ingredients are *process* and *rhetoric*. These two, I would argue, are the metatheories of FYW.

Process

It is not easy imagining how writing was taught before process theory took over, because for decades process has been the water we fish swim in. Even though there were dynamic and rhetorically savvy scholars of writing studies before the 1960s, the standard version of FYW, according to some of the scholars who endured it (Clark 2012, 3–4), expressed indifference to the process by which students wrote. They (the students) wrote on their own time, and then their work was "corrected." "The best way, indeed, to become a good writer," wrote someone in *Century Magazine* in 1896, "is to be born of the right sort of parents" (cited in Brereton 1995, 240). Failing that, your best bet was to take a college writing class in which you were assigned to read a British novel and a book on the History of England and write a "theme" on "How a Rosebud Uncloses" (494). Your overworked instructor would then "mark" your theme in red ink in esoteric codes indicating your vulgarities, and then you'd write another one. How you did the writing was mostly up to you. I'm caricaturing a bit for rhetorical effect, but this description isn't far from the average old-school writing course.

In the 1960s and '70s, composition folks turned the field's attention from the products of writing to the process of writing—to the way students use writing as an act of discovery in the service of learning something more important than how to write an error-free essay. Writing instruction, then, was imagined as a series of interventions in a writer's process: helping students come up with ideas, draft them, get meaningful feedback, and then try again to discover what they want to say. The focus shifted from the final, always inadequate text to the kinds of capacities students develop to produce those texts (Anson 2014, 217). In some sense *the students*, as learners, become the texts, capable of being revised. Early on, these interventions were canonized into a linear process of prewriting, drafting, and revising, and this three-stage process is still popular. (I learned it in high school; I taught it as a graduate student.) Subsequent research on writers at work revealed that writers did not follow these linear models. Different writers do different things for different situations and tasks, often in a recursive process that reflects messy creativity rather than instructions to put together an Ikea dresser.

Almost all writing courses have adopted process as metatheory. A more sophisticated list of the assumptions behind process can be found in *Naming What We Know*, a book on threshold concepts in writing studies (Adler-Kassner and Elizabeth Wardle 2015; more on this in chapter 2). If the concepts listed in *Naming What We Know* accurately describe what research tells us about the writing process, then process teachers (like yourselves?) believe that writing is

"a knowledge-making activity";

"a technology through which writers create and recreate meaning";

both a "cognitive" and "metacognitive activity";
"performative."

They also believe that

"writing involves the negotiation of language differences";
"writers' histories, processes, and identities vary";
"a text is an object outside of oneself that can be improved and developed";
"revision is central to developing writing";
"reflection is critical for a writer's development."

A course drawing from process pedagogy will lead students through strategies of invention, prewriting, drafting, collaborative review, revision, and reflection. Process is now "deep in the discipline's bones" (Anson 2014, 226). This book's marrow is process through and through.

Rhetoric

The second metatheory that informs how writing is taught is *rhetoric.* And let's admit at the outset that the word in popular usage is unquestionably toxic. In an unpublished analysis of the word using digital corpora of global and contemporary American English, a grad student and I discovered—really, confirmed everyone's hunch—that most of the time when the word *rhetoric* is used, the speaker means empty, deceptive, or inflammatory speech. The word has experienced pejoration, a term linguists use to describe when a word goes through a gradual semantic souring into infamy over time.

Well, that's a shame. The word is just too dang useful to throw out. In fifth century democratic Athens, when an assembly was called to debate an issue, the people gathered in the Pnyx, an outdoor amphitheater that could seat 6,000 people. Once everyone was in place and a pig had been slaughtered and its purifying blood thrown around the Pnyx, the official cryer would open the meeting by praying "a curse (*ara*) upon any speaker (*rhetor*) who should attempt to lead the people astray." Any citizen brave enough to stand on the speaker's platform to put forth an argument was called a *rhetor* and crowned with a laurel wreath "as a mark of his dignity" (Hansen 1999, 142–44). The noun *rhetoric* may have been coined by Plato to criticize his rivals, but after Plato and Aristotle's treatments, the word came to describe a theoretical body of work concerned with the art of public discourse—the "available means of persuasion," as Aristotle famously put it (Aristotle 2007, 36; Schiappa 1999).

It is important to think meta about Aristotle's *Rhetoric.* Ignore what he is saying in the text: What is the man trying to *do*? He (through his students' lecture notes) is trying to construct a systematic accounting of what people do when they try to persuade other people—how they reason, establish credibility, draw from common categories of thinking, evoke emotional responses, cater to audience types, organize a message, turn words into art, influence attitudes. Those who followed Aristotle in "the European tradition" of education expanded, refined, and sometimes repudiated his enduringly stubborn categories of thinking about these issues (Conley 1990). You can read about the fortunes of this tradition in a number of books; it wouldn't hurt to start with Susan Jarratt's encyclopedic article on the subject (2007). Rhetoricians have also sought to transform, transpose, or throw out this European tradition in an effort to develop international, decolonial, transcultural theories of communication (Wanzer-Serrano 2018). Fundamentally, and to simplify the topic recklessly, I think of rhetoric as the study and practice of how we use symbols to influence the attitudes, judgments, and behaviors of others in culturally situated communication. Writing, of course falls into this study of symbolic artfulness. Rhetoric is never really rhetoric, as in one thing, but *rhetorics,* a variety of culturally contingent practices and assumptions about how we use language in social action in any field of human (and maybe even animal?) interaction.

In writing studies, we have embraced rhetoric as a pliable theory of discourse for a modern, multicultural student body. The Writing Program Administrators' Outcomes Statement (version 3.0) reads: "*Rhetorical knowledge* is the ability to analyze contexts and audiences and then to act on that analysis in comprehending and creating texts. Rhetorical knowledge is the basis of composing. Writers develop rhetorical knowledge by negotiating purpose, audience, context, and conventions as they compose a variety of texts for different situations" ("WPA Outcomes Statement" 2014). We write for specific people, and we write to accomplish something. This truth seems so self-evident that it's hard to describe what the alternative would be. (The lyrics to "Nowhere Man" come to mind.) Since James Kinneavy's 1971 masterpiece *A Theory of Discourse,* writing studies folks have sought to flesh out a theory that turns classroom writing into more than double-spaced fodder for the grade machine. Taking as a starting point that writing is a social act, writing instructors use rhetorical theory to enhance the way students think mindfully about writing projects. If we turn again to *Naming What We Know,* we see a variety of concepts from rhetorical theory about genre, audience, and purpose. We want our students to think of themselves as actors situated in a social milieu, writing to other people in a manner those other people, for whatever reason, might find acceptable, even actionable. Rhetorical thinking requires writers to construct in their minds social imaginaries in which their writing plays a part.

* * *

Process and rhetoric—the metatheories. Beyond that, there are dozens of approaches to FYW that offer often competing *axiologies*; that's Richard Fulkerson's term to describe the "theories of value" our courses present to students (Fulkerson 2005). Some courses emphasize creative nonfiction to develop voice, without much concern about audience or rhetorical need. Many teach a version of what Ann George describes as "critical cultural studies" meant to "revitalize students' conceptions of freedom and inspire them to collectively re-create a society built on democractive values and respect for [cultural] difference" (2014, 80). Other cultural studies classes focus on consumerism and the value of resistance through analysis; others focus on nondominant identities of race, gender, ethnicity, sexuality, ability. There are still approaches that assign literature (as in fiction and poetry); more common, though, are those that foreground public discourse or multimodality as the ultimate expression of rhetorical agency. Many courses focus on argument, others on what's been called "academic writing," or the writing expected in learned communities; others teach linguistics and the politics of language to engage diverse language users and learners (Matsuda and Hammill 2014). There's been a recent surge of interest in a "writing about writing" approach, which assumes that writing studies itself—a subject usually reserved for rhet-comp nerds (like you?) in graduate programs—is a "relevant subject of study" for FYW students (Downs and Wardle 2012, 131).

I'm not just talking about content here. If you use a reader focused on the environment, your axiology is not "the environment." The axiologies of FYW are more philosophical than that. They represent theories of how and why writers write: how writing reflects or refracts or otherwise constitutes reality, how people learn to write from and for others, how language functions descriptively and prescriptively in social situations, and so on. You can have a class on the environment with an axiological bent to creative nonfiction, or public argument, or collaborative writing, or writing with sources. You can adopt theories of writing that could work nicely in a variety of teaching contexts (students, assignments, texts, etc.). As I said in the introduction, this book presents a theory of metacognition and writing that I hope can be applied to a variety of learning contexts, using a variety of topics and texts as support.

If this is your first semester teaching, you might not give two hoots about axiologies of composition. You want to know what to do in class *tomorrow*. I understand that concern. But surely it is not too early to think about the theoretical assumptions that inform your teaching. Practice, after all, whether intentional or not, is theory on the move. What do *you* believe about how students make knowledge? Or learn to write? How would *you* define rhetoric? What assumptions about language, power, and literacy do *you* bring to the classroom? There are very good researched reasons why these metatheories have endured as long as they have. I'd encourage you to take advantage of this generous legwork as you develop your own theory for teaching writing.

Let me see if I can nutshell what is most important about what I've said in this chapter. Teaching writing has a long history, and it hasn't meant the same thing in every historical era. The modern first-year writing course has been influenced by undergraduate requirements and the common practice of using contingent (non-tenured) labor to cover all those required sections. Historical practices, program interests, research findings, textbooks, student population dynamics, and technological change all exert a force on the FY curriculum. The FYW course takes different shapes based on the assumptions we bring to it. In the 1960s and '70s a *field* called composition studies emerged, with a professional apparatus pushing for interdisciplinary inquiry into best practices. Competing theories of value create different "brands" of FYW, like critical cultural studies or argument, but most programs teach the two metatheories of *process* and *rhetoric*.

What, then, does it mean to teach college writing? It depends on the assumptions we bring to it. On a grander, more philosophical level, teaching people to write is helping them *self-actualize*. Language is power. Learning language is empowerment. In the best cases, students walk away from our classes with improved judgment, sharpened skills, and greater confidence in their ability to tackle writing tasks with the kind of mindful orientation that psychologist Lev Vygotsky believed was at the heart of all language learning (1978, 26). In the next chapter, we'll talk about what it means for students to be mindful writers, no matter what axiology we eventually adopt.

2
THE CONTENT OF/IS WRITING

This book is about how to teach students to be mindful throughout any and all major writing tasks—during your FYW course and beyond. We'll get into the details of mindfulness in the next two chapters. For students to be fully mindful writers, I'd argue, there are principles (theories, research findings, best practices) they need to understand, and these principles constitute the content of the course, as we discussed in the last chapter. I'm using the word *understand* here in a specific way. In the 1950s, educational psychologist Benjamin Bloom proposed a taxonomy of learning levels, from simple knowledge through application and eventually evaluation. When the ed bureaucrats talk about "deep learning" or "higher-order learning" as teaching goals, they are talking in some way about Bloom's taxonomy of learning.

In a revised version, favored by metacognition scholar Saundra Yancey McGuire, the hierarchy of learning goes in this order: remembering, understanding, applying, analyzing, evaluating, creating. The assumption behind this "hierarchy," if we can call it that, is that each level requires just a little more from the "ol' dog's breakfast" (novelist Kurt Vonnegut's term for our brains). At the lowest level, you can spit out info you've memorized without really understanding it. (Like that one time when I was three and sang Rick James's "Super Freak" in front of my mother's church friends, though I didn't know what a *kinky girl* was.) At the highest, you can "come up with your own ideas about solving different kinds of problems" (McGuire and McGuire 2015, 35). The language from our course outcomes often follows Bloom's taxonomy ("Students will *analyze* professional writing for rhetorical strategies . . . ," "Students will *evaluate* the writing of a peer using course criteria . . ."), though in writing studies we haven't been too interested in hierarchizing our threshold concepts by assuming one is more sophisticated than another.

McGuire recommends we teach students directly about Bloom's terms to improve their metacognition. Grant Wiggins and Jay McTighe see understanding as the governing term of learning: "the ability to

DOI: 10.7330/9781607329374.c002

marshal skills and facts wisely and appropriately, through effective application, analysis, synthesis, and evaluation" (2005, 39). It is clear in almost every discipline that students cannot analyze, synthesize, or evaluate if their content knowledge is shallow (see Lang 2016).

In taking up this topic, we're flirting with what I think is a fundamental debate in all education: What is the relationship between the subject matter and the student? Often we think of learning as knowing stuff or mastering disciplinary factoids. As a young college student, I took a biology course to fulfill a general education requirement. As you can imagine, the course was about, you know, biology—textbook, lectures, ill-designed slides, and multiple-choice tests. Yet my affective relationship to biology—as in, what it had to do with my life and how I might use what I learned—was immaterial in the frantic covering of the material.

The American education philosopher John Dewey made the very strong case throughout his career that the subject matter of schooling is important only insofar as it leads to intellectual growth and "trained capacities" of being and acting in the world, capacities he called "social intelligence" and "social power" (1972b, 75). He believed education should lead to the self-realization of everyone, a power to act with our own skills in harmony with other actors and their skills. In 1902, while serving as professor of education at the University of Chicago, he wrote an essay titled "The Child and the Curriculum," in which he argued that the subject matter of schools should be "psychologized," meaning that it should be presented to students as integral to their own experience, as an "outgrowth of present tendencies and activities" (2008, 287). Specifically, content should be presented to students as equipment for solving "intellectual, practical, or ethical" problems (287). You solve the problem of student motivation, in part, by framing content this way. In this way, understanding, as we've defined it, means discovering how content gives you dispositions for acting in the world.

Therefore, in order to be mindful writers—to apply, evaluate, and create—students need to *understand* the principles they will use as writers, in this Deweyan sense. They need some pragmatic content knowledge about writing process and rhetoric, our two metatheories mentioned in chapter 1, which together form the theoretical and philosophical core of FYW.

There is some debate about how much students need to know about rhetoric and writing studies to be successful writers. ("Stop Using Rhetoric to Teach Writing," reads the title of an *Inside Higher Ed* piece from 2008—which was then swarmed by rhetoricians in the comment section.) Some of what we teach as rhetoric scholars seems like banal common sense. ("You say I should think about my audience when I speak or write. And you went to how many years of grad school to learn that?") Either common sense, or Greek nonsense. ("The President used *apophasis*, not *antiphrasis*, when he insulted the journalist.") Both views are caricatures of what rhetoric is and can do for our students.

Several decades ago, when scholars with PhDs in literature started running college writing programs, they cast about looking for theoretical underpinnings for their practice, and they found rhetoric—a 2,500-year-old tradition of teaching and theorizing about the power of language to influence the attitudes and judgments of others. Turns out that rhetorical principles had always been there, in both speech and writing education—we just needed to find and formalize all of it. This interest has led to a rich body of work on classical rhetoric, rhetorical theory, rhetorical criticism, comparative rhetorics, and the relationship between rhetoric and teaching student writers. Over the years we've used insights from classics, philosophy, poetics, education, linguistics, cultural studies, political science, and psychology (cognitive, social, and moral) to inquire into language practices of all kinds, with particular concern for teaching, which in my view is rhetoric's most important and enduring heritage.

How much of this stuff do our students need to know? Answers to this question have varied. If you gather up all the "rhetorics"—textbooks that aren't handbooks or readers, the ones that teach writing principles through a rhetorical lens—you'll find some commonalities across the texts. They often begin by pointing out the ubiquity of writing—heck, it's everywhere—and describe its situatedness in social contexts. Students are then introduced to the word *rhetoric*. But since the word, as I said in the last chapter, has experienced dramatic linguistic pejoration over the years (connotations—empty! inflammatory! dishonest!—have become almost universally negative outside our little circle), the textbooks have to explain what the word really means and how it emerged from the language practices of the classical world.

From that point, some form of Aristotle's *pisteis*—the appeals of ethos, pathos, and logos, often overlaid, confusingly, on "the rhetorical triangle" of writer, audience, and text—appear, and, alongside a description of the writing process, some form of the classical rhetorical canons is presented, most likely invention (coming up with stuff to say about whatever), arrangement (organizing), and style. Some texts make explicit the connection between classical rhetorical theory and contemporary writing instruction (Corbett and Connors 1998; Crowley and Hawhee 2011). Others hide the Greek terms but keep their salience (why say *kairos* when you can just say *timely*?). Many texts with a rhetorical bent talk about *argument* and use principles from informal logic. Recently *genre* has become a god-term in rhetorical instruction, for good reason, but the theoretical source is more contemporary rhetorical theory, particularly Carolyn Miller's 1984 groundbreaking article and subsequent work in what has been called rhetorical genre studies (RGS) (Bawarshi and Reiff 2010; see also Fulkerson 2005 for a review of all these approaches, and others). We use rhetorical theory as a method of inquiry, invention, assertion, identification, art.

So what? The point is that we have a rich disciplinary literature on effective communication, spanning more than 2,500 years, to draw from when we teach the content of mindful writing. However, if we're not careful with the scope, students will not be able to see the forest for the trees. In fact one online teaching source, the excellent "Forest of Rhetoric," compiled by my colleague Gideon Burton, plays with that forest/trees metaphor directly when introducing several hundred Greek and Latin terms (like *epexegesis*, or *restrictio*) for rhetorical strategies.

Thou shalt not commit coverage (see chapter 6).

While instructors should learn all we can about language, rhetoric, and the writing process, we should probably keep our content teaching in FYW limited to a handful of essentials. (No *bomphiologia*?) In addition to rhetorical theory as pedagogical content, we also have *writing theory*—or the cognitive, metacognitive, linguistic, orthographic, institutional, grammatical, technological, social, and stylistic perspectives we bring to bear on writing as a human activity.

It's too much. Even graduate programs can't cover it all. Thankfully, as we saw in chapter 1, writing studies scholars have started talking about "threshold concepts," or the "concepts critical for continued learning and participation in an area [like writing] or within a community of practice" (Adler-Kassner and Wardle 2015, 2). The "continued learning" part is key to our discussion of metacognition. We assume that if students understand (in the more advanced Bloomian sense) key concepts on writing, they will be able to apply those principles in any writing setting they encounter after our class. Again, Wiggins and McTighe think of "understanding" as the ability to explain key concepts and "use them *mindfully*" (2005, 39, their emphasis). Hardly trivia.

Members of the writing studies community have proposed a few dozen concepts that make up a somewhat provisional, but solid, base for a content for FYW. In table 2.1, I have synthesized three organizing categories of threshold concepts (rhetorical situation, genre, and writing and the writer) from three publications: *Naming What We Know*

Table 2.1. Major threshold concepts from three publications

	Naming What We Know	*Writing about Writing*	*Critical Transitions*
Rhetorical Situation	Writing is a social and rhetorical activity.	"Good" writing is dependent on writers, readers, situation, technology, and use.	Writing always occurs in context, and no two contexts are exactly alike.
		Writing helps people make meaning and get things done, but there are always constraints.	
Genre	Writing speaks to situations through recognizable forms.	Genres: writing responds to repeating situations through recognizable forms.	Genre awareness contributes to successful transfer.
Writing and the Writer	Writing is (also always) a cognitive activity.	Writing is a process, all writers have more to learn, and writing is not perfectable.	Prior knowledge, experience, attitudes, and beliefs set the stage for writing and shape new writing experiences and learning.
	Writing enacts and creates identities and ideologies.	Writing is impacted by prior experiences.	Reflection is critical for a writer's development.
	All writers have more to learn.		Writing is an activity and a subject of study.

(Adler-Kassner and Wardle 2015), *Writing about Writing* (Wardle and Downs 2017), and *Critical Transitions: Writing and the Question of Transfer* (Anson and Moore 2017). Each of the five concepts in *Naming What We Know* has several subconcepts that could develop a student's transferable writing power even more. I also want to point out that the concepts in the *Writing about Writing* column come from a popular textbook, which means that Elizabeth Wardle and Doug Downs catered the wording specifically to understanding on the part of undergraduate writing students. Their textbook is a thousand pages of sweet writing studies goodness.

How do we want our students to understand these concepts? Recitation would be simple enough; give them a handout of the above table and then a quiz the next day. But that's a low-level learning activity—not "understanding," as we've defined it, and certainly not metacognitive. We want the students to feel these truths in their bones, to drag them out of long-term memory three years after we've taught them and they're sitting down to write a literature review for a dietetics class. We want them to understand how these concepts work in practice, how they inform and circumscribe and strengthen any writing task. An effective writing course will have these concepts woven into the fabric of the entire course, making appearances in class discussions, supporting documents, comments on student writing, and reflective activities. (Wardle and Downs 2017 include "Meta Moment" discussion activities after their readings.)

More practically, I would propose reserving two class periods to introduce students to these concepts more thoroughly before they jump into their first writing task. In addition to all the important stuff you need to do on the first day, you could engage the students in a conversation about their experience as writers (see the interlude between parts I and II). In their Teaching for Transfer model, Yancey, Robertson, and Taczak encourage their students to "articulate a *theory of writing*" from the beginning of the semester using key rhetorical terms such as audience, discourse community, and circulation (Yancey, Robertson, and Taczak 2014, 58). When I talk about the writing process with students in the first few days, I often have them draw a picture of their composing space—where they write, under what conditions, and with what technologies—so they can hover above it and describe what they see and don't see.

On the second day, you can introduce students to the rhetorical situation as our workable theory of communication. You should develop your own vocabulary for this instruction or find a free source students can consult for their key terms (maybe from Joe Moxley's online *Writing Commons*). Although I find acronyms embarrassing, I use GRAPE to describe the rhetorical situation: genre, rhetor (speaker, writer), audience, purpose, and exigence (the sociohistorical event that "called forth" the writing).

On GRAPE day, I assign students to read something—and, really, it can be anything interesting; how about a fortune cookie message?—and then in class we talk about how that text is embedded in a social situation governed by rhetorical dynamics. Specifically, I ask students to work in groups to describe how each dynamic of the rhetorical situation is reflected in the text. This activity helps them understand key terms but also *analyze*, in a Bloomian sense, how those terms "relate to one another and to an overall structure" of a text (McGuire and McGuire 2015, 35). I've found in these conversations that terms that seem straightforward such as purpose or audience become rich and complicated and confounding, in a good way. (How is the assumed purpose of a fortune cookie message different from its actual purpose?) These conversations lay the groundwork for a semester-long discussion about rhetorical theory, with these terms as workable heuristics for new texts and situations.

I've also found it useful to focus students' attention on the rhetorical situation separate from rhetorical strategies. Let me be more specific: I feel like *ethos*, *pathos*, and *logos* have killed rhetorical literacy in the United States. Many states use those terms directly in their Common Core standards for high school students. The triumvirate sticks. When young writers think about rhetoric, they often think of these appeals, and often think of them poorly. Logos is the worst. My heart leapt when my son, a junior in high school, dropped the term in a dinner conversation one night, but then my heart plunged when he told us it meant "facts." Well. We have to start somewhere. Aside from my snooty concern about the proper usage of Greek terms, my beef with the appeals—which I am here categorizing under the term *strategies*—is that they easily can be reduced to just another close-ish reading exercise ("this fact here in King's 'I Have a Dream' Speech is logos") that elides language as social action. Maybe I'm being a curmudgeon. At any rate, I want my students to delay questions of strategy till they've grasped fully the dynamics of situation.

All this is to say that the content of writing is writing—how and why writers use rhetorical strategies in social contexts to achieve whatever it is they're trying to achieve. No matter what you choose to read, talk, and write about (climate change! guns! social media! immigration! donuts!), the core content of FYW should be fashioned around the ways and whys people communicate to get things done in the world. A carefully selected, and short, list of these threshold concepts can orient a semester's worth of teaching. Specifically, mindful writing can help students reflect on how their prior experience with these concepts is being reshaped and repurposed for present writing tasks.

3

METACOGNITION AND MINDFUL WRITING

So: You're a writing teacher. The teaching of writing has a millennia-long pedigree. While there have been a variety of approaches, some more soul crushing than others, the most powerful approach at the moment is to combine rhetorical knowledge and writing process as the metatheories of learning to write with power. We will now add to this content knowledge the engine of self-directed learning itself: metacognition.

PULLING OUR HEADS OFF AS WE WRITE

This one night as I was buttoning up the house, I spotted my fourteen-year-old daughter, Lydia, sitting on the couch staring out the window into the darkness. She had her winter coat on (indoors?) and headphones over her ears. I tapped her on the shoulder. She looked startled and pulled off her headphones.

I asked, "How's it going?"

She said, "I'm working on my story."

She was not typing. She had no paper or pencil in hand.

She explained that she had discovered that all her good ideas for her fantasy writing came not while she was actually sitting in front of the computer typing but while she was daydreaming—just walking around or sitting in the quiet of the house, listening to Approaching Nirvana, an electronic band, and letting her mind do whatever it had a mind to do. The point was that she knew this about her creative process, and she was intentionally placing herself in what photographer Dewitt Jones calls "the place of most potential" for creative work. I don't know when or how she learned to do that. Somehow, she figured out how to gaze into the workings of her own mind.

On the western facade of the Notre Dame cathedral, in Paris, France, there is a sculpture of St. Denis, standing between two angels, holding his own severed head in his hands (figure 3.1). Wikipedia tells me that Denis was bishop of Paris in the third century and was martyred by

DOI: 10.7330/9781607329374.c003

Figure 3.1. St. Denis—professional cephalophore, Notre Dame

decapitation. This did not slow down Denis, who, according to popular legend, picked up his head and walked around with it in his hands, preaching sermons, thus becoming one of several famous *cephalophores* (Greek for "head carrier").

I've thought about this delightful image of St. Denis—holding his head in his hands as if inspecting it with eyes that aren't there anymore—as I've thought about *metacognition*, or the act of thinking about our thinking, which is central to my model of teaching writing. How nice it would be to get that kind of critical distance from our own heads, to examine our assumptions, thoughts, impressions, memories without being so wrapped up in them. To examine ourselves, to be aware of ourselves, to act intentionally in the world with this awareness, for the benefit of ourselves and others—this seems to me the sign of a philosophical life, a purposeful and mindful life.

That word *mindful* is quite trendy ("What Mindfulness App Is Right for You?" asked one *Huffington Post* article in April 2015; *The New*

Mindfulness, shouted the title of a magazine at the grocery checkout last week), even though it was coined by professor of medicine Jon Kabat-Zinn back in the 1970s. One brand of mindfulness, borrowing from Eastern philosophy, particularly Buddhism, teaches us to "come back to the present moment" through intense concentration on breathing and the current state of the body, while resisting judgments about self or affective states (Nhat Hanh 1973, 64). Another brand, made popular by psychologist Ellen Langer, is more about learning, about having "a limber mind" (1989, 70) attuned to new categories of thought and experience. In both approaches, mindfulness is transformative because it invites the practitioner to stop the incessant flow of life and take control of the moment.

While I want to capitalize on the mindfulness movement, I think it's important to distinguish the kind of mindfulness I'm talking about from other kinds. For instance, the approach to mindfulness popularized by the Vietnamese Buddhist monk Thich Nhat Hanh is about being fully present in your body, living and breathing only in that very moment, without judgment, and learning how living in the present leads to what the classical Stoics called *euthymia*, or tranquility. Its methods have been used as a mental health practice to reduce stress—in elementary school children, for example (L. Davis 2015)—and foster overall emotional and spiritual well-being. From an education standpoint, this kind of mindful practice is like recess: Even if it is not directly related to learning, it helps students produce a state of being conducive to learning. And three cheers for anything that will do that.

On the other hand, mindfulness conceived as metacognition is more intimately connected to the learning process itself. In fact, you could say it *governs* the learning process, like a TV producer running a big awards show. For me, mindful writing requires being present in the moment of writing (as creative writer and practicing Buddhist Dinty Moore conceives it) *and* projecting or reflecting across time as a way to realize writing power. For me, mindfulness is a purposeful, deliberate awareness of what we are doing and how we could do it better—right now, and in the future.

My argument in this chapter is that first-year student writers (or any writers, for that matter) benefit when they learn metacognitive strategies for taking their heads off, so to speak, and paying attention to what they're thinking and doing as they move purposefully through a writing task. (The chemist Saundra McGuire tells her students to think of metacognition as having "a big brain outside of your brain looking at what your brain is doing"; McGuire and McGuire 2015, 16.) Learning about metacognition—understood as a writer's habit of mind—will help us be better teachers. It will also lay the groundwork for the model of mindful writing I'm suggesting is at the heart of a writing teacher's strategies.

A NEW SET OF SKILLS

Much of our education culture has been informed by what journalist Paul Tough calls the "cognitive hypothesis"—the belief that learning means mastering certain cognitive skills that help you on quantifiable exams (recalling facts, writing clear sentences, analyzing, solving math problems, and the like). We need cognitive skills, obviously, but Paul Tough (2012) describes a recent movement in education that has questioned the cognitive hypothesis by suggesting that learners need "a very different set of qualities" to succeed in school and life: "persistence, self-control, curiosity, conscientiousness, grit, and self-confidence" (xv). Economist and Nobel Laureate James Heckman is one of many scholars hoisting up data to support the conclusion that *character development*—as old, at least, as Aristotle's *Nicomachean Ethics*, and once the primary concern of American public education—is just as important to the future success of students as cognitive abilities (Heckman and Kautz 2014).

For the past ten years or so, learning science and writing studies have converged on a novel vision for teaching writing that responds to this call to engage more fully with the whole learner. The vision is novel because it draws our attention more to what student writers become as a result of taking our classes rather than what they produce (i.e., writing). If we adopt this vision, we focus on the "habits of mind" or "dispositions" students "cultivate" as a result of our instruction as much as, or actually more than, the double-spaced essays they crank out (Behm, Rankins-Robertson, Roen 2017, xxiii; Driscoll and Wells 2012). We will care as much about how students will succeed as writers in (say) a future microbiology class as we do about their research papers for ours, because we're interested in portable dispositions more than current writing performance. To that end, the 2011 "Framework for Success in Postsecondary Writing"—developed jointly by (big breath) the Council for Writing Program Administrators, the National Council of Teachers of English, and the National Writing Project, all our big hitters—adds to the standard outcomes (e.g., writing process knowledge) eight new "habits of mind essential for success in college writing": curiosity, openness, engagement, creativity, persistence, responsibility, flexibility, and metacognition ("Framework" 2011). Alice Horning argues we should add critical reading skills to this list as well (2017).

While this list is no doubt exciting to teachers, it is no easy task trying to articulate what "creativity" or "persistence" might look like or how we help students cultivate them. A habit such as "openness" sounds virtuous, but then the fact that it sounds virtuous becomes a liability: Are we teaching writing or ethics, or somehow both? In sixteen weeks?

This is a daunting task, this "cultivating habits" business. In the *Nicomachean Ethics,* Aristotle equates habit with *ethos,* a term that means much more than credibility—it means identity. For Aristotle, we become who we are by habitual behavior; we are "habituated" by "doing the acts that we do" (1947, 953). Habits, in this sense, are not slavish acts (like biting your fingernails) but deliberate acts of attunement—self-driven decisions about "what is good and expedient" for ourselves (1026). When we teach, we invite students to habituate themselves to certain ways of being. In the literature, this way of being has been called *self-regulated.* Self-regulated learners are fully in charge of their learning. They know what they want to achieve, they believe in their abilities, they set goals, they stay focused and committed, even when everything goes sideways, they are motivated, they seek help when they need it, they pay close attention to how it's all working, and they make necessary adjustments to their behavior and environment to get what they want (Nilson 2013; Zimmerman and Moylan 2009).

It can be intimidating thinking about our jobs as writing teachers in terms of cultivating habits. Nevertheless, since the act of writing "enacts and creates identities" (Scott 2015, 48), we cannot ignore this dimension of teaching writing.

The writers of the "Framework" have argued that writing students should be habituated in a variety of ways, but one of the most important is in *metacognition.* Through metacognitive habituation, writers learn how to take control of their writing tasks and become self-directed learners. We can teach them how to do that. And if we do, they might take what they've learned when they leave our course. In the rest of this chapter, I will describe what metacognition is, how it works in writing, and why it is important for our model for mindful writing.

METACOGNITION

The term *metacognition* appears last on the "Framework" list, but it may very well be the one disposition to rule them all. Metacognition is an attribute of mind that distinguishes an expert from a novice (National Research Council 2002, 47). By some accounts, the term was coined by child psychologist John Flavell in 1976 in *The Nature of Intelligence.* Three years later, in *American Psychologist*, Flavell (1979) explained that while studying developmental differences in schoolchildren, he discovered that most children "do relatively little monitoring of their own memory, comprehension, and other cognitive enterprises" (906). Even though Piaget found evidence of sophisticated dual processing in children as young as two, Flavell noted that, on the whole, schooled children didn't know whether they were learning, or how or why. Often they don't know what they know or don't, and they don't know how to make their knowing work better for them. It may not come as a surprise to discover that college students likewise struggle to pay attention to their learning and improve it (Nilson 2013, 2–3).

These twin challenges are presented in the research as *monitoring*—"assessing or evaluating the ongoing progress or current state of a particular cognitive activity"—and *controlling*—"regulating the ongoing cognitive activity" (Dunlosky and Metcalfe 2009, 3). Some scholars also include a third aspect, *knowledge*, which is essentially epistemological: knowing how things are known and why (Dunlosky and Metcalfe 2009; Tarricone 2011). Metacognition, then, is the act of monitoring and controlling your own mental activity.

According to another classical text by Jacobs and Paris, the goal of metacognition is to be able to plan learning, evaluate how one is learning, and make changes to improve, both during tasks and for future ones (McCormick, Dimmitt, and Sullivan 2013). In essence, metacognition is used to improve performance, and in fact dozens of education studies assert that this is precisely what it does (see McCormick, Dimmitt, and Sullivan 2013; Santangelo, Harris, and Graham 2016). One major metastudy has revealed that metacognitive teaching strategies have an effect size of 0.69, ranking 14 out of 150 studied influences on student achievement (Hattie 2012, 266). (Effect size refers to the difference between one type of instruction and a comparison group. Any positive number suggests that the type of instruction had a positive effect compared to a control group. Effect sizes at 0.5 or above are moderate to strong.) Clearly, teaching students how to think metacognitively is a best practice.

It could be said that all learning is metacognitive in the sense that in pursuing our goals we experience feedback that teaches us something about how we're doing. However, philosopher Joelle Proust argues for a more active and purposeful view of metacognition. Metacognition activates a "cognitive subsystem" that works as "an independent form of mental agency"—a kind of second self, a monitoring self, a self attuned to the values that lead to success (2013, 7). This kind of self-investigation was popular in Greco-Roman philosophy and education. However, the nineteenth-century French philosopher Auguste Comte had his doubts about its viability: "The thinking subject cannot divide himself into two parts, one of which would reason, while the other would observe its reasoning" (in Dunlosky and Metcalfe 2009, 12).

True, there is something spooky about metacognition if we entertain the idea that one part of our cognitive self can be more perspicacious than another part. (The cephalophore, presumably, looking at her own head is somehow wiser than her own head.) And yet recent neurological studies support the idea that self-reflection is not only possible but neurologically distinct from other cognitive activities, such as memory retrieval (Dunlosky and Metcalfe 2009; Schwartz, Scott, and Holzberger 2013). Our metacognitions—much like the maladaptive "automatic thoughts" (Beck 1979) that make us mentally ill—have "epistemic authority," meaning that they can influence our "judgments, memories and intellectual performances" (Nelson, Kruglanski, and Jost 1998, 77; see also Dweck 2006). What we think about ourselves as learners has persuasive power. Metacognition is an act of self-persuasion, inviting us to transform the conditions of our work.

I've been saying "we." Who's *we*, really? Does everyone, no matter where or how you live on earth, use the same metacognitive processes? Seems like the answer is *yes*, and *no*. I'm punching dangerously above my intellectual weight class here, but the most recent research takes two positions on the question: (1) If metacognition is defined as the monitoring and controlling of mental processes, then every culture (studied, at least) has methods for explaining and refining this process; (2) but epistemological practices such as metacognition are meant to select, transmit, use, expand, and teach information "relevant to a [particular] group" (Proust and Fortier 2018, 2). Any time we talk about metacognition, we are talking about a universal practice with culturally specific operations and values. Thinking—along with speaking and writing and reading—is an activity meant to "enact specific socially recognizable identities engaged in specific socially recognizable activities" (Gee 2012, 152).

METACOGNITION AND WRITING

In writing studies, metacognition is considered one of the dispositions or habits of mind of successful writers—along with other attributes related to metacognition, such as self-regulation, self-efficacy, motivation, attribution, meta-awareness, and the other "Framework" habits (e.g., flexibility). And in fact, this understanding of metacognition has been part of the mental model from the beginning of cognitive writing studies in the 1970s. While the earliest models (Hayes/Flower; and Bereiter/Scardamalia) did not use the term *metacognition*, they distinguished the act of writing (i.e., thinking of words, writing words, reviewing those words) from the social environment in which the writing takes place (the audience and purpose) and the *task schema* writers use to monitor and control the writing process (McCutchen, Teske, and Bankston 2008).

Schemata are mental models we apply, deliberately or automatically, to solve problems. Carl Bereiter and Marlene Scardamalia used the term *intentional cognition* rather than *metacognition* to describe how a writer has a "self-directed mental life" that is "carried on consciously and purposefully" as they write (1987, 336). Expert writers show "deliberate control" through "goal setting, planning, memory search, problem solving, evaluation, and diagnosis" (xiii). In a recent refiguring of this complex model, John Hayes, an emeritus psychologist at Carnegie Mellon, placed metacognitive skills on a "control level," separate from the "process level" (i.e., the act of writing in a social context) and the "resource level" (i.e., cognitive resources such as long-term memory and attention) (Hayes 2012). In short, this research showed that expert writers can separate themselves from the act of plinking out words on the page in order to set goals, make plans, monitor their process, make adjustments as they go, and reflect on the value of the product and the experience—all in the service of their craft. Expert writers are cephalophores.

As you can imagine, the knock on this research was that it was too obsessively focused on how the three-pound universe between a writer's ears produced the writing. But why do people write in the first place? As Charles Bazerman argues, "writing is a technology designed to communicate among people," and it is "learned and produced in social circumstances, establishes social relationships, changes the writer's social presence, creates shared meanings, and accomplishes social action" (2016, 11). As I said in the last chapter, before children learn to scratch out real words, they often write rows and rows of squiggly lines on notepaper and expect friends and family to read it. Their need to communicate in writing develops faster than their ability to do so. What's the point of all that monitoring and controlling and taking off our heads if we're not communicating with others?

Here's the point for writing teachers: The habits of mind mentioned in the "Framework," including metacognition, are established, maintained, and deeply enhanced by our motivation to speak to others. These dispositions spring into action in social contexts—with genres, audiences, and purposes all embedded in the relationships that give them *telos*, the ultimate aim of writing: communion. The mindful writer wants to refine the process of being together through language.

We can see this rhetorical awareness in action when as children we learn how to speak with the people we live with. However, in unnatural and schooled writing, we develop socially motivated metacognition over years of practice. According to one study, our "cognitive apprenticeship" as audience-centered writers takes twenty years or more of deliberate practice as we develop control techniques that can juggle both the text and a representation of a reader's needs (Kellogg 2008, 3). Our young students may struggle to understand how to plan, execute, and evaluate their own writing as an addressed, pragmatic act in a social world (Beach, Newell, and VanDerHeide 2016), especially if we continue to give them writing tasks that do not have any imagined audience beyond a teacher with a gradebook. "The only true education," wrote American philosopher John Dewey over 100 years ago, stimulates a learner's powers through "the demands of the social situations" they find themselves in (1972b, 84).

METACOGNITION AND TEACHING WRITING

So, where are we? Let's review: For a writer, metacognition—a kind of mindfulness—is the act of monitoring and controlling your own mental activity as you write in social contexts for social goals. It is a habit of mind separate from other writing processes (e.g., typing syntactically clear sentences or drawing from what you know about a topic), and it can be developed through deliberate practice. And research tells us it *should* be developed, since writing performance is influenced by the writer's ability to monitor and control the writing process purposefully, considering the audience and rhetorical goals.

There is another reason for teaching students metacognitive strategies—a biggie. Recent research suggests that students who develop metacognitive strategies are more likely to transfer important writing skills to new settings. Being the bearers of bummer news, we tell our students that after they leave our sixteen-week crash course on writing, they will find themselves once again in a situation that calls for them to write. (Turns out that writing is a life sentence. Pun intended.) And it's likely that the new writing task, whether in school or out, won't look much like the ones we throw at them in first-year writing. ("Write a literacy narrative," says no boss ever at no engineering firm.) But if students can see how all writing tasks share certain attributes across contexts, they can write with the power of their metaminds. We call this trick of abstraction *transfer*—when a writer can "repurpose or transform prior knowledge about writing for a new audience, purpose, and context" through "mindful abstraction" (Moore 2017, 2).

The research on writing transfer is deep, rich, and growing like kudzu. (See Beaufort 2016 for a nice synthesis; also Anson and Moore 2016; Moore and Bass 2017; Yancey, Robertson, and Taczak 2014.) Here's what a writing teacher needs to know from this research:

- Transfer is the ultimate goal of all learning, if we think of learning as developing powers to understand and act in new situations.
- Transfer is easy and somewhat automatic when a new situation is identical or near-identical to a prior situation (which is why you can drive a rental car you've never sat in before); but higher learning, including learning to write, requires a significant degree of abstraction—learning to see in novel situations what might apply from dissimilar prior experiences.
- Transfer is hard to detect in research studies, and often in writing studies students show *negative transfer* from one writing situation to the next, meaning (for us) that what they learned in first-year writing interferes with new writing tasks, because prior learning plays a commanding role in new learning.
- Transfer is aided by metacognitive habits that help students become aware of themselves as learners and writers, monitoring and controlling the writing process in a new social context.
- The list of "abstractable" schemata writers need varies, but a good starter list would include genre knowledge, knowledge about the writing process, and knowledge about how writing works as "a social and rhetorical activity" (Adler-Kassner and Wardle 2015).
- Students can develop metacognitive habits of mind more effectively if we (a) teach them about metacognition and transfer explicitly during the course (as in, "Hey students, this thing I'm teaching you about genre: You'll need it every time you get another writing task"), (b) give them multiple opportunities to practice metacognition, particularly as they transition from task to task, and (c) provide feedback for their metacognitions.

In this chapter, I've tried to establish a little of the theory behind what I will now call, without much poetry, the "learning cycle for mindful writers." Metacognition is at the heart of it. In the next chapter we'll take a brief look at this cycle.

4

THE LEARNING CYCLE FOR MINDFUL WRITERS

We know that expert writers have very good metacognitive skills: They monitor and control the writing task in its social context. We know students don't necessarily come to us with all those skills, but we know we can intervene and teach them to develop habits of mind that will help them as lifelong writers. How, exactly, do we do that?

We can start with the insight that effective metacognition in writing, or any other kind of learning, flows through time in a *sequence.* Barry Zimmerman, one of the most important figures in this line of study, calls this sequence the "personal feedback loop," and for him it rolled out in three phases: forethought, performance, and self-reflection (2009, 300). Others have suggested plan, monitor, evaluate (Nilson 2013, 8). Susan Ambrose and her research team suggest five steps in a "cycle of self-directed learning" (assess, evaluate, plan, apply, reflect), and I am greatly indebted to their work for my own learning cycle for mindful writers (Ambrose et al. 2010, 193). For a writer confronted with a project, the three-step sequence might look like this: (1) You analyze what this writing task is asking you to do, set goals, and make a plan; (2) you write the thing, using whatever strategies you know, all the while monitoring yourself to see how you're doing, making adjustments when necessary, with the help of others; and then (3) you finish, looking back and assessing how you did, making sense of it all in the context of life, liberty, and the pursuit of happiness.

As we've established, this kind of self-directed writing does not happen naturally. And the traditional model of teaching writing—one that I imagine is still quite popular—shortchanges the forethought and self-reflection phases and shoves all its chips onto the performance (i.e., drafting + revising) phase. We can help writing students build mindfulness during major writing assignments by asking them to practice thinking metacognitively—in writing—at various stages throughout the process.

DOI: 10.7330/9781607329374.c004

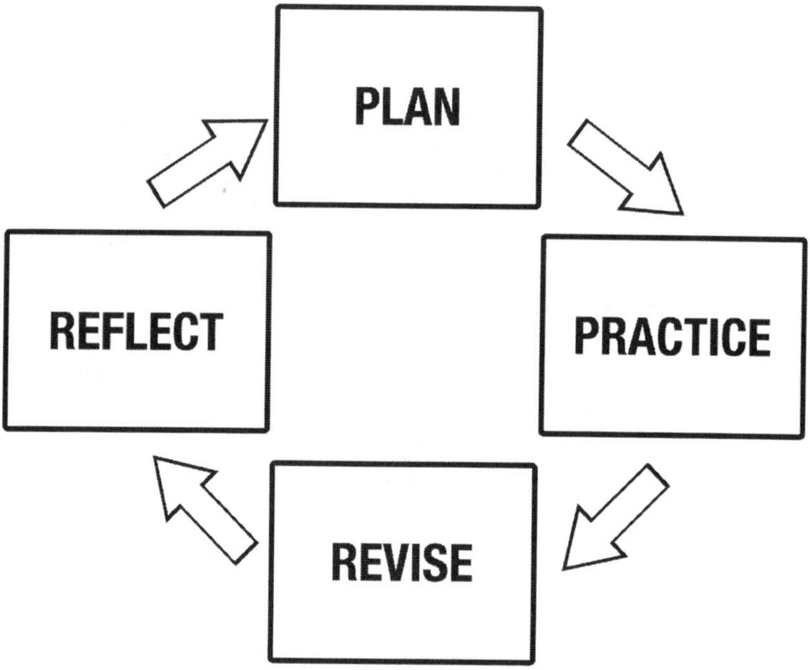

Figure 4.1. A learning cycle for mindful writers

As I imagine it, the learning cycle for mindful writers (figure 4.1) has four phases that more or less map onto the models mentioned previously. I call it a *learning* cycle because by the end of the experience, we hope our students will have learned something about themselves as writers and the processes most useful to them. Again, we're not interested entirely, or exclusively, in *what* students write; honestly, most of our students will never write these kinds of essays again in college, or anywhere. Rather, we're hungry for their *souls*. We want each of them to be a different kind of writer when they walk out of our classes (and go burn all their notebooks and papers and sell their textbooks back for pennies). This learning cycle requires students to manage writing tasks more strategically and intentionally than they have before. And it requires them to employ explicitly—by putting into words, in writing or speaking—a metacognitive learning process that they may have experienced only subconsciously before. (How many high school projects did *we* reflect on when we finished them?)

The word *cycle* suggests an apply-rinse-repeat formula. That's not necessarily my intention. Writers develop idiosyncratic processes that work for them. I'd argue, however, that unless you teach in a tesseract, we teachers live and work only in three dimensions, and today's teaching follows yesterday's. In other words, students are taught metacognitive strategies in a sequence of experiences meant to prepare them to own their own sequence one day. I have found from my reading of the research and from my teaching that this learning cycle for mindful writers creates powerful interventions into the writing lives of students.

In subsequent parts of the book, we'll spend time on each phase. Here's a quick preview:

Plan. As soon as you give students a new writing task, they can start thinking mindfully about what the task is asking them to do. In the planning stage, students assess the task (its rhetorical situation) and set goals.

Practice. In the practice stage, students use writing strategies and get feedback. The strategies are informed by research in writing studies and rhetorical theory. The students put these principles to work on a writing project in beta, so to speak, so their work can be reimagined in future iterations. During this phase, you will instruct students on important writing principles and share models. The students will discuss principles, read texts, and put into practice these principles and various writing strategies they've learned from instruction. In the practice stage, students make the "demo tape" of their writing.

Revise. Revision can be a metacognitive activity, or it can be a cosmetic chore. In this stage of the learning cycle, students evaluate a full draft in light of their genre, audience, and purpose and the effective feedback they receive from you and their peers—an effort requiring both monitoring and controlling their work. Much of their disposition for revision will come from your careful feedback.

Reflect. Reflection is central to all purposeful thinking. In fact, John Dewey used the term *reflective thinking* to describe any kind of thinking that is orderly, deliberate, and focused on "controlling purpose and end" (1986, 117). Kathleen Yancey, one of our leading scholars on the topic, sees reflection as the central governing activity, start to finish, that makes students "*agents of their own learning*" (1998, 5, Yancey's emphasis). In this book, I will use the term *reflect* in the conventional sense of looking back on a completed project to evaluate the quality of the writing and assess what has been gained in the process. Reflection is a looking-backward to move forward.

As writing teachers, our job is to design powerful writing experiences for our students—powerful because they (re)create rich rhetorical situations, engage students' critical-thinking skills, permit topic exploration, use an interactive writing process, or invite personal application and passion (Anderson et al. 2015; Eodice, Geller, and Lerner 2016; Melzer 2014). There are many resources for new teachers on how to create effective writing tasks. (I recommend to anyone and everyone John Bean's indispensable book *Engaging Ideas*.) Once you have established the course outcomes and the major assignments, you can use this four-step learning cycle to design how you will use major writing tasks to build your students' metacognitive skills. That's what the rest of this book is about.

A few practical application points in closing:

- For this model to be effective, you will need to budget time in the semester to teach it, and accountability (points, or whatever reward system you use) for evaluating the work students will do as they practice metacognition.
- Students can practice metacognition in speaking (as in, speaking with peers about writing plans) or writing. Mindful writing is better because it commits students to put their metacognitions in a document, so they can curate all those statements and reflect on them later in portfolios.
- Therefore: Students will develop metacognitive skills through a variety of writing interventions, starting at the moment when you give them a new major writing task. These interventions—we'll call them writing-to-learn activities (W2Ls) in chapter 7—can be collected online or on paper. I've had students write some of them on 3 × 5 notecards and turn them in at the end of class. Other times I've had them keep a document in Google Drive that they use for metacognitive writing.
- Motivation is tricky for this kind of work. I've learned to hate the word *points*, even though I just used it a moment ago. If you don't assign "points," students may not do the assignment; if they don't do it, they don't learn the habits. I try to follow Daniel Pink's advice about motivation: explain the rationale, keep the point payoff low and muted, give students freedom of voice, make it part of the culture of the class by letting them share their metacognitions, and provide feedback in the form of genuine dialogue with them about what they've written (2009). I refer to their reflections in the comments I write on their graded work.
- I've designed this model to fit any kind of first-year writing course, wrapped around any topic using any kind of reader and doing any kind of writing. However, this model represents (in my view) best practices in the field of teaching writing. There are aspects of the model that might suggest certain assignment models or classroom exercises over others.
- Although the model is designed for any going brand of FYW, it assumes that students will be taught some amount of content from rhetoric and writing studies—enough, for example, to know what a rhetorical situation is, or what a writing process looks like. We'll talk more about that in part III on practice.

By inviting them to adopt metacognitive ways of being, the learning cycle can help students take control of their development as writers. Instead of being spectators, falling into assignments and completing them one painful paragraph at a time, they can become self-regulated strategizers who know how to take charge of a task, and take meaning from it as well.

Although we do not talk nearly enough about our students' emotional well-being, there is an invitation in this cycle to help students manage what could be called the affective ecology of writing. Writing is an emotionally fraught experience. Projects intimidate us. When I started this project, I would go to my study office in the library and curl into a ball on the floor for ten minutes and contemplate returning to my post-high-school job painting apartments.

But as my therapist says, "Don't stew—*do.*" Planning invites students to look ahead to a project with strategic purpose. Planning asks students to think about what they know so far and what they need to know. It invites them to begin a project with calm, not chaos; with goals, not groans. It invites them to choose what they want to learn. And at the other end, reflection gives them an opportunity to think about what they learned, to channel their satisfaction or frustration into the next iteration of their writing self, with transformed beliefs and attitudes.

The rhetorical critic Kenneth Burke (1897–1993) believed that life is art, that is, that living life is a work of imagination made pliable by what he called "the comic frame." For Burke, when we live and act in the comic frame, we act with philosophical self-consciousness: "In sum, the comic frame should enable people *to be observers of themselves, while acting.* Its ultimate would not be *passiveness,* but *maximum consciousness.*" Through the comic frame, we transcend ourselves "by noting [our] own foibles" (1984, 171, Burke's emphasis). Ultimately this kind of maximum consciousness, this mindfulness, provides "important cues for the composition of one's life," which requires us to accommodate the lives of others (our audiences) as well (173–74). Can we design learning experiences that help students construct a comic frame for themselves?

5
MEANINGFUL WRITING TASKS

When I was in graduate school teaching the second semester of a first-year writing sequence, I joined forces with two colleagues—one teaching tech writing and the other business writing—to stage a three-class role-play based on a local conflict. A copper company had its unblinking Sauron-like eye on a little patch of land near Superior, Arizona, a small town in a semiarid plot of the Sonoran Desert beloved by recreationists and environmentalists alike. My colleagues and I thought the public debate about the proposed mine presented an opportune rhetorical moment. We planned a collaborative project called *Showdown in Superior!* to dramatize how competing interests present written arguments in public discourse to influence public judgment.

My first-year students took the role of Superior's townspeople; Eric's class of business writers became special interest groups, such as conservationists or rock climbers; and David's tech students represented the mining company's managers and engineers. Each class created and shared documents. *Showdown in Superior!* culminated in a simulated town hall meeting in which each group presented arguments in documents and speeches, and then my students—the town of Superior—voted whether or not to permit the company to mine the copper cache in the hills near the town. They voted "no."

In running the role play, we were trying to accomplish a variety of things. Most important, knowing that much of the writing that students do in college is directed at no one for no reason, we wanted to give our students real—"real"—audiences and purposes as writers. You pluck low-hanging fruit if you point out that college students write in an environment sealed off from the real-life purposes of writing in the real social situations that call for writing. It's a common, and compelling, argument.

At the same time, it's kind of a lame argument. Unless we want to give up teaching and grading writing—writing, as we've established, is, like reading, an unnatural act requiring years of explicit instruction—we're stuck with teaching it in classrooms that are somewhat (so-called)

DOI: 10.7330/9781607329374.c005

artificial. Any time you assign students to write and then grade them, no matter how authentic you think you are making the assignment, you are creating an environment that contrasts with the "everyday writing" people do at work or for pleasure for their own purposes (Brandt 2015). In spite of these limitations, in *Showdown in Superior!*, we wanted to create as much as was possible an authentic environment for writing for our students: a situation in which students were called to write for specific people in specific genres for specific purposes, even if the situation was manufactured. We wanted students to be motivated to write by the *answerability* of a rhetorically rich context.

I've since rethought the value of role plays such as this (Jackson 2009). Several years ago I tried to create a role play for first-year students about cyberbullying—they were staffers for the state governor working on a white paper. It bombed. While I still want to believe that gaming the writing class can transform student experience (see Carnes 2014; McGonigal 2011), I had much more success with engagement when I taught a course on "The Millennials" and had students prepare a conference on subtopics of their choice, acting as themselves speaking to a handful of real guests (who, maybe, role-played being interested). It was hard for my cyberbullying students to feel authentic pretending to be state staffers writing about a topic they didn't choose to a pretend audience they couldn't begin to understand. No matter the framing, it is perennially difficult for students to feel like authentic writers writing for grades in a school environment.

MEANINGFUL WRITING

Since this book is about the dispositions of the writer, I thought I'd make a suggestion or two about how to create meaningful writing assignments for your students before we get to the planning stage of the learning cycle for mindful writers. Not all writing assignments are created equal. As a longtime writing center director, Muriel Harris talks about her experiences with AFH: Assignments from Hell. "Analyze the problem of gender in *Hedda Gabler* and *Uncle Tom's Cabin*," commanded one assignment. "Remember to consider other relevant factors such as race, social conditions, economic class, and author's nationality" (2010, 187). Another, as an example of what Harris calls "intimidating the novice," reads, "You are expected to be in control of your subject, to think with analytical skill, not to pad with unnecessary words" (196). Examples of the AFH have confusing criteria, too many questions, too critical a tone, too broad a topic, and too vague a description of purpose or criteria.

As I said in the introduction, I assume you are new-ish to a writing program that may not give you much freedom to choose the kinds of writing assignments you give your students. The program may give you a prewritten assignment sheet for the major tasks, which is perhaps quite useful for the rookie teacher. Or, they may not. Or, they may give you guidelines without being prescriptive. Since at some point you will need to design your own major assignments, I offer the insights below on meaningful writing tasks based on research in writing studies.

Meaningful Writing Situates Students in a Rich Rhetorical Context

In the language of our list of threshold concepts, or the concepts students need to understand to be mindful writers in all settings, "writing is a social and rhetorical activity" which "addresses, invokes, and/or creates audiences" by "speaking to situations through recognizable forms" (Adler-Kassner and Wardle 2015). Meaningful writing tasks have a specific genre (more on genre in part II), an audience to address, and a purpose for the writer (i.e., how the writer should work to influence the judgment of the reader).

We can help students develop their metacognitive skills by helping them think about their readers—and not only think about them, but in a sense "invent" them, call them into being, imagine their needs as they write (Lunsford 2015). In his study of over 2,000 college writing tasks (including written essay exams), Dan Melzer discovered that most of them (82 percent) were designed with the instructor as the only audience, most often playing the role of grader (2014, 28). There's no faster way to kill the spirit of writing than to make its telos a grade rather than meaningful communion.

But hey, we all know the game: You *will* grade their writing! So why the charade? Students know how this works. They know who they need to please—not some imagined, invented audience, but *you*. Fine, let's admit that and move beyond it. In spite of the necessary constraints imposed by school teaching, our writing tasks can help students think mindfully about audiences beyond graders. For example, the writing in the disciplines movement encourages us to help even first-year writing students think of themselves as apprentices in a specific field of knowledge making, such as biology, in which specialized audiences (called *discourse communities* in writing studies lingo) use particular genres (for instance, lab reports or lit reviews) to get group-specific work done.

In an FYW course focused more on publics than on academic communities, I have found it helpful to let the genre goad the students into thinking about audience. For example, I've often asked students to write an opinion editorial for the student newspaper or a newspaper of their choice. Before they write, they have to imagine, based on their experience and an analysis of previous op-eds, who their audience is and what their needs are. Easier said than done. It's often harder for my younger students to imagine a diverse student body that does not think like them. Digital and multimodal writing present even more interesting challenges for students as they imagine, invoke, and invent audiences for their work. (Social media "followers" constitute an audience, of sorts.) We should create tasks that invite students to think rhetorically, and therefore mindfully, about their writing context by designating—or asking students to designate—a rhetorical situation, with genre, audience(s), and purpose.

But what if I want to assign a rhetorical analysis—a synthetic school genre that nobody writes in real life, with nowhere plans for nobody? Yes, this is a challenge, and many a writing scholar has wrestled with the a-rhetorical problem of what Elizabeth Wardle calls "mutt genres" (2009). Some mutts are adorable and we can't live without them. Some assignments, while not obviously "real world" genres, help students learn important writing principles. School genres are still genres; school, in fact, is a social world in a place called *real life*. It is appropriate, though not entirely satisfactory, to tell students their audience is composed of their instructor, classmates, or a general audience of intelligent, somewhat informed people who would like to be enlightened. You may need to get inventive. When I've taught rhetorical analysis, I try to show students how analysis, like any cultural criticism, contributes to what the Greeks called *phronesis*, or public wisdom. By writing an analysis, they teach an audience how to read and value a text.

Meaningful Writing Asks Students to Do Meaningful Thinking

As an undergraduate, I took a course titled Modern Africa. Near the end of the semester, we were divided into groups and assigned a country in Africa. A whole country. My group was assigned Liberia. We were asked to write a report. That's all the instruction we received—you know, just write a report on Liberia. Each of us took a historical period, hit the books, and then barfed up what we learned in a twenty-five-page paper. That was not a meaningful experience (beyond teaching me how to cut and paste in a word processor, a skill that in 1997 I'd never used before).

In a recent study of data from nearly 70,000 students, it was discovered that "meaning-making writing tasks"—tasks that required "students to engage in some form of integrative, critical, or original thinking"—correlated on a national survey with deep learning experiences (Anderson et al. 2015, 207, and *passim*). According to Dewey, all meaningful thinking "occurs when things are uncertain or doubtful or problematic" (1985, 155). Problematic-in-a-good-way writing—or "ill-structured" writing (Bain 2012, 134)—asks students to work through problems, raise questions, take a stance and support it, synthesize dissimilar things, complicate the all-too-easy.

I once had a student who wanted to write about abortion for a research project. He was morally opposed to it, and he wanted to prove through research that it was morally wrong. Although abortion is a topic on my "never never never never never let students write about this thing" list, there was something in his earnestness and good nature that made me think he could learn something from the project if—a *big* if—he avoided the abstract question about abortion generally and focused on a single specific question he did not know the answer to. The assignment required him to answer the question with credible support. He chose, "How do abortions influence the emotional well-being of the patient?" He assumed he knew the answer. It seemed so obvious to him that women who had the procedure subsequently suffered mental trauma.

What he discovered surprised and dismayed him. To his credit, he wrote the paper answering the question with the available evidence. "All thinking involves risk," wrote Dewey, and also powerful moments of growth (1985, 155). Students can learn to persist in difficult tasks that may not be immediately interesting to them if the task itself is challenging, and if it leads to discovery. I want my students to ask compelling questions, not merely pick topics.

Meaningful Writing Is Social

We've already established that meaningful writing is addressed to an audience. It is equally true that meaningful writing, for our students, takes place in a nurturing social environment that invites students to discuss writing with instructors, classmates, peer tutors, friends, or family (Anderson et al. 2015). Students' motivation to write is greatly enhanced by this kind of interactive writing process (Boscolo and Gelati 2013). The authors of *The Meaningful Writing Project* confirmed through a study of 707 college seniors that students considered writing meaningful and engaging when they interacted with others about their writing (Eodice, Geller, and Lerner 2016).

Why is this the case? It seems to me that asking students to talk about their writing with others turns the writing task into a collaborative intellectual enterprise. *This is what I'm trying to do,* we say to our peer reviewers. *What do you think?* Talking to other people—about whatever, but particularly about our work—is one of the easiest ways to feel happy in this life. It may be that students will more easily develop the habits of mind necessary for mindful writing if they can learn to share their work-in-progress as part of the monitoring aspect of metacognition. We need to build into our major assignments opportunities (no, requirements) for students to conference with us, get feedback from us and peers, and/or visit with peer tutors. A deep interaction with a mentor can fundamentally transform the college experience for a student (see Bain 2012; Chambliss and Takacs 2014; Light 2001).

Meaningful Writing Does Not Necessarily Give Students Complete Freedom to Choose Their Own Topics or Projects

Often we believe that students need to be interested in the topic to enjoy writing. If that's the case, then they're in for a life of misery, since much of the writing they will do on the job will not be so self-directed. While it is true that students who are interested in their topics show more motivation in research studies—aren't we happier and more focused when we're interested?—their interest did not necessarily lead to better writing performance. Knowledge about the topic, in fact, is a stronger factor of performance than interest (Hidi and Boscolo 2006, 147).

Sometimes it's more important to assign students an interesting problem to write about, or a project that they perceive as being useful or relevant to their goals. Many of the students in the *Meaningful Writing Project* reported that they found writing projects meaningful even when they were "*required* or *forced*" to write in genres or about topics they did not choose (Eodice, Geller, and Lerner 2016, 22, their emphasis). It's far more important to make writing interesting than to find an interesting topic (Boscolo and Gelati 2013, 290). (Some of my students tell me they're not interested in *anything* we talk about in class.)

The terms *self-directed learning* or *student-centered teaching* are misleading. They lead us into thinking that students will be better off if we give them little direction and let them come up with whatever the heck they want. It's tempting to think that giving students minimal instruction on writing tasks (no topic, no genre, no expectations) will draw out the best from them because they are free to choose their own writing path. There is simply no evidence for that, and there is significant evidence to the contrary (Hattie and Yates 2014; Hillocks 1986). In the massive study I mentioned before, student engagement and learning were correlated strongly with "clear writing expectations," by which the study meant "instructors providing students with an accurate understanding" of the task and "the criteria by which the instructors will evaluate" it (Anderson et al. 2015, 207). At the risk of sounding like Thomas Gradgrind, I submit that meaningful writing instruction is direct instruction—with *some* degree of freedom for topics and approaches.

Meaningful Writing Invites Students to Make Connections

Finally, meaningful writing directs students to make connections between the current writing task and their previous tasks, and other classes, future classes, their careers, their lives. Again from *The Meaningful Writing Project*, students reported that writing was meaningful when it "connects to previous experiences and passions and to future aspirations and identities" (Eodice, Geller, and Lerner 2016, 108). After interviewing 400 Harvard undergraduates, Richard Light made this discovery: "The faculty members who had an especially big impact are those who helped students make connections between a serious curriculum, on the one hand, and the students' personal lives, values, and experiences, on the other" (Light 2001, 110).

Meaningful writing experiences show students how their writing has real-world applications outside our classrooms—in their personal, professional, and public lives. In my experience, it is unlikely that all the students in an FYW class will make these connections themselves without prompting. Once you get into a writing project, you tend to put your head down and think of nothing else till the wretched thing is done.

That's why the learning cycle is so important. Students will make these connections if we invite them to—if we require them to by giving them reflective writing prompts. The cycle is meant to help students become what Rebecca Nowacek calls "agents of integration," drawing from prior experience with writing to address a present problem, and then thinking about how what they are learning as writers might help them in other contexts (2011). These connections will make what students learn in your class transportable.

Practically speaking, every major writing task will have *the deliverable*—you know, the final Big Thing students draft and revise and turn in—and then a constellation of smaller, less formal writing tasks that answer questions such as "When in the past have you used research in your writing, like you will need to do now?" or "What about your writing process might need to change next time you write?" We will talk more about these questions soon enough. Those prompts will help students act metacognitively as they grapple with your writing assignments. Assignments come and go; the habits of mind remain. And one important subhabit is making connections.

THE ASSIGNMENT

How do you choose what major writing tasks to assign? If you're a brand-new teacher (relax—you've got this!), you will more than likely be asked to teach specific assignments created by the writing program. These writing tasks were created so that students would learn specific things that your institution wants them to learn. We call these specific things *outcomes*. An outcome is a new capacity students will gain by taking your class. Often outcomes are posted right at the top of the syllabus as a kind of "behold your future powers!" statement. At one institution, I was not required to list any outcomes; at another, the outcomes, drafted by the office of the Dean of Undergraduate Education, popped up on my online syllabus whether I wanted them to or not. If you can choose your own outcomes, you will want to review the Outcomes Statement composed by the Council of Writing Program Administrators. I have taken one of the CWPA outcomes and adapted it for my class in my own words: "By the end of FYW, students will develop mindful, flexible, and collaborative strategies (e.g., planning, drafting, revising, editing, and reflecting) for writing in a variety of technologies and genres."

You can introduce your students to the major writing tasks with an assignment sheet. There is no way to make the phrase "assignment sheet" sexy. "Rubrics" is another buzzkill of a word—essential, but unpoetic. In the famous teaching movies, you never see an action shot of the teacher passing out an assignment sheet. Embrace them. Make them part and parcel of your nerdy teacher self. They are teaching tools. They will help you establish the rhetorical situations that make writing meaningful. They will lay out the task for students and set expectations. Harris suggests that our assignment sheets list our goals for the assignment, a few clear competencies students will need to show, and the grading criteria. They should be short and designed clearly (2010, 203–5).

After I introduce students to a writing task, I include a rubric (grrr-rowl!) so the students see how I will evaluate the assignment. Later, as I will explain, I have the students use the rubrics to evaluate previous students' work (anonymized—and I get the ex-students' permission in the semester I taught them) and spark conversations in peer review. If

I'm really on the ball, every major writing task's supporting documents (assignment sheet, rubric, peer review instructions, and previous student examples) will all be posted on the learning management software at the beginning of the semester. (*Learning management software*—another hot term.)

Below, as a mini-appendix to this chapter, I have included an assignment sheet I've used for the major research component of FYW. Some people (Muriel Harris!) might feel that I've been too thorough here; they're probably right. I was hesitant even to include this because I know how idiosyncratic writing assignments can be. But notice how I have made clear the three essential components of the rhetorical situation (genre, audience, and purpose), and I direct them (too much, Mr. Overdetermined?) to think about audience in a certain way. I can imagine how productive it might be if an instructor coauthored with students the assignment sheet, and even the rubric, to give them an opportunity to analyze a target audience. You'll also notice that I've scaffolded the assignment so that they complete it in increments, giving me a chance to give them feedback early in the process.

AN ATTEMPT AT WRITING A MEANINGFUL ASSIGNMENT: THE CONFERENCE PAPER

YOUR SITUATION

Imagine that you've been invited to attend an undergraduate student conference titled "The Good, The Bad, the Ugly: College Life and Well Being." The conference has been convened by a non-profit organization whose mission is to promote student health, as well as academic discussion, public speaking, and civic engagement. How can undergraduate college students, even first-year college students, address contemporary social problems in fresh and interesting ways? They believe that bringing all of you together will help strengthen society by creating aware citizens who can communicate with each other peacefully and effectively.

They've invited students like you from colleges and universities across the U.S. to gather in the Tampa Marriott Waterside Hotel and Marina, in downtown Tampa, Florida, to give 15-minute academic presentations on issues of particular interest to college students. The conference is an exciting opportunity for you to hear ideas and arguments from students from all walks of life—and to share your own.

Here's your exigence: You have been invited to come to the conference, stay in the Marriott hotel for a couple of days, and present an exploratory but persuasive paper to your peers about the health and well-being of college students.

YOUR GENRE

Conference presentations are live performances. Conference coordinators will put you on a panel with other students presenting on a topic similar to yours. When it's your turn, you will stand at a podium with a microphone and present your research. To make your presentation as compelling as possible, you will prepare a script for your presentation (around 2,000 words, or over around eight double-spaced pages). Your script should be engaging, considering your live audience, but it should also include credible and timely sources cited in MLA format, with a works cited page with around eight sources. (The conference conveners will ask students to submit their papers to be published on the conference site.) In other words, you will produce something that is both a script and an academic paper.

The genre of an academic presentation varies by discipline, but since you're writing to an audience of college students interested in your topic, you will make several moves in your paper. You will

- capture your audience's attention with an anecdote, news event, personal story, question, problem, paradox, or common (but interesting) human experience;
- review several perspectives from credible people who have researched or written about your topic to create a research space;
- pose a question about the issue—a question to which, at least at the start, you don't know the answer;
- explore multiple perspectives on this question, but present an argument for a particular perspective, policy, or ethical position;
- support your argument with evidence your audience will accept;
- conclude by suggesting how your research matters to your audience (its implications, the "so what?" of your presentation).

For this genre, you will write in a comfortable but intelligent style suited to the college students in the audience. Think about the kind of presentation you'd like to hear, and give that presentation.

YOUR AUDIENCE

Imagine around 100 college students seated in a conference center ballroom, ready to hear your presentation. The audience is relatively young (the average age is 23) but certainly diverse: The only thing bringing you together is your interest in contemporary issues and a desire to hear exciting new ideas about how to understand or address its social challenges.

What can be said about such an audience? You can safely assume that those who chose to attend your panel session are interested in your specific topic. After all, they chose your topic over many others happening concurrently with yours. However, it should go without saying that your audience may not share your views. In fact, assume some degree of skepticism in the audience as you write your paper. You can also assume that the crowd will be politically liberal to the degree that Americans currently under 30 tend to be politically liberal. (More on that from Derek Thompson, from *The Atlantic*, if that helps.) All political perspectives are welcomed at this conference.

Because of the diversity among your audience, it will be a challenge to imagine an exact audience. You know this much: They are undergraduate college students interested in engaging in academic conversations with other students. (Not everyone gets invited to the conference.) Among you all, there is energy, hope, optimism mixed with anxiety for the future, and goodwill. You see yourselves as engaged citizens, collaborators, creators, future leaders, problem-solvers. This crowd is not interested *only* in getting a degree quickly and earning money; they want to make a difference.

YOUR PURPOSE

For this project, you will have a specific purpose related to your topic. As rhetor, you'll want your audience to feel, think, or do things *specifically related* to your topic; remember that rhetoric is about influencing attitudes and judgments about shared concerns. That does not always mean changing their minds. More generally, your purpose is to share something of value to your audience, give them a cool intellectual experience with your topic, present alternative opinions respectfully, and convince them that you know what you're talking about and that your argument is credible. As in every other writing task, you'll use rhetorical strategies you've learned in this class to connect with your audience and make allies of them.

POSSIBLE TOPICS

The conference organizers decided this year on a topic broad enough to encompass all kinds of ideas and interests. For example, on the call for papers, they've listed the following topics as possibilities for panels of four presenters giving papers on similar topics related to college life and well being:

student finances and debt
student health and sexuality

mental health
ability and disability
political identity and activity
the value of general education
relationships and dating
volunteerism
alcohol
sexual misconduct and violence
sports programs
social life (including fraternities and sororities)
academic challenges
spiritual life
multitasking, study habits, academic challenges
cheating

While they are open to a variety of topics, it is important to them—and to your writing teachers!—that each student picks a topic with three essential characteristics: (1) they feel passionate and personally invested in it, (2) the topic is sufficiently narrow for a brief paper and presentation, and (3) it will interest other college students.

All good research presentations begin *not* with a topic, per se, but a question, a narrow question that can be answered in a brief presentation, like this: "How has Tinder influenced the 'hookup culture' at elite colleges?" or "How can dorm meal plans do a better job of improving first-year student health?"

As we discuss possible topics, you may want to join with 3–4 other students to form panels on similar topics for the conference.

WHAT IS MEANT BY *RESEARCH*

The word *research* means different things to different people. A physicist might imagine shooting electrons through a cathode ray tube to study the way particles behave. An economist might gather census data and perform statistical analysis on investment decisions. An anthropologist would think of research as collecting data from careful observations of human behavior in everyday life. Historians or literary scholars will visit archives for their research.

For this conference, however, *research* means *finding effective sources to help you answer an engaging question*. As you prepare your conference script, you will read deeply and widely on your topic and find around 6–8 key sources that are credible, timely, convincing, and with limited bias. Some, but not all, of these sources will come from peer-reviewed academic journals. You'll present these sources as evidence that your argument is acceptable, and you'll weave those sources into your argument using a citation style guide (in this case MLA), which is a common practice in academic writing.

6
ORGANIZING WRITING TASKS

As we've established, mindful writing means monitoring and controlling your writing process before, during, and after writing tasks. To be a mindful writer, you have to understand core ideas from rhetoric and writing processes because these ideas provide the theoretical language we use to reflect on our experience. Our students' experiences will be enhanced if we create meaningful writing assignments, as we discussed in the last chapter. In this chapter, we'll talk about how to organize those writing tasks at the start of the semester.

AN ARCHITECT OF LEARNING

When you show up to class on the first day (see the interlude chapter), you'll need to present students with a syllabus. Syllabi are learning contracts that tell students what to expect and establish policies that will help them behave themselves and get the work done. What to do with late papers is up to you, but if you don't write down a policy, students will find ways to push the limits of the possible (Comer 2016). Your syllabus will include required texts or materials, outcomes, official policies (about sexual misconduct, for example), your personal policies (e.g., laptops in the classroom?), brief descriptions of the major writing tasks, a grade breakdown (what percent gets a B+, which, to many of my students, is the new D+), and the course schedule. Your program will likely require you to use a learning management software that will organize all this stuff for you. The learning management software (LMS) takes away to some extent your ability to design your syllabus and make it your own, but I've found that harried students want, and expect, me to use the default LMS because it aggregates conveniently all their courses and schedules together in one seamless corporate interface. Yuck.

As I said, I won't get into too many details about the syllabus. (Check out *First Year Composition: From Theory to Practice* to see examples from the all-stars. The *St. Martin's Guide to Teaching Writing* is a great source as well. You can find a bunch online. Dartmouth has outstanding online

DOI: 10.7330/9781607329374.c006

teaching material; google "dartmouth first year writing pedagogies.") You will have to make some important decisions long before you step into the classroom. And for you first-year graduate students who have only one week (or less) of training before teaching for the first time, "long before" means, like, *a few days before.* Crazy, but all too common. At any rate, good learning design begins with the end in mind—your outcomes, and then the major tasks that will help students achieve those outcomes. As a reminder, I'm assuming here that you will get help on that part of your teaching from your program.

In the syllabus, you'll have a schedule of all the stuff you'll do together. That schedule will be organized around three to four major writing tasks and a handful of minor ones. This chapter is about how and why you organize a *unit,* or a series of several days set aside for one major writing task. By "major" I mean the writing assignments that will go through a writing process and count significantly toward the students' grades in the class.

Now, I suggested earlier that the metacognitive activity students do while writing a thing is as important as the thing itself. Even so, you want their polished writing to demonstrate that they understand rhetorical principles. Your institution likely will demand that you consider their polished writing as evidence of their learning. In chapter 7 we'll talk about the more informal metacognitive writing your students can do to develop these necessary dispositions while still creating a product worth paying attention to. Process is essential to writing teachers. To employers and grant evaluators and claims adjusters and reading publics, *products* are essential. In fact, outside school and its patient pedagogues, products are all there is.

We can think more creatively about "product" when we evaluate student portfolios, which are student-curated collections of writing across time (in a course, or a series of courses) with a significant reflective component such as a personal essay. In portfolio assessment, the product *is* the process—the process by which students write, learn to write, and reflect critically on their writing. The evidence of their learning is not a single product (a research paper), but a series of products that illustrate an even more important process of becoming.

At any rate, we don't just sit around and metacognize; we need an activity to metacognize about. Hence, the major writing tasks. You, my friends, are architects of learning. For each major writing task, you will organize a sequence of events that build on each other to help students develop their metacognitive abilities and writing skills. What should this sequence look like?

BEGINNING AT THE END

Let's begin at the end. What do you want your students to learn from the major writing tasks? Let's say you assign some kind of textual analysis—a close or rhetorical reading of a text. Why are you doing that? What do you hope they will accomplish by writing it? Maybe you want students to learn to read "for inquiry, learning, critical thinking, and communicating in various rhetorical contexts," or to "read a diverse range of texts, attending especially to relationships between assertion and evidence, to patterns of organization, to the interplay between verbal and nonverbal elements" ("WPA Outcomes" 2014). In *Understanding by Design*, Wiggins and McTighe teach us that this kind of "backward design" helps us focus less on the content of our courses and more on the results—the "explicit performance goals" we want students to achieve when they finish writing the thing we asked them to write (2005, 17). Their backward design model looks like this:

1. *Identify desired results* that answer the question, What should students be able to understand or do when they finish this major assignment? I like how Wiggins and McTighe avoid using the word *know*, as in, "We want students to know X or Y." Rather they use the word *understand* to refer to higher-order learning from Bloom's taxonomy: To understand means to know why something is important and how to use it (Wiggins and McTighe 2005, 39). Other "action" words for student outcomes could be *apply, analyze, synthesize, explore, support, discover, inquire,* or *evaluate.* To identify desired results, we review the outcomes of our university, program, and course and decide how best to articulate those outcomes for the specific unit we're designing. It's important to note here that the students themselves, as cephalophores, will have their own desired learning outcomes, and sometimes their desires might clash with the goals of the establishment. You will want to articulate how these desired results will empower students for their personal, professional, and public lives after your class.
2. *Determine acceptable evidence* that the students have learned what you (or the institution or the program or—imagine!—even they) hoped they'd learn. Here the perceptible evidence will appear in the student writing. For example, we'll see from a student's textual analysis if they have attended "to relationships between assertion and evidence," if that is our emphasis. Their writing will tell us the degree to which they understand how to analyze the rhetorical support a text gives for a claim. Again, portfolios with multiple drafts, finished and unfinished, and reflective writing can constitute acceptable evidence.
3. *Plan learning experiences and instruction* that will help students create the evidence showing that they have learned those things (Wiggins and McTighe 2005, 18). For the outcome listed in #2, our writing students need first to learn the difference between assertion and evidence.

They'll need some whole-class practice on identifying assertions and evaluating the evidence that supports the assertion. Then they can learn how evidence can be evaluated using principles of rhetoric or informal logic. During this third part of your planning, you plan what you will do each day in the unit to help students develop the trained capacities you identified in #1.

This system is based on the entirely reasonable and yet shockingly difficult principle that students learn what we teach them. If we want students to "adapt composing processes for a variety of technologies and modalities," as the WPA Outcomes Statement suggests, then we need to (a) decide what we'd take as evidence that they could do that, and (b) set up learning experiences that will help them learn to do it.

I know that outcomes can make teaching overdetermined. My university just completed a seven-year freak-out over accreditation and assessment. A group of professional external reviewers descended on campus like Seal Team Six and set us straight. Each course, program, and academic unit had to have a list of objectives and direct evidence from students showing to what extent our students were achieving them. I like the joke about Americans and educational assessment: It's like planting a seed and then digging it up every ten minutes and asking, "Is it growing? Is it growing?" Sure.

However, my experience observing teaching suggests that the opposite is just as likely: We often teach *underdetermined* lessons that lack meaningful goals or outcomes. When grading, we may identify desired results we didn't prepare our students to deliver. We need to be clear about what we want students to be able to do *and why* it will be useful to them to be able to do those things. Otherwise, we're just a social club. Our students don't need us to organize a social club for them.

LAYING OUT THE UNIT

Okay, let's put backward design into practice.

Let's imagine that our program requires us to assign a research paper. Never mind that the genre of "research paper" is much like Spam—a synthetic product not found in the wild. Ours is not to question why! We'll keep the genre of the assignment generic so we won't get distracted from the design focus. We want this writing task to teach the students a number of things but here's the most important one (again from the "WPA Outcomes" 2014): "Our students will 'use strategies—such as interpretation, synthesis, response, critique, and design/redesign—to compose texts that integrate the writer's ideas with those from appropriate sources.'" Looks like we have one desired result of the unit, with several little results embedded in it. (no. 1: Identify desired results.) This outcome has been adopted by the Council of Writing Program Administrators, and it turns out that the (imaginary) program we teach in has adopted it as well.

This outcome is informed by a more philosophical assumption about learning that Wiggins and McTighe would call a "big idea"—a concept that is "both central to coherent connections in a field of study *and* a conceptual anchor" extending the student's writing power beyond the classroom (Wiggins and McTighe 2005, 68, their emphasis). In writing studies, as we've already established, we call some of these big ideas threshold concepts. It turns out that knowing more about these principles correlates with strong writing performance (Harris, Santangelo, and Graham 2010).

In our scenario, the threshold concept providing the theoretical ballast for the outcome we've identified is "texts get their meaning from other texts" (Roozen 2015, 44). As students write a research paper for us, we want them to think about how their own text is in dialogue with a variety of other texts that they will interpret, synthesize, critique, and work into their own—hence enacting the dialogic imagination of discourse itself. Our students might be more enthusiastic about writing a research paper if they understood how this work of synthesis is at the heart of all writing. Learning to interpret, synthesize, etc., etc. will help them do the things they want/need to do in life.

Having established the outcome, we decide on a "performance indicator" (Wiggins and McTighe 2005, 47) that will show that students have learned strategies for integrating other texts into their own (no. 2: Determine acceptable evidence). Wiggins and McTighe explain how this sequence—goals, and then evidence—does not come naturally to teachers who want to jump right from goals to planning activities to meet those goals. The novice teacher might use an "activity" approach to planning: once I've got my topic, I need to come up with "fun and interesting activities" to keep the students interested in the topic (151). But backward design compels us to think through what students will produce as a result of our teaching *before* we plan what we teach.

In our imaginary case, the performance indicator seems fairly straightforward: We decide that the "research paper" is that evidence, the standard eight- to ten-page research paper in which students summarize, paraphrase, and/or quote other writers and end with a reference page. Of course we want to use what we learned in the last chapter about how to make writing meaningful: We want a rich rhetorical context, critical thinking, a social process, and opportunities to connect what they are learning. But we need to develop standards of success for the major paper.

You'll notice that this step sounds like rubric building. We start with a list of target capacities:

Students who successfully interpret and synthesize and respond to texts in their research paper will . . .

- use sources appropriate for the genre, audience, and purpose;
- introduce other texts to demonstrate their relevance or credibility;
- distinguish clearly between their own ideas and the ideas of other writers;
- explain, represent, or summarize other texts accurately, but in their (the students') own words (see Harris 2006, 15);
- limit the amount of direct quoting of other texts;
- describe how their stance or position or perspective differs from the perspective presented in other texts;
- treat other writers civilly, even while disagreeing;
- use an acceptable academic citation style;
- avoid "patchwriting" or plagiarism;
- fill in the blank: ________________.

Step 2 in the backward design model is a good time to draft a rubric. Designing a rubric is a useful way to determine not only acceptable evidence but a range of student performances based on our criteria. We'll talk more about rubrics in chapter 20.

Above we've listed the writing indicators we will accept as evidence that our students have used strategies like interpretation, synthesis, and so on, to integrate their ideas with other texts. This is dangerous business. By so doing, we have committed ourselves pedagogically to supporting the students in their quest to achieve those aims. We can't be like Monty Python's Knights Who Say "Ni!" and command our students to chop down the largest tree in the forest with a fish without helping them do it. We must now design "a particular sequence" of learning experiences that will help students take on the task (Fink 2003, 130).

This sequence is what you end up doing every day in class (or every lesson in an online class) over the several weeks (or months?) your students work on a major writing task. Only now are we ready to think about the learning experiences we want students to have each day.

As an undergraduate English major, I took several classes whose daily schedules were presented to me in this form:

Tues, Jan 6—Ellison, *Invisible Man*, 3–70
Thurs, Jan 8—Ellison, *Invisible Man*, 71–150
Tues, Jan 13—Ellison, *Invisible Man*, 151–250
Thurs, Jan 15—Ellison, *Invisible Man*, 251–332

And I loved them. I loved reading *Invisible Man* and coming to class having no idea at all what we were going to do that day (talk about *Invisible Man*—duh!) and why we were doing it (because *Invisible Man* is awesome!). But some of these courses, in hindsight, were committing what Wiggins and McTighe call the "twin sins" of course design: activity ("hands-on without being minds-on") and coverage ("march through a textbook") (16). Now that we've described our outcomes and imagined what it will look like when students achieve them, we have a focused orientation to class time that will be less tolerant of waste.

The learning cycle I introduced in chapter 4 can help us arrange a self-directed learning process for each writing task (i.e., each unit in an FYW course). The overall picture of the unit, then, might look like this:

Day 1—Plan: assess the task (cue prior knowledge, analyze genre)
Day 2—Plan: assess the task and set goals
Day 3—Practice: learn rhetorical strategies (related to genre)
Day 4—Practice: learn and apply rhetorical strategies
Day 5—Practice: apply rhetorical strategies
Day 6—Revise: prepare for peer review
Day 7—Revise: conduct peer review and student conferences with teacher
Day 8—Revise: learn and apply revision strategies
Day 9—Reflect: evaluate writing task and plan for the next one

Of course, the amount of days you spend on each of the parts will vary depending on your own needs. I don't want to set this up as a definitive schedule; it's meant more to *suggest* what the architecture of a unit might look like. Throughout this book, we'll do our best to inject specific learning activities that would support this generic schedule.

(A confession: I feel all kinds of anxiety about setting up the class schedule. I can never get it right. I end up getting out of the plane midflight and banging on the wings. As carefully as I plan the amount of days for each task, I end up moving, delaying, switching around, or canceling teaching sessions as I see how the students are responding to my teaching. After seventeen years, you'd think I would have it right. On the first day of class, I can't make myself give the students more than about two months or two major tasks of the schedule because I know it will change, and I tell them so at the top of the schedule in the syllabus.)

Remember that Stage 3 in backward design is *plan learning experiences and instruction* that will lead students to produce the acceptable evidence of learning. The cycle will ensure that much of this learning happens as a result of the sequence. For example, in the planning stage (which we'll discuss in part II), students will look closely at successful examples of the target genre. In our imagined scenario, we show students A+ research papers from the past and point out, for example, how these documents *synthesize* or *respond to* other texts effectively or *limit the amount of direct quoting* (a hard one to learn!). In the practice stage, we might give other models for integrating texts—describing, maybe, the moves made famous in the templates in Graff and Birkenstein's best-selling textbook *They Say/I Say*—and ask students to practice those moves by themselves or in pairs or groups. (This teaching strategy assumes students have already found sources to integrate.) On revision days, maybe we give students direct feedback in our conferences related to how they have designed, and how they may need to *redesign*, their integrations to follow appropriate conventions for the genre. And for reflection activities, we will ask students to analyze how well they responded to their rhetorical situation by writing with sources. Each of these activities (we hope!) will support our students as they learn to "use strategies . . . to compose texts that integrate the writer's ideas with those from appropriate sources."

To conclude this chapter, I want to point out that the best-designed units have characteristics that I think are implemented quite nicely by the learning cycle. Using insights from Wiggins and McTighe, we can say that each writing unit should be designed to be engaging (a design "that the (diverse) learners find truly thought provoking, fascinating, energizing" and "worthy of intellectual effort") and effective (helping learners "develop greater skill and understanding, greater intellectual power and self-reflection") (2005, 195). We begin the unit with *purpose*, introducing students to compelling ideas and questions and rhetorical applications for what they will write. We *model* effective rhetorical strategies. We *organize* the experiences in a meaningful way, so that principle builds on principle. We *coach* the writing process with opportunities to practice and receive feedback. We give students opportunities to mindfully *reflect* and *redirect* their efforts.

7
WRITING AS (META)THINKING

As I've tried to capture it, mindful writing is the creative and empowering scrutiny of rhetorical action in the narrative arc of the action itself—in its before, during, and after. In the last chapter we talked about how you can use backward design before the semester starts to plan major writing experiences for your students. As promised, this chapter describes a parallel track of before-semester (or before-next-unit) planning to create specific metacognitive interventions during a major writing task.

WRITING AS THINKING

When I started teaching writing, I was not prepared to think of writing as a form of thinking. Rather, like many people, I thought of writing as the completed product of thinking. Yes, there was brainstorming and outlines and drafts, but I didn't think of all that as writing.

In chapter 1 we talked about how the process movement transformed our understanding of college writing. It oriented writing teachers to the idea that we write to *discover.* If there is a manifesto of this orientation, it's Donald Murray's short essay "Teach Writing as a Process Not Product." Murray writes with an open, matter-of-factness that is immediately accessible; it has the ring of Truth. "What is the process we should teach?" he asks. "It is the process of discovery . . . [,] of exploration of what we know and what we feel . . . It is the process of using language to learn about our world, to evaluate what we learn about our world, to communicate what we learn about our world . . . We should teach unfinished writing, and glory in its unfinishedness" (2003, 4). Other early acolytes of process, such as Ann Berthoff, wrote that writing is "how we make meaning"; it is "an instrument of knowing" and "our chief means of shaping and communicating ideas and experience"; it is "a means of discovering what we want to say" as well as "the saying of it" (1981, 5, 19, 20). In *The Making of Meaning,* a work I've seen on a short list of books all new writing teachers should read, Berthoff talks about this writing-to-discover as "learning the uses of chaos," which she presents as a "theory

DOI: 10.7330/9781607329374.c007

of the imagination," the chaotic, recursive, experimental, dialectical process by which we find our voice and fill the page (39). To paraphrase Funkadelic, free your mind and your prose will follow.

This is a powerful idea. It opened up the writing classroom for *play*—for experimenting with words and meaning in a risk-free environment. What students wrote on the way to completing a writing task—their outlines and rushwrites and prewrites and lists and drawings and reflections—became an archive of their thinking and learning. Early research by James Britton and Janet Emig revealed that we use speech like we use thought: to solve problems in a recursive, often messy, self-directed, self-correcting process (cited in Bazerman et al. 2005, 58). The writing class became a site for exploring and cultivating this process.

Over the decades since, we have come to see the value of the writing we do in order to do our writing. To continue the tautology, we attend to the texts we create in the process of creating texts. Earlier I made the argument that what we ask students to think and write about before, while, and after they complete a major writing task is just as important as that final product they turn in for grading. Why? Because we can use the writing that supports writing to help students develop those important metacognitive skills we've talked about—"deliberate, strategic control" over writing processes (Bereiter and Scardamalia 1987, 6).

CATEGORIES OF WRITING TO LEARN

As you design your major writing tasks, you will want to create interventions into the writing process so that your students can write to discover and write to reflect. So, I suggest we divide the kinds of writing tasks we do in FYW into two larger categories: (1) We have the major writing task that students turn in—the final, graded product of their labors—in a specific genre, directed at a specific audience for a specific purpose; and (2) We have dozens of other minor, shorter, informal, exploratory, low-stakes, unstructured, and personal texts students will write in order to become mindful writers through the act of writing.

You may have seen this second kind of writing labeled *writing to learn* (W2L). I have found from my study of the literature that it is useful to divide W2L into three different categories, each serving a different pedagogical purpose:

Content W2L. Across all disciplines, instructors can use minor writing activities to bring students to a higher level of understanding about the content (e.g., chemistry) of the course. For FYW, the content is *writing* and *rhetoric*. As we've established, some knowledge of these theories and their practical applications strengthen student writers. Content W2L could include student explanations or definitions, recalling principles from reading assignments (Brown, Roediger, and McDaniel 2014), writing summaries of other texts (Graham and Perin 2007), keeping reading journals, and so on. We assign Content W2Ls in FYW to help students master the theories they will apply in future writing tasks.

Metacognitive W2L. These writing activities ask students to exercise their metacognitive abilities when they write plans and goals, craft theories of writing, articulate what they are learning, reflect on what they have completed, make connections with their personal lives and other classes, or otherwise pull their heads off and wax philosophical about their process. In one metastudy, these W2L activities were "significantly more effective than other kinds of writing prompts" in improving student writing (Klein and Yu 2013, 168). Metacognitive W2L is meant to strengthen students' ability to think critically and reflect meaningfully on their writing process.

Task W2L. While students work on a major writing task, they can use informal writing as a way into the task: for prewriting or brainstorming or outlining or starts-and-stops or lists or notes or whatever they need to do to make the writing happen. Task W2L represents the iterative design process of doing and making. You're using writing to develop a prototype—a draft, as we call it—that will be "tested" by users to see if it's doing what it needs to do. All prewriting and drafting activities could be categorized as Task W2L, which is our primary method for teaching students what the research literature calls "writing strategies." In another metastudy for the Carnegie Corporation, teaching writing strategies was shown to have an aggregated effect size of 0.82, which means that it's one of the most effective teaching methods available (Graham and Perin 2007, 15).

Now, these categories might bleed. That's the thing about writing process; it's learning the uses of chaos! Still, these categories might help us realize the purpose of informal, exploratory writing as a tool for learning different things at different times. In later chapters, I'll have specific examples of how you might assign this kind of writing (see chapter 14, e.g.).

SETTING UP W2L IN YOUR CLASS

How do you set up these activities before your students are sitting there in front of you, bright-eyed and eager, waiting for the magic to happen?

I've struggled for much of my career trying to convince students that W2L writing isn't "busy work." From one perspective, busy work is work that is irrelevant or useless or rote. In my experience, however, students label "busy work" anything that isn't graded that they don't want to do.

John Bean speculates that students see W2L as busy work because they are either "closure oriented" and therefore dislike "goalless" writing or they are grade oriented rather than learning oriented. He refers to a study indicating that around one-third of students see ungraded written assignments as "a waste of time" (2011, 123–24). Whatever the reason, we need to do a better job convincing our students that W2L activities will empower them in ways that other activities can't. These little micro-bursts of meaning make the Big Project powerful.

On my syllabus, I explain to students that throughout the semester I will ask them to respond to questions that will build their metacognitive skills as writers. I consider these responses *informal writing* (i.e., W2L) because I do not require them to be drafted, peer reviewed, revised, and proofread. In these exercises, students can use alternative language practices that might not be rhetorically appropriate for larger projects. I want to hear their own voices as they write mostly for their own benefit to learn and explore their own thinking. But I also want them to give meaningful responses. Like all writing, metacognitive writing, even if informal, is rhetorical. The students need to explain to me, and to themselves (Yancey 1998, 24), how they are thinking about their writing tasks. In order to be true "agents of integration," writes Rebecca Nowacek, students need "to *perceive* as well as to *convey effectively to others*" those connections that will stay with them beyond our class (2011, 38, Nowacek's emphasis). No matter how well you feel you've set up W2Ls, your B.S.-O-Meter will flutter from time to time as you read some of these responses.

You might think about including something like this in your syllabus:

> *Informal writing:* Throughout the semester I will ask you to think metacognitively about your own learning and writing process by writing brief answers to prompts—both in class and out. These activities will help build habits of mind (like rhetorical thinking) that I hope you take with you when you leave my class. Some of the informal prompts will ask you to recall or summarize readings; some of them (e.g., prewriting tasks) will lead to our major writing tasks. I call these writing tasks *informal* because they don't need to be polished (i.e., revised and heavily edited; you should still proofread them). They do need to represent your best thinking on the questions I ask: You will be trying to convince me, and yourself, that your reflective thinking is authentic and thorough. We'll do some of this work in class. Sometimes I will collect your writing, sometimes I won't. Sometimes I'll write back to you, and sometimes I won't. Sometimes I'll just highlight parts I like or ask questions. Sometimes I'll just put a check at the top indicating I have read your work and you seem to be on track.
>
> I want you to have the freedom to respond as you wish, in a voice and manner that pleases yourself. However, I want you to take these exercises seriously. I've set aside around 15% of your grade for these informal

writing tasks. If you write nothing, you get nothing—that's a given. If your response doesn't really address the question, or if your response does not convince me you are taking these questions seriously, I will give you partial credit. At the beginning of the semester, I'll show you examples from previous students so you can see what effective responses look like.

In addition to this kind of informal, free-response writing, you may ask students to write more formal reflective documents after they complete drafts or at the end of the semester to include in a portfolio of curated work. For a final, maybe. Kathleen Yancey calls these documents "reflection-in-presentation," and we'll talk more about them in later chapters (1998, 70). These culminating reflections could be weighted more than other informal assignments. While in this chapter I have thought of metacognitive writing as informal W2Ls, in approaches such as Teaching for Transfer and Writing about Writing the instructor will assign metacognitive writing as full-blown writing tasks, with drafting and feedback and revision. In 2018 I experimented with this approach when I required students to write a longer (1,000-word) formal genre analysis for the first major writing task, and I liked the results.

A final note about collecting. You have a variety of options for collecting your students' informal writing. Many of the instructors I know use writing journals—handwritten, mostly. Since all my students recently have had laptops, I use Google Drive for both in-class and out-of-class informal writing. I still require handwritten reflective writing in class the day a major writing assignment is due. In a rhetorical studies course I taught a few years ago, I required the students to write "reading captures," or reading responses, on 4 × 6 notecards. Some of the students thought it was old fashioned. Heck, *I* thought it was old fashioned, having them write with pens and stuff when we had computers and response options on our LMS. I tell ya, though, I really liked having all their responses in a small stack in my hand, skimming through them quickly and writing comments on the back. I felt like I could get a global sense of their reading practices rather quickly. That said, the LMS (or a shared document on Google Drive, or even a blog) can make responses public and collaborative in a cool way. Students can respond to each other (most likely if you require them to), and often you can grade their responses right there in the system, rewarding them their coveted points. I'm not going to say I'm agnostic about response medium, but the questions I ask matter more to me than the medium the students use.

So, big picture: Major writing assignments supported by minor W2L assignments that build content knowledge, develop mindfulness, or support the major writing task. You could decide at the beginning of the semester the exact amount of these assignments, or you could tell students they'll make up 15 percent of their grade and then you can assign as many as you want and adjust their percent value accordingly. Like other writing tasks, students will find these exercises more meaningful if we invite them to share them with each other, to read them aloud in class, to read others' responses and comment on them, to make them part of the interminable play of writing.

Interlude
THE FIRST DAY

You can do so much on the first day. You can teach the students that your course is about writing and social connection. You can teach them to think of themselves as writers—writers who think and talk and reflect about writing. You can also start forming important emotional bonds with your students.

On the first day of class, the world is remade. No matter who they were or what they were doing before, when students step across the threshold of your class (or gather up online) they become *your* students, in *this* particular course, working on *these* projects, together. Their sociality, though not entirely random, is constituted of the accidents, requirements, and conveniences of registration. You gather as strangers. But by the end of the first day, you, the teacher, with your hocus-pocus, have constructed a league of learners, theorists of the writing process and amateur rhetoricians in a "protopublic," to use Rosa Eberly's term (1999). When the semester ends, you scatter to the winds like dandelion fluff.

The first day can be one of the best days and yet one of the easiest days to squander with housekeeping that the students surely will forget. The temptation, especially for new teachers, is to introduce yourself; read down the roll and make little check marks (which, admit it, you've always wanted to do); "go over" the syllabus with them in a linear, but unscripted fashion; and then turn them loose a little early. Do the students need to know what they need to buy? Yes. (They'll need to know how many hours they will need to put in at work to afford the *n*th edition of Fancy Handbook, retailing at $95, with the updated style guide trivia.) Do they need to know your policies? Surely. Do they need to be oriented to the schedule? Of course. Do they need to know the outcomes they should expect? Well, *we* think they do.

Do they need to have *all those things* read to them on the first day? Nope.

Then, what do we want to accomplish on the first day?

Imagine two classrooms on Day 1:

In Classroom A, students sit quietly waiting for teacher to arrive. Teacher arrives and writes her name and the section number on the board. (You've seen movies.) Teacher introduces herself in a professional manner and takes roll. (Reads, and sometimes mangles, student names and makes checks.) She passes out a syllabus or projects on a screen the course syllabus from the LMS. "This is Writing 101," she says. Then she reads the syllabus, often turning her back to the students to read from the screen. She goes over the required texts, major assignments, and the policies ("**I DO NOT ACCEPT LATE PAPERS**" is in all caps and bold, each letter half a foot tall on the screen). "Any questions?" The students know the drill. They'll review the syllabus after class. Teacher reviews the first week of class and dismisses the students early. If the students haven't read anything yet, what is there to discuss? We're all a little freaked out here and could use the time to get our bearings.

In Classroom B, Teacher is already in the room as students arrive. Maybe some cool instrumental music plays in the background. In her hand she holds a class roll with student pictures (most schools, I'd bet, have this feature). Before the bell rings, she walks around the room matching pictures and faces and introducing herself to each student—an excellent way to make emotional connections in any class period (see Lang 2016, 180). When the bell rings, she introduces herself and writes her name and section number on the board, just as we saw in Classroom A. (One confused student stands up and races out.) Then she says, "Since this is a writing class, I want to start with a little writing. In fact, we'll write every day in this class, so please bring your [whatever this teacher permits as writing tech in her class] every day." She gravitates to the middle of the room, making warm eye contact with each student. "I want you to think about a writing experience that was particularly meaningful to you as a writer. Could be in school or out of school. 'Meaningful' here can mean a number of things: you felt passionate about it, you immersed yourself in it, you learned a lot from it, it was about a topic you loved, or it helped you connect with someone or something. Take a few minutes and describe this writing experience to us. Give us as many details as you can. Don't worry about making mistakes; you're not getting any 'points' for this. You'll share what you wrote with me and just one other person." The class falls silent except for pen scratchings or the tap-tap of computer keys. The teacher sits down and also writes an answer to the question. Five to six minutes later, she stands and says: "Now, I want you to pair up with someone next to you. Introduce yourselves to each other. Tell each other your first name, where you are from, what you want to study here, and then one thing about yourself that is unique, memorable, or otherwise distinguishing. Then share with each other what you wrote." Instant loud chatter. The teacher circulates, listening as unobtrusively as possible to the conversations. After about ten minutes, teacher invites the students to introduce their partners to the rest of the class. Everyone takes a turn at that; the class gets a

> few good laughs at the answers to the "unique" question. Teacher explains: "This class is about writing as a social activity." She comments on a few commonalities among the responses to the prompt, describing how these commonalities suggest various theories about writing. "I want each of you to think of yourselves as writers who have more to learn about writing. Take a moment and write *one goal* you hope to accomplish as a writer this semester." Students write a goal on their document. "Now," says teacher, "I want you to know where you'll be as a writer by the end of this course, and why that's important to you . . ." She reviews outcomes and the first week of the schedule.

Yes, Classroom A is a bit of a caricature, but from my experience in writing programs, there is a kernel of truth to it. (Confession: On my first day teaching, in 2001, I took roll, drew the rhetorical triangle with its Greek terms that I did not fully understand, went over the syllabus, and dismissed the students early.)

The teacher in Classroom B uses the first day to do several important things. She establishes, first, that FYW is a course on *writing* and not other topics. Second, she asks the students to write about a meaningful experience; by so doing, students tap prior experience and think as a mindful writer. When you collect this little writing sample, you can get a sense of the range of abilities. Third, the students then share that meaningful experience with someone else, thus emphasizing audience and creating a community of writers. Finally, we will assume that, yes, at the end of those more important activities, the instructor explained how the course would be guided by outcomes, policies, and schedules. You'll need to wax bureaucratic on the first day about the syllabus, schedule, prerequisites, policies, and enrollment (if students show up wanting to add the class). I ask students to read the syllabus before the first day and give them a "no points" quiz to help remind them of my policies.

The first day is the first time you can, and should, prompt students to mindfulness. On the first day of his basic writing course, Jeff Sommers writes *credo* (belief) on the board and tells his students, "Please make a complete sentence out of each of the following three sentence-starters[:] 'I believe writing . . .', 'I believe revising . . .', 'I believe writing courses . . ." (2011, 103–4). This activity gets students exploring what they've come to believe about writing. Expressing belief makes belief more an object of consideration rather than a wispy, invisible essence.

CONSTRUCTING ETHOS ON THE FIRST DAY

On your first day, you begin the challenging process of constructing a teacher *ethos*. What should this ethos look like? There's no single recipe, but I'd say there are three essential ingredients: credibility, humanity, and passion. In *The Skillful Teacher*, Stephen Brookfield defines credibility as "the perception that the teacher has something important to offer" that will empower students (2006, 56). We project credibility by showing the students that we know our stuff, we know why it's important to them (i.e., rationale), and we know why our approach to teaching it is useful. Credibility also means being honest about what we know and don't know (see Dannels 2015, 35–39, on this point). Credibility can be hard to perform on the first day of the first semester you teach. You're going to have to fake some of it; we all do, in our own way and throughout our careers. Hence Therese Huston's fantastic book: *Teaching What You Don't Know* (2009).

However, before you doubt your credibility as a rookie teacher, listen to Deanna Dannels's pep talk: "You were chosen to teach for a reason, and that reason has something to do with your ability and expertise" (2015, 38). Chances are quite good that you've been a writer, learner, and thinker for longer than your students. Stand and speak with that confidence. Your expertise will grow. I find it interesting that Brookfield suggests we avoid constant self-deprecation ("Shucks, I'm just stumbling around up here 'cos I don't know what I'm doing!") because it might be all too effective at convincing students you actually *don't* know what you're doing (2006, 66).

You can also project humanity on the first day. By *humanity* I mean a variety of things, for instance, being authentic, which Brookfield defines as "being open and honest" in our teaching (2006, 56). We project humanity when we are consistent, open to making mistakes and correcting ourselves, supportive of all kinds of learners, merciful and decent in the face of the foibles of young students, overly enthusiastic about nerdy stuff such as rhetoric. Get out from behind the tech podium, stand as close as you can to the students, look at them, one at a time, once or twice during the first day, and smile. If it's your thing, use fitting storytelling and humor; psychologists have determined that "a positive mood," particularly laughter, "prepares the brain to solve complex problems" (Bain 2012, 84).

Too many of the grad students I worked with felt like they needed to be cold and stern on the first day to establish credibility (and scare away people to reduce the workload). We have this entirely reasonable assumption that it's better to go hard at first and then soften up. While I understand the impulse, especially among young women teachers, who, because of enduring sexism, often need to establish clear boundaries on the first day, I think with a little practice we can become the "warm demander" Elizabeth Bondy and Dorene Ross write about. The warm demander is a "teacher stance that communicates both warmth and nonnegotiable demand for student effort and mutual respect" (2008, 54). It is customary on the first day to bring out the Bad Cop to make sure students are *darn clear* that they will "lose points" if they step out of line or that we "do not tolerate" this and that behavior. I've read syllabi that sound like an orientation to a juvenile detention center.

We can balance warmth and openness with professionalism. The research in higher ed isn't as clear, but there is significant research in K–12 learning that "close, supportive, and nonconflictual teacher-student relationships" lead to student learning gains (Capella, Aber, and Kim 2016, 274). I don't want to make this a Sunday School class, but I believe, quite ardently, that our students will have a stronger learning experience if we *love* them, treat them kindly, seek after their good and gain, commit ourselves to their growth, expect more from them, and take interest in them as individuals with significant intellectual potential. In an excellent article on "teacherly *ethos*," Marshall Gregory describes the warm demanding stance as *befriending*, in the classical sense of drawing close to someone else to seek their benefit, even if that means calling "a bad job a bad job" (2001, 83) or even becoming "indignant over time that is wasted" and "talents that lie fallow" (85).

Finally, we can show the students on the first day that we're juiced up about this whole writing and rhetoric thing. We can show the students that we *enjoy* talking about writing and rhetoric for the power they give us to make sense of the world and act in it. Again, Gregory explains teacherly enthusiasm so fittingly he deserves to be quoted at length:

> If the teacher exhibits an ethos of passion, commitment, deep interest, involvement, honesty, curiosity, excitement, and so on, then what students are moved to imitate is not the skill or the idea directly, but the passion, commitment, excitement, and interest that clearly vivifies the life of the teacher . . . Such enthusiasm justifies our efforts as learners because *we, too*, want to know things that will make us love our lives more. *Then*, at that point, and only at that point—when we are moved as students to want what the teacher has and is as a person—do we as students begin to place high value on the skill or the idea that the teacher is trying to teach us. It's never just for the sake of the skill or idea alone that the learner learns it, but for the sake of the life that is heightened, vivified, intensified, and enriched *by means of* the skill or idea. (Gregory 2001, 77–78, his emphasis)

I love what Gregory says here because it provokes me—makes me feel sheepish for my 65 percent efforts, for those times when I let the curriculum talk more than my heart, for those moments when the bureaucracy of my courses (the syllabus and policies and points and all that mess) speaks louder than my passions. And of course Gregory is speaking here of a semester-long labor of teaching, but each semester begins with one day: the first.

PART II

Plan

8

PLANNING AND THINKING

A writer in the act is a thinker on full-time cognitive overload.

—Linda Flower and John Hayes,
"The Dynamics of Composing" (1980)

The next three chapters cover the first part of our self-directed writer's learning cycle: planning (figure 8.1). Now, a snag: From the very beginning of our process Renaissance, writing scholars argued that writing, as a creative act, was not linear but recursive (with strategies repeated not in any particular order), idiosyncratic (unique to the writer), and context specific (dependent on the writing task and the rhetorical situation that provoked it). Any effort, then, to teach a linear, step-by-step method (prewriting! drafting! revising!) is doomed to drain the creative energy from writing. As a writer, I see the wisdom in this orientation.

On the other hand, as a *teacher* I see how important it is to use a sequence of learning that provides a scaffolding for novice writers. We can't tell our students, "Writing is idiosyncratic, and therefore I can't teach you any set sequence for a process. Go look up all these writing strategies and choose what you'll do first." The very idea of metacognition and self-directed learning, as we get it from John Dewey through Susan Ambrose and colleagues' *How Learning Works* to Linda Nilson's *Creating Self-Regulated Learners*, is that mindful learning takes on a natural sequence once a task has been assigned: there's planning, there's contingent performance, there are adjustments, and there is a looking back on what's been accomplished.

It may be that the four steps I'm sharing with you can be repeated, reversed, skipped, or whatever. I suppose that's up to you. I'm presenting them here as a natural sequence of metacognitive working-through in a writing class. In this first brief chapter, I present a little of the theory behind planning.

DOI: 10.7330/9781607329374.c008

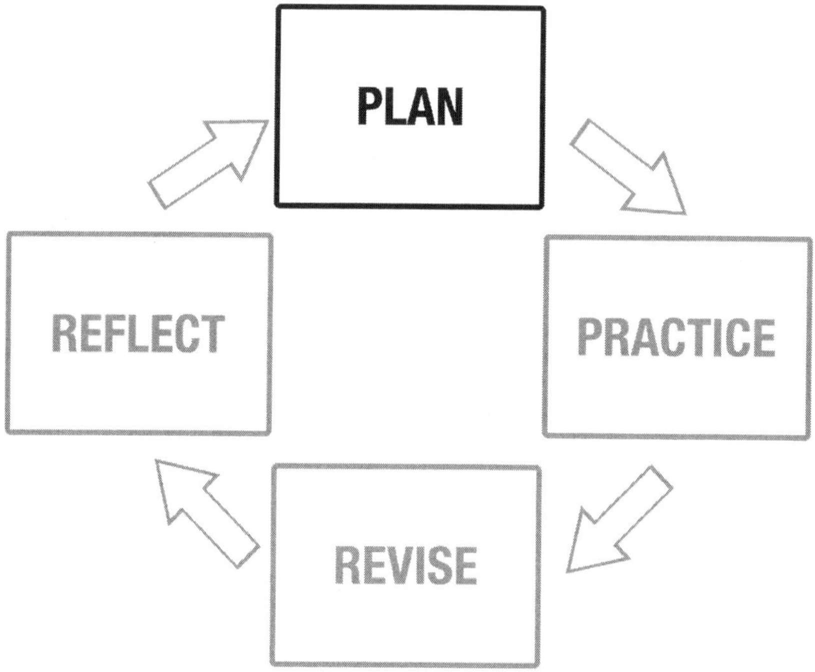

Figure 8.1. The planning stage

PLANS

I was at a close friend's wedding reception in a church gym a few years back, when, with no warning whatsoever, he called me to the mic to give an impromptu speech. Maybe he thought, *Brian teaches rhetoric; he'll have something cool to say about our friendship and the meaning of marriage!* I didn't. I had nothing. My mind folded in on itself like a camp chair and disappeared. My hands shook. I could feel my lower back tighten up as my adrenal glands kicked into high gear. The audience, sitting at tableclothed rounds, blinked at me in expectation. Words tumbled into the microphone in what could be technically classified as syntax, but I had no idea where I was going. I recall mentioning that my friend, as a ball boy for the Utah Jazz, had seen several all-star NBA players naked. It was one of the many times in my life I started saying something I knew was stupid but couldn't stop myself from saying. The words pranced out on their own volition like wild colts.

I had no plan. The social magnitude of the moment, and my emotional ecology as speaker, doomed my improv.

Some people are good at filling an empty, unscripted moment with extemporaneous art. Most of us are not. Most activities we'd consider important could be improved if we first thought mindfully about our approach, using what psychologist Daniel Kahneman calls "System 2" thinking: slow, deliberate, reflective, focused (2012). If some of your students are like some of mine, they have been conditioned by standardized tests and automated essay scoring to have a "starting gun" model of composing: the test begins, the prompt drops on them, and they write whatever is at top of mind, necessity fueling invention as the clock ticks away. Research shows that entering college students are oriented to a "test-motivated, single-draft writing practice" (Yancey 2017, 315). While many novice writers have useful task schemata for completing essays (five paragraphs or otherwise), they often have no plan, or they have an impoverished plan. And once the words are there, they're loathe to change them because of the cognitive price they feel they've paid to produce them. Who can blame them? Slow thinking isn't rewarded in timed exams or machine-scored essays.

If we can get students in the habit of planning their writing projects more effectively, we'll enhance both their thinking and their writing. Planning is an essential part of self-directed, metacognitive learning. Students who plan writing tasks and monitor their own process from the higher vantage point of their mindful brains will succeed as writers. Several research studies, including two metastudies, support this conclusion about planning (Graham and Perin 2007; Kellogg 2008; McCutchen, Teske, and Bankston 2008; Santangelo, Harris, and Graham 2016; Torrence 2016).

However, students' ability to plan depends to a great degree on *our* planning as teachers. In the traditional model of teaching, we hand out an assignment sheet for a major writing project, and then we start teaching specific writing strategies that will help students finish the job. In contrast, the model for mindful writers invites students to delay what we've called "drafting" until they have thought about the project and planned their route. We'll need to require them to do that and give them a little time to do it. The goal is to cultivate in the students a planning habit of mind similar to the one expert writers use. Had my friend given me a heads-up on the wedding speech, I would have asked myself several global questions about what I wanted to accomplish in such a situation. These concerns—integrated into a planning task schema—are fundamental for planning a response to any rhetorical situation. They constitute part of the metacognitive strategies we hope students take with them when they leave our writing class.

PLANNING AND THINKING

Clearly something happens, up there in the three-pound universe, before someone writes. Wikipedia tells me that the wife of poet William Butler Yeats was one of the many people who feel they can produce "psychography," the kind of spooky writing someone does automatically and beyond will, as if possessed. The rest of us have to think about it first.

In the research, then, planning is often synonymous with thinking, specifically with the pauses that precede "bursts" of writing. In one study, participants produced "a mean burst length" of twenty-five words for every three-second pause they took to think (Torrence 2016, 74). One popular model proposes a psychodynamic, of sorts, in which a Planner character proposes vague "thought things" to a Translator, who fashions those neuroclouds into morphosyntactic chains and sends them to a Transcriber, who puts on the phonological finishing touches in words ready to be typed or scribbled. And all this happens ostensibly before we write a single word.

Another, more practical way to think about planning is to think of it as a self-regulation strategy a successful writer uses before, and even during, a writing project. Planning helps us attune ourselves, intellectually and emotionally, to writing for social ends. Researchers who have developed and refined cognitive models of writing situate planning in the "motivation/affect" realm of the writing experience (Hayes 1996). In this model, writers orient themselves to the writing process in an environment of their own dispositions, beliefs, previous experiences, goals, and social purposes. Effective writers use this affective framing from the beginning of a writing task. Effective writers, like effective learners in general, learn to "*monitor* and *control* their learning," as we've established (Ambrose et al. 2010, 192). Planning helps students manage mindfully the emotional ecology of writing, thereby giving them confidence (Bruning and Kauffman 2016).

Novice writers—and students should consider themselves novices who have more to learn about writing (Sommers and Saltz 2004)—direct little of their attention "to what they want to accomplish" or to "the needs of the reader" (MacArthur and Graham 2016, 33; Sommers 1980). Novice writers lack task schemata, or practical models, for planning a writing task (McCutchen, Teske, Bankston 2008).

Why do we need such models as writers? Because writing is dang hard. You know this, and it wouldn't be a bad idea to let your students know you know this. We have to master a mechanical process to learn to write in the first place, a process that can take six or seven years or more. Our previous writing experiences afford and constrain us; our students write in the astral presence of every writing teacher they've had. We write in a social environment that places demands on how and when and to whom we write, and how fast we have to write it. While we write, our brain has to juggle two separate processing systems—one for the immediate process of cranking out words, phrases, clauses, and sentences (working memory) and one to draw from our (hopefully deep) well of discourse types and subject knowledge (long-term memory). And there's yet another harried mental character—called by some cognitivists the *central executive*—overseeing the entire process, much like Bob Fishman, legendary director of CBS Sports, would direct over 100 TV monitors of a football game, shifting live shots every three seconds for three straight hours (Bowden 2009).

Planning can reduce the demands on the central executive, the goal of any kind of expertise (Kellogg 2008, 3). Planning makes the goal-oriented nature of writing more explicit, more mindful. Planning orients students to a performance task rather than a grade, and research suggests that this kind of planning leads to higher student gains (Pulfrey, Buchs, and Butera 2011).

TEACHING STUDENTS TO PLAN

In college writing classes, our students don't have to write sweaty timed essays, but they still hear a starting gun—say, the night before a draft is due. They may not think much about it till the pressure to produce it is urgent. The two-part planning strategy, detailed in chapters 9 and 10, helps students gain more control of their writing tasks from the beginning, which is what it means to be a mindful writer. At the end of a recent semester of teaching FYW, many of my students said in their reflections that planning was the most novel, and ultimately most useful, writing strategy they learned in my class.

9

ASSESS THE TASK

For each major assignment, ask students to assess the writing task before they start drafting. By "ask students," I mean ask them to use informal writing or speaking to respond to any or all of the prompts I suggest below. The material they produce can be used later in the "reflect" stage of writing or at any other time during the major tasks. Remember that while this planning process could be called reflection (and is so called by John Dewey and Kathleen Yancey, among others), I've found it useful to separate planning from reflection to emphasize the sequence aspect of teaching for metacognition. All the parts of the learning cycle can be operating, in varying degrees, during any stage of writing.

READ THE ASSIGNMENT CAREFULLY

You've taken the time to write out a nice assignment sheet for your writing task; the students should take the time to read it. Encourage them to find out what you want them to accomplish. College challenges students to be in a constant process of attunement; every new teacher has a new set of assumptions and expectations about writing. (Gerald Graff [2003] calls this bouncing back and forth the "volleyball effect.") Ask students to

- read the assignment sheet;
- notice key terms related to the kind of writing expected (define, apply, analyze, contrast, assess, explain, describe);
- enter the scaffolded due dates (early bits such as outlines, full draft, peer review, final) in a phone/planner;
- review evaluative criteria (the rubric—it would be nice if they could see it from the beginning of the task);
- check overall understanding of what is being asked and ask questions.

DOI: 10.7330/9781607329374.c009

ANALYZE THE GENRE

Genres, according to Carolyn Miller, are "typified rhetorical actions based in recurrent situations" (1984, 159). While we'll talk more about genre in later chapters, we should unpack Miller's definition here. Miller is working against the standard understanding of genres as literary form (e.g., the epic poem, or a paranormal romance set in the gothic Northwest). Genres, from a rhetorical perspective, are not forms but sociological phenomena. They are semiformal but adaptive (typified) texts (rhetorical actions) meant to respond to events that happen over and over in a community of rhetorical practice (recurrent situations). In this sense, then, any writing we do is in a particular genre: an opinion editorial, lab report, grant proposal, thank-you note, Wikipedia entry, white paper, incident report, whatever.

Writers write in a particular genre (or socially situated "genre sets") because cultural groups have come to expect a certain kind of response to a recurring need, and writers attune themselves, one way or another, to what is expected. By writing genres, writers participate in patterns of knowledge making in these contexts of practice (Bawarshi and Reiff 2010). Genres themselves evolve with the needs of communities. As in the use of a planchette board in a seance, all users have a hand on the genre, but somehow the genre moves itself mysteriously to the music of time, forming and conforming to a social context. (As you've probably guessed, I'm skipping over fantastic research literature on genre theory. Go get some.)

A few years ago I submitted a grant proposal with two colleagues to the National Alliance of Concurrent Enrollment Partnerships. (I almost fell asleep just writing that title.) A grant proposal is a genre pretty set in its ways. We'd written them before. When we heard back from the NACEP, their rejection email was curt: *no budget.* Yikes. Even after several rounds of revision, we'd forgotten to tell these guys how we'd spend their money. And that was a genre no-no.

Students need a sense of the affordances and constraints of the genres we ask them to write. We need to teach them to be students of genre who learn to abstract from various examples the practices common in a rhetorical community. So, part of planning is analyzing the genre of the writing task.

Scholars of genre—specifically Amy Devitt, Mary Jo Reiff, and Anis Bawarshi—have described a useful three-step method for teaching students how to do this:

1. *Gather examples.* If you assign a literacy narrative, put some examples of literacy narratives into the hands of students. I assign students to read 2–3 professional examples (from Malcolm X, say) and 2–3 student examples reflecting a range of accomplishment. We want them to see that there are conventions, but also deviations. The professional examples give students something to aspire to, surely, but student examples, especially good ones, provide the kind of "vicarious experience" students need to help them develop self-efficacy (i.e., confidence) as writers (Bruning and Kauffman 2015).
2. *Analyze the rhetorical situation.* As students read various examples of the genre you've assigned, they should ask themselves questions such as, What kind of problem (or exigence) "calls forth" this genre? Who writes this genre, and what authority do they have as knowledge makers in that community? What kind of audience does this genre call out to? What discourse community or activity system or community of practice does this genre serve, and why? What is its purpose? What does it want its audience to feel, think, believe, do? At this stage, you may want to have students perform a *critical* assessment of the rhetorical situation, in which students describe the power dynamics inherent in the genre's context: How does the genre create asymmetrical power relations? Who controls the genre—and how, and why? How does a genre invite, inscribe, hail, or permit some rhetorical identities and not others? To what extent can writers resist, refuse, or reimagine the conventions of the genre?
3. *Analyze rhetorical strategies.* Each genre uses various strategies of influence that students can analyze as they read examples. This aspect of genre analysis is important because we know that using models to teach students to write is one of the most effective methods of teaching writing we have. As they look at models, they can use analytical principles they've learned in language arts classes in their pasts, but with a new rhetorical twist. They can ask, How is this genre organized, usually? What kind of style or argument or document design or evidence or diction do I detect across examples? (You'll notice I placed "style" in the *revision* section of the learning cycle, even though a mindful writing style can begin here, with careful analysis of stylistic decisions by other writers.)

This process will give students a powerful habit of mind that will help them in any writing situation they find themselves in (Devitt, Reiff, and Bawarshi 2004).

There's one catch, however: If we do invite students to find multiple examples, we need to be flexible in the way we grade their work. I've worked in a program that teaches students to write opinion editorials. Our original assignment sheet told students to write four to six pages, double spaced. We had a section explaining paragraph development, and one about thesis-driven argument. But once we turned the students loose to read op-eds from the popular press, they discovered that op-eds were considerably shorter than four to six pages, often had one-sentence paragraphs, and frequently employed narrative or description rather than thesis-first argument. If we're serious about genre analysis, and I hope we are, we have to accept that students will discover, through their analysis, a spectrum of affordances not normally permitted in academic writing. Such a discovery can help students transcend the confines of school and the "mutt genres" we often teach there (Wardle 2009). I had this lesson taught to me recently when I invited students to write Amazon product reviews for a genre assignment. Considering the crazy range of possible, I had to make a few guidelines about length (no one-liner reviews). We had to have conversations not just about what was possible (anything) but what was *desirable* for consumer audiences.

ASSESS THEIR RHETORICAL SITUATION

After students study some examples of the genre and its situation(s), they can assess their own rhetorical situation. A meaningful writing task will invite students into a descriptive rhetorical situation with its own genre, audience, and purpose. Once students read the assignment, they should be able to answer the following questions based on your description/class conversations:

- Who is my audience? What do I know about them? What are their values and assumptions? What do they want from me? How should I think about them, construct and invent or hail them, as I write?
- What discourse community do they belong to? What conventions will that community expect? What does that community count as evidence? What kind of knowledge am I contributing to?
- What is my role as writer? What do I want my audience to feel, think, believe, or do as a result of reading what I write?
- How am I constrained by the situation? What freedoms do I have to make rhetorical decisions? To what extent can I resist the conventions and expectations?
- (If I've been given this kind of the freedom), What medium will I use to design or distribute my work?

In the planning stage, these questions are orienting questions that set students on the right path. They'll need to consult them again, as a monitoring compass, as they go through the other stages of the writing task.

REVIEW PRIOR KNOWLEDGE OR EXPERIENCE

We learn in paradigms constructed from our experience. Prior experience plays a powerful role in what's before us: We "construct new knowledge and understandings based on what [we] already know and believe" (National Research Council 2000). As I mentioned above, students write for us with the weight of their experience as fifteen-year veterans of the school system; the ghosts of teachers past both help and hinder them (Ambrose et al. 2010, 13). When my students write an eighty-page research report in five gargantuan paragraphs, I have to remind myself that "the prior" is lurking. Kathleen Yancey explains that "the prior" is made up of "processes, knowledge, dispositions, beliefs, values," and also emotional states, previous skill indicators (e.g., grades), and habits of *place* (as in, where we have written in time and space)—all related to the writing students have done in the past, both in and out of school (2017, 313). As I suggested in the interlude between parts I and II, you can start tapping into prior knowledge as a reflective activity from Day 1.

For the major assignments, invite the students to reflect on previous experiences writing things like the thing you just assigned them. Research shows that students' ability to learn to write a new genre depends significantly on "antecedent genre" experiences prior to your class (Artemeva and Fox 2010; Devitt 2004). Mary Jo Reiff and Anis Bawarshi call this genre trace an *income* of teaching first-year writers, rather than an *outcome.* More effective student learners "repurpose and reimagine their prior genre knowledge" to fit a new situation, rather than resist adapting because their understanding of prior genres has hardened (2011, 325).

We can help students become "boundary crossers"—who can use or discard prior learning to fit what's demanded at the moment—rather than "boundary guarders"—who want to protect their current understanding from the pollution of the Now. Reiff and Bawarshi recommend we engage students in "not" talk, meaning that we ask students to think about how this new assignment is like previous writing tasks and how it is *not* like anything they've done before (Reiff and Bawarshi 2011, 328).

If I were assigning a rhetorical analysis, for example, I would give students the assignment and then ask them to write brief answers to questions like these: What is my understanding of the word *analysis*? How does this assignment remind me of previous writing tasks? How is the rhetorical analysis genre like the literary analysis I wrote in high school? How is it *not* like that? Which of my writing tools will help me here, and which won't? How is a rhetorical analysis like the product reviews I see on Amazon? How not?

ASSESS ABILITY TO PERFORM THE TASK

Sometime during the semester—on the first day might be ideal—ask your students to think about their own abilities as writers. Have them answer questions like, What are my strengths as a writer? What are my weaknesses? How would I describe my writing process? How confident am I with writing the genre my instructor has assigned? We know from research that self-perceptions will influence whether student writers work hard, "persevere" when the going gets tough, and bounce back after failure (Pajares and Valiante 2006, 159). This reflective moment might be an opportunity to remind students of our enduring Article of Faith that *writers get better at writing by writing*. (We are evangelists of writing growth!)

I spend a little time at the beginning of the semester warming students to the idea that writing skills, like muscles or a number of other attributes, improve with deliberate practice (Kellogg 2008; Kellogg and Whiteford 2009). I've learned this powerful, but somewhat silly, teaching strategy with my own children. When, in abject agony, one shrieks, "I can't do fractions. I hate fractions!" I encourage them to say, "I have not yet mastered fractions. But with practice, I'll learn!" Yeah, parents are nerds. But this is a powerful Jedi mind trick. We want our students to assess themselves honestly. We also want them to adopt a growth mindset, defined by psychologist Carol Dweck as the belief that skills, abilities, and habits of mind can be cultivated by effort (2006).

ANTICIPATE THE VALUE OF THE TASK

In addition to everything I've said above, we can also invite students to get selfish about their writing. We want them to imagine how our writing tasks will empower them. Ask them to write brief answers to these questions: What am I going to learn from this project? What skills will it teach me? How will it help me do the stuff I want to do in the future? How will I make personal connections to this writing task so that I won't be bored or discouraged?

When you invite students to assess the task in this way—with rhetorical principles and emotional commitment—you give them the wherewithal to monitor and ultimately control the writing process.

10
SET GOALS

The second part of planning after assessing the task is *setting goals.*

I know. The phrase *setting goals* evokes mixed feelings. Students will think about those moments when well-meaning adults in their past compelled them to set goals they had no intention of keeping. I belong to a faith tradition that inundates youth with goal-setting talk, and it can be cloying. On the other hand, goal setting can be empowering because it invites us to daydream (a better word would be *ideate*) about future accomplishment. Goals can be incantations for drive.

The research on goals is clear: Student writing improves if they make goals in the planning stage (Graham and Perin 2007; Hillocks 1986, 23–24; Santangelo, Harris, and Graham 2016). And, again, we should invite students to put their goals in writing for us to review.

As with all writing instruction, neurodiversity and identity challenge us to be flexible with student differences when we help them plan. A few years ago, I worked with an instructor who had one student with Asperger's Syndrome who felt it was too painful to set goals or write outlines because she felt physical pain when her final product didn't match with her plans. While the research on goal setting for ESL students and students with disabilities is quite optimistic (Cumming 2006; Troia 2013), not every student writer will benefit from planning.

There are two kinds of goals students should set for each writing task:

1. *Specific product goals.* Once students have analyzed the genre you want them to write, they'll understand better what their own writing should look like—its shape, moves, conventions. A "product goal" is a statement explaining to yourself what you want your writing to look like when it's done. Genre exerts powerful normative pressure on product goals. For example, if students are writing a rhetorical analysis, they may reason in themselves, *In the best examples I reviewed, the writer organizes paragraphs by describing or quoting strategies from the text and then analyzing the intended effects of those strategies. That's what I'll do in my own analysis.* Or *the student example I really liked concluded with a strong "so what?" statement that made the analysis matter beyond our classroom.*

DOI: 10.7330/9781607329374.c010

Sometimes the assignment you give students will outline explicitly the product goals they should make (like "support your thesis with at least two peer-reviewed sources"). I would argue that if you have worked with your students on genre analysis, it is likely they will come up with much of the criteria for the genre inductively on their own, or in class discussion. Since product goals, like carry-on luggage, can shift in mid-flight, students can revisit them after drafting and adjust them based on the text so far (Dean 2010, 57).

2. *Self-regulating goals.* Being mindful is serious work. Nobel Prize–winning psychologist Daniel Kahneman teaches us that the cognitive machinery we depend on for monitoring ourselves, for evaluating and calculating all the input and making smart decisions, is superlazy (2012). Paying attention, it turns out, depletes us. And it's hard to imagine a more "effortful mental activity" than writing. Which is why, in the midst of writing this paragraph, I have picked up and put down the water bottle on my desk—for no reason, without taking a drink—half a dozen times. (I even pinched the plastic cap strap and gave it a bite.) Skilled writers are confident they can accomplish what they need to, but they also distrust their own self-control enough to check it with self-regulating strategies.

As I mentioned earlier, students may not think about a writing project till they have to, and then they might binge-write a draft the night before, believing, perhaps, that necessity is the mother of invention. However, we know that this method of cramming—called "massed practice" in learning research—is not as productive as consistent, shorter periods of daily writing that help students achieve a writer's flow (see Brown, Roediger III, and McDaniel 2014). Binge writing has been shown to cause writer's block and even "dysphoria," meaning "general dissatisfaction" in the writing task (Kellogg and Whiteford 2009, 257). We don't want that kind of shade. Self-regulating goals will orient students to a higher, and happier, level of performance.

There are three different kinds of self-regulating goals. Below I use language I share with my own students in documents I give to them (and yes, I give them these citations):

Environmental. Environment goals establish the *when* and *where* of writing. Write down a specific plan for when you'll write and where. Block out time *each day* to write or even just think about your project. Write every day, and then when you get stuck, you can quit without freaking out that the paper's due tomorrow; you'll let your work percolate subconsciously while you do other things (see Benedict Carey's chapter "Quitting before You're Ahead" [in Carey 2014]). Suspending closure can serve as a powerful motivator (Cialdini 2016, 86–88). Choose your writing spot carefully. You want to find a quiet place with as few distractions as possible. Surprisingly, there is some evidence that varying where we write might actually help us make useful mental connections (Carey 2014, 61).

When you sit down to write, turn off your cell phone so it makes no noise at all, or, better yet, put it out of sight. Decide for a period of time that you will be unavailable. There is research showing that the mere presence of a phone, whether on or off, causes "brain drain" (Herrera 2018). Additionally, when you multitask across various screens and programs, you are making more work for yourself, even if you think you can get away with continual partial attention ("Multitasking: Switching Costs" 2014). Even listening to music while writing, especially music with lyrics, can throw you off your writing groove because of your "selective attention" (Hattie and Yates 2014, 191). Just trust Uncle Brian on this one: You'll get more writing done if you're not shifting attention from your words to your phone to an irrelevant web page, unless, of course, you're using your phone to write, read, or research related to your task (which I don't recommend, unless you have to).

Personal (or behavioral). Set a goal to check your own progress—this is called "self-monitoring." Set deadlines for yourself for increments of the work, but adjust them if they don't work for you. Decide how much or for how long you want to write. After each day or writing period, reflect on how well you're doing and decide what you need to do next. Start each new writing session by reading what you wrote last time, making changes as needed. Reward yourself. For example, tell yourself, "As soon as I write 500 words, I'll check sports scores on ESPN," or "If I write for one hour today, I will go buy myself a mango pineapple smoothie."

Social. Talking about your work out loud with anyone willing to listen can be a powerful writing tool. Your instructor will likely assign you to work with peers to review each other's writing. Set a goal to have more people than your peer group review your work. Take your writing to a tutor (in the Writing Center, e.g.) or a trusted roommate, or maybe a family member with some word skills. Set a goal to form a writing group in which the members hold each other accountable for producing a certain amount of writing each week.

* * *

In this chapter, I've argued that we need to spend more time working with students on *planning* their writing tasks as part of an instructional model meant to foster mindfulness. Specifically, for each writing task we assign, we should ask students to assess the task and set goals before they begin prewriting (though surely these planning strategies are a kind of prewriting). We should require students to take these steps through informal writing assignments—in writing journals, for example—that we review in some way without grading for quality. Planning helps writers become self-directed from the beginning, even when their best-laid plans change as the messiness of writing takes over.

PART III

Practice

11
THE ESSENCE OF TEACHING

Buckle up. Here's where my tidy mindfulness theme is going to take a scenic detour. In part I, I described the history and content of writing instruction, metacognition, and the learning cycle. I explained how you can design and organize meaningful tasks, including informal W2L activities, that help students develop mindful writing practices. In part II we jumped right into the learning cycle with planning strategies, including assessing the task and setting goals. So far, so good.

Here in part III, I hope to share with you some teaching strategies you can use to (a) teach students principles from rhetoric and writing studies, and (b) invite them to practice applying those principles to a major writing task (i.e., practice—figure 11.1). In that effort, I will be sharing teaching strategies focused just as much on *your* mindful methods (such as leading class discussion) as the students'. Again, to be mindful you need an activity to monitor and control, and that activity is *rhetorical action.* Teaching writing is an invitation to rhetorical action; the better the teaching, the better the action. So, some of part III will sound much like a standard teaching guide you can consult throughout your career. Still, I hope you'll be able to see the thread of mindfulness woven through the practices I describe here, practices both for you and your students.

TEACHING THE MOONWALK

My daughter Louisa sees this YouTube video of a popstar moonwalking across a stage during a live performance. And just like every other ten-year-old kid who sees the magic glide, she wants to learn how to do it right this second. Luckily her Dad grew up in the 1980s and knows how to breakdance—or at least can't stop insisting he knows how to breakdance. (His breakin' name, back in fourth grade, was *Berzerker.*)

Louisa and I took off our shoes.

I said, "Watch me," and then I moonwalked across the kitchen floor in my socks. "Now you try."

DOI: 10.7330/9781607329374.c011

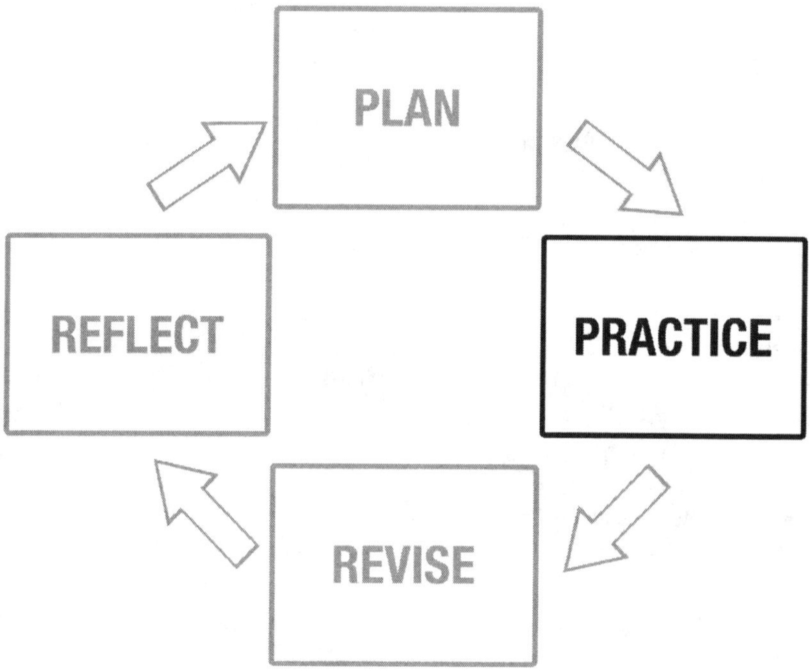

Figure 11.1. The practice stage

Louisa did her first ever moonwalk. It needed work.

"Watch me again," I said. And moonwalked, more slowly now. "Do you see how I end up on my toe each time? Like this?"

"Like this?" said Louisa, moonwalking again, but this time sliding each foot on her toes.

"Close," I said. "Don't come up on your toes till the end of the slide when your foot is back, like this." And I moonwalked again, even more slowly.

"Ah!" she said. "Like this!" And she moonwalked across our floor like a champ.

Doesn't this corny little anecdote somehow get at the essence of learning? Louisa wanted a new power. She found someone—luckily it was Berzerker—to show her how to do it. She gave it a try and received immediate feedback. She adjusted, tried again, got more feedback, adjusted again, then nailed it.

I can imagine a writing class stripped down to this moonwalking lesson. You show the students what they need to write and ask them to analyze the model (genre analysis!). They write it. You give them feedback.

They write again. And so on till they nail it. Everything else that may happen in the classroom is just garnish.

Teaching writing is more complicated than a moonwalking lesson—and of course it should be. I remember sitting down after gathering my first batch of papers as a new teacher and despairing at all the everything they didn't know how to do, the everything that I had not yet taught them—in part because I didn't know how to teach them, in part because I still didn't have the language of expertise with which to tell them. Writing is a multidimensional human activity with a multilevel complexity compounded by an imperfect social matrix. As we've established, it takes more than one shoeless lesson in the kitchen to master it. And what, frankly, does "master" even mean in the context of writing?

In part III I tackle the complicated, multidimensional aspect of daily teaching that gives students opportunities to practice mindfully and receive feedback. I'm imagining here that you have already introduced students to the assignment, they have written informally about its rhetorical situation and genre, and they have set goals. (The necessary caveat: because writing is an imperfect, recursive, idiosyncratic process, you may find that students need to do some of the work of planning in the midst of practice, and vice versa.)

Remember that we are building metacognitive abilities through a self-directed learning cycle of monitoring and controlling that begins with a planning stage. Monitoring and controlling can be complex when we're dealing with a symbolic system that makes meaning on multiple norm-governed levels, from the social purpose down to the semicolon. Students need opportunities to practice getting words on paper while holding in their minds their genre, audience, and purpose (Kellogg 2008). We expect so much from our students, many of whom are in the throes of a neurological conditioning that will not be completed till their mid- to late twenties (Johnson, Blum, and Giedd 2009). Our best longitudinal research shows that students do grow as writers throughout college; however, that growth is not always detectable in a semester or in a clear sequence of powering up, like you do in a video game (Carroll 2002; Haswell 1991; Sommers and Saltz 2004). Because of this complexity, I recommend you reserve instruction and comments on sentence-level stylistics or error for *after* the practice stage. As I say far too often, more on that later.

Part III tries to answer the question, What can I do as a teacher to instruct students on the principles they need to become mindful writers? To answer that question, we'll discuss lesson plans, daily writing, using models, class discussion, collaborative work, and reading. In the practice stage, students put their learning plans and writing theories into action to achieve some kind of social end. Gregory summed up nicely the practice stage of mindful writing: "What students need is time to make mistakes, to correct them, to fail and try again—and they need teachers who can help them view each failure as merely interim, as merely a *halt* in forward progress, not as a terminal judgment on their abilities" (2001, 76, his emphasis).

12

THE LESSON PLAN

The novelist Norman Mailer called writing "the spooky art." Teaching and learning are no less spooky. The outcome is often unpredictable. We cannot be sure that our efforts will yield the results we want. What students take away from our teaching is often not what we had hoped they would. That's still learning. If we want them to be self-directed, then we have to be open to the possibility that they will repurpose what we've given them for their own goals, sometimes in ways that we may find frustrating. It's misguided of me to be so overdetermined as a teacher. Let a thousand flowers bloom.

On the other hand, the best teaching, like the best writing, is goal directed. Our courses are nested in outcomes: outcomes for the university at large, for general education, for the department, for the course. And then for each assignment there are more outcomes. At this point the word *outcomes* might turn your stomach. Nevertheless: Each time you meet with students, you should have a purpose—an objective you want them to achieve by the end of the day, whether they end up achieving it or not. What do you want your students to be able to do? Or understand? In about an hour? And how does the day's outcome mirror, support, and strengthen the outcomes leading all the way back up the outcome chain?

We've already established ourselves (in chapter 6) as architects of learning who reverse engineer a series of classroom interventions that build students' abilities to complete a major writing task mindfully, and incrementally. Before you focus on daily *teaching techniques*, as Dee Fink calls them, you'll need to understand the *teaching strategy* for the major writing task and how it breaks down into a series of "knowables" and "doables" that you work on each class period. We've established that this "backward design" or "beginning with the end in mind" is an essential component of designing learning (Davis 2009; Fink 2003; Hattie 2012; Wiggins and McTighe 2005). Remember, from Wiggins and McTighe's *Understanding by Design*, that we begin with desired outcomes, imagine what kind of evidence (i.e., student writing) would demonstrate that

DOI: 10.7330/9781607329374.c012

those desired outcomes were achieved, and then set up learning experiences to support those goals. Daily lessons fit into this master plan as tactics supporting the Big Strategy.

By the practice stage, students have analyzed the target genre—let's say it's an opinion editorial—so they should have a sense of the range of the available means of persuasion. If, for example, they've read more than a dozen or so published op-eds, they may have noticed the way in which some writers use personal experience, humor, brief paragraphs of no more than three sentences, other internet sources for support (included as embedded links, not a "works cited" page); they may have also noticed, most of the time but not always, the prevalence of a little thing we call "opinion," voiced firmly and with the kind of A, B, C support we see in other genres like timed essays. This analysis has been part of their metacognitive habituation. After all that analysis, what do students need to learn to be able to write their op-eds?

It depends on you or your program's outcomes and interests. Let's say you have adopted for an outcome the following from the "WPA Outcomes Statement":

> By the end of first-year composition, students should learn and use key rhetorical concepts through analyzing and composing a variety of texts.

You see how the words *learn* and *use* reflect the Bloom terms we mentioned in a previous chapter: specifically, *understand* and *apply*. Let's say in this scenario you want to introduce the students to *ethos* as a key rhetorical concept (threshold concept: "writing enacts and creates identities and ideologies") because you want them to build their credibility mindfully as they write their op-ed.

We're now approaching an objective for the day:

> Today in class, students will understand the key term *ethos*—specifically credibility—and apply strategies of ethos to their op-ed.

The objective then becomes the governing principle for the day's lesson plan. Most of the media, the discussions, the questions, and the practices should reinforce this power in the students. They should leave the classroom understanding (again, in the mindful sense) *ethos* and knowing how to build credibility in their own writing.

Once your objective is established, you plan your day by writing out an actual lesson plan to follow. Lesson planning, while not a particularly exciting subject to talk about, is the essence of design thinking and learning. In my experience doing observations, instructors often overestimate their ability to deliver significant learning by the Seat-of-the-Pants method or the I-Just-Show-Up-and-the-Magic-Happens method. This last year we learned that some of our second-year grad instructors were telling the first-year instructors during in-service meetings that, having taught the course twice, they didn't need to write lesson plans anymore because they knew what they were doing.

Balderdash. Unless you are a gifted impromptu teacher, you need to design a day's teaching with a significant end in mind and activities that support that end. Without a class goal and a plan to achieve it, we're not empowering our students with the dispositions they need to be mindful writers. Save the improv for the Upright Citizens Brigade. I suspect that those who teach without lesson plans are teaching favorite readings, video clips, or cherished activities instead of students. Remember Wiggins and McTighe's warning against the "twin sins" of lousy instruction: activity-oriented instruction (fun, cool stuff leading nowhere important!) and coverage instruction (gotta get through all this stuff or we'll get cancer and die!) (2005, 16).

A lesson plan can take a variety of forms. In the 1980s Madeline Hunter, a UCLA education professor and one of the most influential thinkers on education in American history, proposed an eight-step lesson design that became so entrenched that she herself had to repudiate it in *English Journal* (Hunter 1989). More recently, in *Understanding by Design*, Wiggins and McTighe suggest seven parts of instructional planning that reflect quite nicely the self-directed writing model I've presented here (2005, 197–98). Granted, these two sources are more popular with K–12 teachers, but they are based on sound principles of learning design that apply just as well to emerging adult and adult learners. Wiggins and McTighe, specifically, use these principles in workshops with college professors across the disciplines.

MAPPING OUT THE LESSON

Considering these and other sources on designing learning, I suggest the following sequence for lesson plans, with one *big* reservation, which I will express now. Learning is organic; it grows from the needs of students in a specific learning context and with the help of a teacher's own brand of teaching skills. There's no formal recipe. As Madeline Hunter (1989) warned, any model of learning design should not be followed slavishly and without concern for the needs, goals, and talents of you and your students. Just recently, while in the thick of a research task, I showed up to class with a lesson plan on argument and evidence, and I discovered to my dismay that the students were still wrestling with their topics, for goodness sakes. That lesson plan went into the bin, and instead I had to reinforce a previous lesson on finding narrow and timely topics.

The Big Question the lesson plan answers is, *What activities should I do in class to help students achieve X?* Here, then, are seven possible components for effective lesson plans:

1. *Objective.* What do you want your writers to learn in the lesson? The goal should support the class outcomes. Today's goal is *students will understand the key term* ethos*—specifically, credibility—and apply strategies of ethos to their op-ed.* During a class period, students should know the objective and why it's important to them. You could write it on the board (after the "hook," see no. 3) and explain how learning the concept will help them as writers.
2. *Homework.* Assign homework—writing and reading—that will help students learn the principle and its application, so they come to class primed. You can see how impossible this sequence may seem the first time you teach, when, out of necessity and scarce time, you end up assigning a text you haven't read for reasons you can't begin to guess. (I'll say more about reading homework a little later.) It's okay. This will come with time. Ideally, we will assign texts not merely because we like them or need to cover material but because we want students to learn a specific principle. As homework, we'll assign students brief reading and writing activities to cue prior knowledge and teach principles.
3. *Hook.* Begin the lesson with some kind of hook—an image, a video clip, a good story, a problem or question, a writing activity—to engage students in the work of the day. I'm a firm believer in taking the first few moments of a lesson to cue the "pleasure brain" (Bain 2012, 82–85). However, recently I learned from cognitive psychologist Daniel Willingham that I've been using hooks ineffectively over the years. He warns us that attention grabbers work only if they get students thinking *beyond* them, to the goal of the lesson (2009, 80–81). For example, for the ethos lesson I have shown students that part in *The Lego Movie* when Emmet, the accidental hero, gives a speech before all the Master Builders in which his clumsy self-deprecation destroys any chance of convincing his audience of his point. After having read Willingham, now I'm concerned that the example, though hilarious, is too obvious, or maybe too distracting. We engage with content more deeply when it is presented to us as a "conflict" (2009, 84) or a "messy problem" (Bain 2012, 133). An opening story left unresolved can also be a powerful cognitive engine. The hook primes the students to the engaging value of the day's lesson. James Lang suggests that we spend time at the beginning of each class inviting students to (a) review, retrieve, or reconstruct something they have learned previously in class, or (b) predict, based on reading or homework or past classes, what today's lesson will help them do (2016, 53, 83).
4. *Instruction/Discussion.* This next part answers the question, What key concepts or skills do students need to understand to achieve the

objective? For this lesson, students need to understand what *ethos* is and how a writer can construct it while writing an op-ed. In the instruction phase, we often break down a concept such as ethos into subcategories: a definition, for starters, and then two to three varieties in which ethos presents itself (credibility, shared values, experience, etc.). When we think of teaching broadly, we often think of instruction, and we think of it unidirectionally—teacher talks, students listen. But you already know from experience that monologues knock out the lights in students' eyes. Keep direct instruction short and clear. Ask questions to make sure students understand the principles the way you want them to. Texts can teach, and students can teach each other. Full-class discussions fall under the instruction portion, if the point is to help students develop declarative knowledge on rhetoric and writing topics. Remember that instruction is meant to move students to an understanding of *why* a principle is important to them as writers and *when* and *how* it can be applied fruitfully. Only then will it reinforce our learning cycle for mindful writers.

5. *Modeling.* After you've taught the principle for understanding, show students how the principle works in real-life texts. Maybe this is the homework you assigned. Maybe you bring a handout or project an additional text to reinforce the principle. For the ethos objective, I might assign Amy Chua's incendiary article in the *Wall Street Journal* "Why Chinese Mothers are Superior" (2011) (if I can find a way to breach the stinkin' paywall), so we can talk about the way she constructs her credibility effectively, and not. Or, more usefully, I might show them how students like themselves from previous classes have constructed their ethos. Modeling is one of the most effective strategies for teaching writing that we have (see chapter 14). With practice (next step), it makes up the one-two instruction model I suggested with the moonwalking anecdote.
6. *Practice.* Madeline Hunter divided this portion of the lesson into "guided" and "independent" practice ("The Madeline Hunter Model"). The difference, I think, is that guided practice receives immediate feedback. If the students are working on evaluating ethos in a text or if they're starting to practice developing credibility themselves in draft writing, you stop the work and ask a few of them to report and give them feedback on the fly in front of the class (or in one of those more private but surely awkward whisper sessions while crouched by a student's desk). That's guided practice. Independent practice is when students work on their own or in groups without us interfering. Either way, at some point in the lesson, you'll want students to take off their shoes and try that moonwalk themselves. This is *key*. I've seen so many teaching sessions that are wonderful in about every way other than this: The instructor did not give students time to practice the writing strategies they discussed so passionately in class.
7. *Connection and closure.* This is the moment when metacognition takes over. You want students to think about what they've learned, ask themselves whether they've learned it thoroughly enough to practice it, and

anticipate how what they've learned can be used for the major writing task or other settings. You can do this in a brief class discussion in the last five minutes or ask them to write a "one-minute paper" (Light 2001) or an "exit ticket" (Lemov 2010) that asks students to reflect on what they've learned and what they still don't understand. This brief reflective component reminds the students to be mindful learners of writing as well as mindful writers.

Again, this model is not the end-all, be-all. There will be many days when you do not follow this model because you're answering the "How do I help students do X?" question differently. Doug Hesse shares five different ways he spends class time to help students do X, and only some of them would be open to this lesson plan model. For example, his "presentation/application/demonstration" class is a good fit, as is "class invention or revising." But he also reserves class periods for "open studio time," in which students work on their own projects and he circulates (2014, 62–63). Sometimes I will follow the above lesson model for about fifteen minutes and then let students take the rest of class to practice what we just talked about. Hesse calls this "focused studio/problem solving."

No matter what you pick for the day's architecture, budget your time wisely. I feel like such a hypocrite saying that. I can be profoundly lousy at managing class time. I can blow through ten minutes on housekeeping issues (e.g., features of the LMS or how to set up peer review for the Nth time) without meaning to. When I get excited because students are excited about a text, I keep discussions going even though I know the students need time to process and practice. In effective lesson plans I've reviewed, instructors write out the precise minutes (overdetermined!) they want to spend on each of the categories above (e.g., "Instruction—5 Minutes"). Even if the time frames are squishy, I find that if I stick to my lesson plan, I'll at least get to the most important parts of the lesson: specifically, modeling and practicing.

"Ants are creatures of little strength," says the Proverb, "yet they store up their food in the summer." Writing lesson plans your first semester teaching is kind of like storing extra food you can use when you teach again—up-front intensive labor that frees your future self. Next time you teach that lesson, you can be more mindful in your approach, watching the students' responses and making revisions to the plan to suit their needs. The lesson plan invites us to be accountable for moving students in the direction of growth rather than merely spending a pleasant hour with them.

AN EXAMPLE OF A LESSON PLAN

I used to write out all my lesson plans on 4 × 6 cards. But problems with this method persist: The cards are not searchable, they take up space in my filing cabinets, and frankly I forget where I've stored them. So I've moved to using Google Drive for all my lesson plans. I type them up before class and print them on a single page I take with me to class. The next time I teach the same course, I review the lesson and make necessary adjustments.

Although I hesitate to provide examples that I do not consider exemplary or universal, here's what a fifty-minute lesson plan might look like for the *ethos* day we talked about above.

Table 12.1. An example of a lesson plan

Objective	Students will understand the key term *ethos*—specifically, credibility—and apply strategies of ethos to their op ed.
Homework	*Reading*. Students read chapter 8 of textbook on ethos and Amy Chua's *WSJ* article "Why Chinese Mothers are Superior"; *Writing:* In around 300 words, and citing specific instances in the text, describe how Chua establishes her ethos in this article using at least two key terms from our chapter.
Hook	*5 mins*. Show video of Emmet from *The Lego Movie*. Project slide with writing prompt: "Considering what we read for homework today, how could we help poor Emmet use strategies of ethos more effectively?" OR, No video clip. Project slide with writing prompt: "Considering our writing task, what is the goal of today's lesson?" Call on two students to share what they've written.
Instruction/ Discussion	*10 mins*. Write today's objective on board or on slide. Today's lesson (I'll explain): understanding *ethos* as a key term in rhetoric and practicing how to apply strategies of ethos in your op-ed. Pair up (or form groups of three) and share what you wrote for homework today about Chua. As a group, identify one place in the text Chua establishes credibility and one place where she develops a relationship with her audience (the text has three substrategies for each). Students discuss in groups, I circulate. *5 mins:* Full-class discussion. I cold-call groups. Ask what they discussed. With textbook open, we establish the substrategies under credibility and relationship. I ask follow-up questions inviting students to anticipate audience response or evaluate the effectiveness of Chua. I ask, Do we want to model our own ethos strategies on Chua's? Why or why not?
Modeling	*10 mins*. Give students draft of previous student successful op-ed with a particularly compelling ethos. Ask students to identify ethos strategies—either in pairs or whole class.
Practice	*15 mins*. Ask students to open their op-ed drafts on laptops or in notebooks. Write (or rewrite) 2–3 new paragraphs in which you practice 1–2 strategies of ethos. If time, they can share what they wrote with a partner and ask for feedback. They could discuss why the revised or new paragraphs are more effective than the first draft in using ethos to convince an audience.
Connection and Closure	*5 mins*. Project slide with writing prompt—have students write on something they can turn in: (1) In the future you'll have to write less-opinionated papers for classes such as exercise science or business management. What role will ethos play in those kinds of papers? (2) What is one thing you're still confused about or frustrated with at the end of this lesson?

13
DAILY WRITING

One of the worst books of all time to read to a child is the Berenstain Bears' *The Bike Lesson.* When I was a kid and mom read it to me, I despised it with little boy passion. Daddy Bear—a cocky blowhard who pretends to know everything but knows nothing, about camping or science or yardwork or anything—teaches Son Bear how to ride a bike by riding it around himself and crashing into everything, while the kid runs helplessly after him, begging, "Can I ride it now?" And Daddy Bear just keeps pedaling, his eyes closed, one pedantic finger in the air: "Not yet, not yet./Before you do/I'll have to give you/lesson two." In lesson two, he nearly decapitates himself with a tree branch.

In a writing class, we write. Yes, we talk of writing, we rejoice in writing, we preach of writing—but then we write. We do not want to give our students lessons without letting them get on that bike and pedal.

While running a writing program, I interviewed potential graduate instructors, and I would ask, "If I stopped by your classroom on a random day, what would I see?" Any answer to this question could be interesting. The answers I most appreciated were the ones that mentioned *student writing.* I would want to see students talking about writing, analyzing writing, and writing. Writing is how students put into practice the rhetorical principles we teach. Writing provides the raw materials of the monitoring and control process of metacognition.

But writing *what?* As we established in chapter 7, we can divide all the writing students do in our class into two major categories: the major tasks (longer genres that go through a process and get evaluated, often as stand-alone performances) and the minor tasks, which have been called writing-to-learn (W2L) activities. This chapter is about how you can use W2L—the daily in-class (or online) low-stakes writing—in two ways: (1) as part of the mindful workflow of a major writing task (Task W2L), and (2) as writing-to-learn activities that build metacognitive skills (Content or Metacognitive W2L).

DOI: 10.7330/9781607329374.c013

TASK W2L

We write in a complicated environment of meaning. If we give students meaningful assignments, they should feel like writers writing in a social scene to merge their purposes with the purposes of a reader. We call this scene the *rhetorical situation.* As words appear on page or screen, they join a constellation of meanings from the social level (i.e., real people trying to talk to each other) all the way down to the syntax of a sentence. As I'm writing these specific words—lining them up in nice little rows one-sixth inch tall—I'm thinking of you, dear reader-teacher, while at the same time, somehow, trying to think about how I'm going to finish this sentence. This rhetorical situation both inspires and constrains me; when I let it, it also terrifies me.

Writing research shows us that professional writers engage more purposefully than novices with this hierarchy of composing. They start the process with a deep engagement with the needs of an audience and the tacit expertise of text types that we call genres (Hillocks 1996; Kellogg 2008; McCutchen, Teske, and Bankston 2008). This is why in the learning cycle for mindful writers we begin with planning—assessing the task and setting goals—before students have written a word of what we often call "prewriting," which often means some kind of brainstorming for the specific content of what needs to be written.

It turns out that process is much more complicated than my learning cycle suggests, with its fairly straightforward arrows going in one direction. In reality, and as plenty of research has shown, the writing process is a recursive, idiosyncratic activity influenced by the skills of the writer and the demands of a "constantly changing, contingently organized social world" (Bazerman 2016, 18). However, novice students need our help "to become," in the words of Chris Anson, "more conscious of themselves as writers and the strategies they use to produce text" (Anson 2014, 226). We want students to get used to composing with a firm orientation to the social goals they're trying to achieve, the audience whose judgment they want to influence, and the genres used in the discourse community they participate in—all before they make little bubble webs on a piece of paper with "the effects of social media" written in the middle.

We can help students through the composing process by assigning Task W2Ls—short ungraded writing activities they can do in class (or outside as homework) that will help them build up to a product they hope to release in the social wild. Here are a few practices you may consider doing for Task W2Ls after your students have assessed the task and set goals. Remember that the genre should dictate the kind of Task W2Ls that will work best.

Content Discovery

George Hillocks makes the strong case that we do not teach "basic strategies of inquiry" enough when we teach FYW (1996, 100). By that term he means all the activities we do to help students build curiosity, understanding, and substantive content knowledge. Students have been conditioned by standardized tests to do "top-of-my-head" writing. Imagine walking down the street and being ambushed by a guy with a microphone (Billy Eichner, for example), a camera operator behind him pointing the lens at you. The guy shoves the mic in front of your lips and asks, "What do you think about a possible trade war with China?" The red *record* light blips on. That's how students are often asked to write.

We don't have time to build students' content knowledge in specific disciplines so they can write like experts. Inquiry activities as Hillocks has imagined them do not require a specific field of expertise, nor are they confined solely to research projects. To a great extent *all* writing engages us in inquiry—in reading, wondering, asking, observing, remembering, searching, interpreting. Educator Debbie Dean talks about her experience reading Mary Roach's book *Stiff* and discovering how many inquiry methods Roach used in her book, from doing a web search on being buried alive to attending a business meeting on composting in Sweden (Dean 2010, 126–27). Inquiry activities invite students to think of writing as an ongoing act of discovery that makes us emotionally engaged and intellectually attuned to the work. Here are a few inquiry activities you might try as W2L activities in FYW or any writing course:

Cue prior learning. Ask students to write about experiences they've had with the subject they want to write about. What do they know about it, and how do they know? What are their relevant assumptions, values, and personal experiences?

Definitions. Have students write definitions for key terms related to the topic. They can think of these terms as "working definitions" that likely will be revised as they draft.

Predictions. Have students write predictions of what they might discover as they write. Ask them to write a "What I Believe about X" statement before a project. They should feel comfortable with the idea that what they believe might be significantly challenged during the project.

Imagining. Hillocks suggests that "what if" thinking/writing can help students discover "developing arguments from various perspectives; role playing to invent characters and their actions in problem situations; writing about being in an imaginary place under certain conditions; writing from the point of view of a literary character or of some inanimate object; playing various games, including signifying, to develop metaphor" (1996, 105–6). I had a student once who wanted to write about what he considered "frivolous lawsuits," and he wanted to use as evidence the case of Stella Liebeck, who sued McDonald's after spilling hot coffee on her lap at the drive-thru. I encouraged him to read the medical report from the incident and imagine the encounter from Liebeck's perspective before he did his research.

Observing or interviewing. You can ask students to take a notebook with them and go see something or interview someone early in their inquiry. One recent semester I asked students to interview at least one person on the topic they'd chosen. Some students took the easy route and interviewed other students on their dorm floor; other students found experts in the campus community or from back home for their interviews.

Interests. Often with open prompts, students don't know what to write about. And often, we will let them write about things that interest them personally. They can become anthropologists of themselves by writing briefly about who they are, what their values and goals are, what they like to do, how they affiliate or identify with various groups. Exploring the self may help them find connections to the writing they need to do.

Google it. No one has time to read every book on a topic. Somewhat aimless web searches can illuminate the terrain. Foraging leads to the cache. Ask students to look up definitions or key terms and jot down what they find. The "Google It" method gets students into the background literature on an issue, which also could be accomplished with books or magazines or online articles.

Invention

Content discovery is an open starting point for topic exploration; invention brings discovery to the rhetorical situation. One of the classical five canons of rhetoric (with arrangement, style, memory, and delivery), invention is the intellectual process of discovering the most successful path to influencing an audience. In fact, Aristotle defined rhetoric not as persuasion but as "the ability, in each particular case, to see the available means of persuasion" (2007, 37). Technically, invention begins when an exigence calls us to speak or write. We start to think about our rhetorical goal—what we want our audience to feel, think, believe, or do based on what we say. For decades, writing teachers have tapped into the classical tradition and a variety of (often competing) cognitive theories to create what Janice Lauer calls "invention pedagogies" or approaches to helping students explore a topic and come up with things to say (2004, 120). In monitoring terms, we know invention strategies are working when they produce ideas we perceive as promising.

Some invention pedagogies are *structured* and others *unstructured.* Using both methods helps teachers and students explore the range of results these strategies yield.

Structured invention. Structured invention strategies invite students to use established *heuristics* or set approaches for generating writing ideas. For example, students can answer the standard "journalistic" questions about their topic: who, what, where, when, why, and how. A more advanced heuristic, taken from classical rhetorical principles called *topoi,* invites students to approach their topic from a variety of frames that reflect the way we organize knowledge and experience. Some examples include definition (What is this thing? How is it classified?), degree (How much or how intense is this thing?), time (When did this thing start? Where are we now?), comparison (What is this thing like? How is it related to other things?), cause or consequence (What happens because of this thing? Who is affected, and how?), authority (Who speaks about this? Who are the experts or stakeholders?), value (Is this thing good or bad? How is this thing valued or evaluated?), or possibility (What can be changed about this thing?). Give students a list of these question categories and ask them to barrage their topic with questions—preferably questions to which they don't know the answer.

Unstructured invention. Every handbook, textbook, and writing guide for FYW will have lists of these practices: freewriting, clustering, brainstorming, or looping. Google them. They all have in common the pedagogical assumption that ideas can be generated most effectively when we shut off the editor and free-associate. Freewriting, popularized by Peter Elbow, prompts students to "just start writing" and never stop for four to five straight minutes, even if their hands are quaking and the students have no ideas. Freewriting reminds me of American novelist Jack Kerouac's kooky, almost incoherent advice about writing "'without consciousness' in semitrance . . . allowing subconscious to admit in own uninhibited interesting necessary . . . language what conscious art would censor, and write excitedly, swiftly, with writing-or-typing-cramps" (1995, 58). Start a class period by asking students to freewrite on their current writing task, ignoring the insatiable needs of the inner editor so they can free-associate about their work. Sometimes when they finish, I ask them to read over what they've written and circle, underline, or question what they see there, to explore what might be a promising direction.

Incremental Composing

Arrangement, another canon of rhetoric, means "organization," or how a text unfolds in time and space—in the air, on the page, or on the screen. Classical arrangements were based on public discourse types that required speakers to state a point and support it. As the centuries rolled on, rhetoric manuals prescribed four or six or more parts to a speech and gave each part a name and discourse function (like *narratio* or *confutatio*). These divisions are still useful, sort of, for generic academic writing, like the five-paragraph essay. We could make good money showing essay-test-writing pupils how to write flash essays about global trade wars using this model. By contrast, modern arrangement strategies tend to focus on the way genres afford and constrain the order in which we present material. Visual and multimodal rhetoric make the words "compose" and "arrange" even more difficult to pin down outside the study of specific genres (Fahnestock 2001).

You can lead students through a major task by prompting them to tackle it *incrementally* based on the arrangement scheme required by the genre. For example, if you're using a traditional academic genre, you can ask them to draft an outline of how the writing might unfold; that's not an exciting practice, but some research supports it as an effective writing strategy (Hayes 2006; Kellogg 2008). If you use the modeling method I describe in the next chapter, you can show students an effective thesis and then ask them to draft one and share it with a peer. After the thesis, do the same with an intro. After the intro, do the same with a few body paragraphs.

When my first-year students write researched conference papers, I introduce them to the "create a research space" method of introductions, developed by John Swales and used by some writing teachers to teach students how to read scholarly genres (Wardle and Downs 2017). I show them a few examples, identify the three moves that introductions make (*roughly*: present the state of the conversation on a subject, pose a question or a gap in the research, and then fill that gap by presenting a thesis or current question explored in the article), and then invite them to imitate those moves in their conference paper. Students draft introductions and share them with each other, looking for those moves and offering feedback.

You do not need to look at all your students' incremental writing. If you've shown them effective models, taught them rhetorical principles, and then asked them to share with peers for feedback, you've given them significantly more than what they would have normally received while struggling through a paper. Of course, your feedback will make W2L writing more meaningful to them. You'll also be able to steer the writing at an early stage when changes are easiest, which is so important for longer research projects.

The point, finally, of Task W2Ls is to let student writers beta-test ideas and first attempts in small chunks so that revision will be easier and more iterative, and not "locked in the stage-process paradigm" that calls for revision only after significant writing has been completed (Dryer and Russell 2017, 60). Any time you ask students to arrest and investigate process, you help them build metacognitive skills.

Drafting in Class

On some days, I will give students the first fifteen minutes or more of class to work on their drafts. No further instruction: Just keep working on those drafts. I then circulate and talk with any student who wants to talk to me about their project.

METACOGNITIVE W2L

Let's revisit chapter 2 briefly. I argued that mindfulness is a purposeful, deliberate awareness of what we are doing and how we could do it better. Through metacognitive habituation to this awareness, writers learn how to take control of their writing tasks and become self-directed, mindful learners. I noted that metacognition has been listed in the "Framework for Success in Postsecondary Writing," along with other attributes—openness, responsibility, flexibility, and the like—as a desired outcome of FYW. Drawing from cognitive research, I defined *metacognition* as the act of monitoring and controlling your own activity.

Howard Tinberg has written that metacognition is "the ability to perceive the very steps by which success occurs and to articulate the various qualities and components that contribute in significant ways to the production of effective writing" (2015, 76). This ability is motivated by, constructed in, and exercised in a social milieu; we write in our bodies, among other bodies, to connect with other bodies (Portanova, Rifenburg, and Roen 2017). And finally—from research by Rebecca Nowacek, Kathleen Yancey, Liane Robertson, Kara Taczak, and others—it seems that metacognitive abilities give students rhetorical power to move across writing tasks more effectively. Metacognition makes the transfer of writing habits possible.

We can use almost-daily informal writing activities in FYW as opportunities for metacognitive habituation as students practice applying rhetorical principles in drafts. To be clear, we apply metacognitive W2L activities from the very beginning, when students start thinking about their past writing experiences (say, on the first day of class), developing a theory of writing (see Yancey, Robertson, and Taczak 2014), and doing the planning activities we talked about in part I. They will also do this kind of writing after completing a major writing task to review what they've learned and prepare for the next task. In other words, informal reflective writing is integrated throughout the course. In this section, I'll share a few ways you can use metacognitive W2L activities in the *practice* stage, as students learn rhetorical principles and put them into action. (I'll discuss several other metacognitive W2L activities in chapter 17, on reading.)

Theories of writing and rhetoric. In the Teaching for Transfer model, Yancey, Robertson, and Taczak require their students to develop their theory of writing at least ten times during the semester (2014, 58). Ask students to write about the process they are using to complete the draft. During a major writing task, students will learn key terms for rhetorical strategies (e.g., argument). Ask students to analyze the value of those strategies—what they are meant to accomplish, for whom, and why. Ask them to reflect on their experience writing and what it has taught them about themselves as writers. In my experience, students need a good definition of *theory* to understand what we're asking them. I tell them that a theory is a set of assumptions, ideas, or values that help us understand something or do something. Theories reflect what we believe about the world and its various systems of knowing and doing.

Audience analysis. At various points in the writing process, ask students to describe their audience, imagining their interests and attitudes. Ask them to describe the ideal audience for their writing—the kind most susceptible to the strategies they've selected. Ask them to describe the strategies they will use to influence the judgment of the audience.

Make connections. As they learn rhetorical principles (like genre), invite them to describe how they see those principles at work in other classes or in their personal lives.

Revisit the plan. As they complete a draft, they may find that their original understanding, as articulated in the planning they did, has shifted. What might that look like? Ask them to write for two to three minutes on how their plans have changed as a result of constructing knowledge in writing. You could also ask them to answer the question, What am I struggling with the most right now?

Defend your decisions. Ask students to defend their rhetorical decisions. For example, once the students have drafted an argument for a persuasive essay, ask them to write about why they chose the reasons they did or why they organized the essay in the order they did.

Explain to an outsider. If they're learning a new rhetorical principle and you want them to check their content knowledge, ask them to explain it in writing to someone unfamiliar with rhetorical theory.

Review to apply. Ask students to review their notes or what they learned that day and write a list of two to three things they will do to apply what they've learned to the current writing task. (As with the other activities I list here, this one can be done collaboratively.)

The "one minute" paper. At the end of class, with just 1–2 minutes left, ask students to answer some or all of the following questions on a sheet of paper they can turn in before walking out the door: (1) What's the most important thing you learned about writing today (or this week)? (2) At what moment did you feel most engaged? Least? (3) What did I, your writing teacher, do today that helped you the most? Helped you least? (4) What is the "main unanswered question you leave class with today?" (Light 2001, 66; see also Brookfield 2006, 42–43). Brookfield suggests, quite wisely, that we find ways to give these reflective papers back to students at the end of the semester so they can review them for more expansive reflection activities.

THE TOOLS OF DAILY WRITING

Writing is a technology, and we write *through* technologies and various media. Writing technologies simultaneously open up and constrain our meaning making (Brooke and Grabill 2015).

I do not want to prescribe any kind of technology for daily writing activities. Many FYW scholars have for years encouraged journal writing in physical notebooks that can be checked periodically. The idea of the journal is powerful, and old school. Greek and Roman rhetoricians-to-be were encouraged to keep "commonplace" notebooks full of their exercises, quotes, and imitations. Ralph Waldo Emerson, the most famous public intellectual in America in the nineteenth century, kept a writing journal for sixty years "for the habit of rendering account to yourself of yourself," he wrote (Richardson 2009, 19). I like the idea of having a physical journal because of what it communicates: a *writing* journal, for a writer, who may at any moment start writing!

Many students write so much faster on keyboards that they'd prefer to write on computers. For this reason, and because I use Google Drive so frequently, I prefer to have students write on laptops, even with the obvious—and research proven—risks of distraction for the writer and for those sitting behind who see the student looking at pictures of dogs on Pinterest (Dynarski 2017; Ravizza, Uitvlugt, and Fenn 2017). Even with its drawbacks, I want them to write in the ecology of technology they already belong to (though I wouldn't recommend students write anything long and important on a phone). In my laptop-rich classroom, I do find myself pacing around the class, trying to get close to the students to keep them focused. Their—or, more honestly, *all our*—tendency toward distraction makes me want to be a better, more engaged teacher.

14

MODELS (OR HOW TO TEACH ANYTHING)

GOOD TEACHING ON THE VERGE OF GREAT

One year I observed two teachers back to back who exemplified the best and not-as-best of rookie teaching. Both writing instructors were in their second semester, which means they'd taught the course only once before. One teacher was a returning student who had raised children and wanted to pursue her passion for creative writing in our MFA program. The other had come back to the academy after a stint as a border patrol officer and planned to get a PhD in American literature. The first teacher was soft-spoken but focused, the second more chummy and jokey, and in both cases their teaching ethos worked nicely. Both, serendipitously, had assigned the students to read George Orwell's "Politics and the English Language" the day I observed. Both cared deeply about teaching and wanted their students to have a good experience.

And both assumed the students were getting more from their instruction then perhaps they were.

The first teacher was preparing students to write a rhetorical analysis. She started class with ten minutes of silent journal writing from a prompt based on the day's reading. Then she led a full-class volunteer discussion (see the next chapter) on what could be called rhetorical semantics—the way words have connotations that reflect the value systems of the people who use them. She wrote the word *patriotism* on the board and asked the students what it meant. They had a variety of answers, none satisfactory to everyone in the class, which was the point. From the back of the room I could see how some of the students struggled with productive dissonance. Does patriotism connote loyalty, or resistance? In the last twenty minutes of class, the teacher led a conversation about the powerful metaphors Orwell uses in his article—ostensibly to introduce the students to the power of style. To conclude, she showed the students a slide with an excerpt from Dickens's novel *Little Dorrit* as an example of effective writing style.

DOI: 10.7330/9781607329374.c014

The second teacher's class started with a student presenting what I assumed was a recurring feature: "Read Good Writing." This particular student had chosen a sample from Dr. Seuss's *Oh, the Places You'll Go!*, a somewhat schmaltzy choice that generated a surprising amount of chatter and appreciation from the class. Seated at the front—a rarity, since most instructors I observe stand for most of the class period—the teacher then introduced the next activity: *Fight Club.*

I've seen this kind of lesson several times over the years, and I never get sick of it. The students wrote their working thesis at the top of a blank piece of paper and taped it to the wall. Then everyone stood up and wandered around the room, picking fights with theses by writing counterarguments or questions on the blank space beneath them. Like the first teacher, the second one ended class with a passionate discussion about style, using a few examples from the class reading (an essay on golf by A. A. Milne) and inviting students to share what they liked about the examples.

In both instances, the assumption seems to have been that a spirited, but somewhat generic and intuitive, conversation about a writing principle—diction or style or counterarguments—would lodge that principle into the minds of the students. Since both teachers had set up an active lesson, the students played along nicely with this plan. When I talked to each instructor afterward, they both pinpointed (accurately, I think) the "magic moment"—that moment in class when all the students were leaning in, when the room was abuzz with learning.

And I agreed with them, to a point. The students were indeed engaged while talking about patriotism or offering counterarguments. I wondered, however, what would happen when the students got back to the dorm that evening and cracked open the laptop and started writing. What would they remember from the lesson? What "trained capacity," to use John Dewey's term, could they now use as writers? It seems the teachers assumed that an exciting full-class discussion on a principle, with active student engagement, was enough to empower the students with a new skill. The discussion was meant to embed a writing protocol meant to be practiced outside class.

In no way am I faulting either instructor for this. They were both fantastic teachers. The students participated energetically in both classes, and, considering the professional circumstances, that may well be the best we can expect. We habitually hire people to teach writing who (a) never taught before, (b) have little professional interest or ability to teach, (c) have no training or coursework in rhetoric or the English language, and (d) are often not confident writers themselves.

Of course, this says more about college writing as an industry than the folks we hire; efficiency covereth a multitude of sins. I'm saying that with all those constraints in mind, it's delightful that we get teachers like these with energy, passion, and intuitional creativity. If I have to choose between passion or knowledge in a teacher, I'm going with passion. But we want both.

What was missing, in both cases, was a method for teaching a specific rhetorical principle: a clear outcome (otherwise, remember, we commit the "activity-oriented" sin), key terms for the students to abstract from examples, a sense of scaffolding (this first, then this builds on that, then etc.), and, most important, an opportunity for students to practice what they'd learned. There is no learning without practice. Over the years, and through the 300 or so class lessons I've observed, I have come to understand how you can change a student's attitude about a concept (like style) without actually giving that student the trained capacity to use that concept, effectively or at all.

Empowerment comes from practice. One of the easiest ways to get students practicing is to follow the "moonwalking" pedagogy I mentioned in chapter 11: provide a model, invite students to practice with that model in mind, and give feedback.

TEACHING WITH MODELS

In 1986 when he wrote his monumental study *Research on Written Composition*, George Hillocks suggested that the research on "the study of models" (examples of writing strategies) as a teaching practice was mixed (1986, 155). However, later in the book he seems to suggest that the problem isn't teaching with models but teaching models in a unidirectional lecture, in which "the instructor dominates all activity, with student acting as the passive recipients of rules, advice, and examples of good writing" (246). Yes, that sounds dreadful. We'll have more success, the research suggests, if we "plan and use activities which result in high levels of student interaction concerning particular problems parallel to those they encounter in certain kinds of writing"—specifically, in models they want to emulate (247).

Subsequent research on models, imitation, and genre analysis supports the conclusion that teaching with models—called "mentor texts" in the secondary school literature (Gallagher 2011; Marchetti and O'Dell 2015)—is one of the best teaching strategies we have (Devitt 2014; Graham, Harris, and Chambers 2016). Think back to my moonwalking moment with my daughter. The student wanted a new power (moonwalking). The student saw that new power displayed (by an amateur moonwalker). She then practiced what she'd seen and was given feedback related to how successfully she followed the model. This kind of teaching could happen almost every day in a writing class.

Modeling is perhaps the most important way we can teach students writing strategies. In one metastudy of adolescent writers, teaching writing strategies was the most effective pedagogical approach studied (Graham and Perin 2007). We can divide writing strategies into two subcategories: writing processes (planning, drafting, revising, and editing—essentially, what our mindful task model presents to students) and rhetorical strategies (genres, introductions, arguments, narrative, paragraph development, etc.). Since the rest of this book covers teaching writing processes, in this chapter I'll stick to using models to teach rhetorical principles and strategies.

I don't mean to be flip here, but the essence of model pedagogy can be summed up fairly quickly: if you want to teach students how to write This or That Thing, show them a few, analyze them together, and then ask them to write their own.

I admit that this approach to teaching sounds reductive. Thinking back to my cutesy moonwalking example, doesn't modeling imply that our students should be base imitators, following a model with their critical thinking switch turned off? What about the messy parts of thinking for themselves and grappling with questions with no clear answers? What about writing that defies models, challenges power, complicates convention, colors outside the lines? What about that messy social milieu? Anne Beaufort recently warned us that the "tell-and-practice (T & P)" format of teaching may not "invite open-ended inquiry, seeking new information, or examining ambiguity" (2016, 26). Plus, it might invite cheating—that is, essentially cutting and pasting someone else's work. Fair enough.

Models (including existing genres) indeed exert normative power over writers. Often they show us what is, not what should or could be. Some genres do not grant writers a significant range of rhetorical agency. That's why it's important for us to choose a motley crew of mentor texts to invite students to think of models as options rather than iron-clad templates (unless, of course, the genre requires iron-clad templates). We need to give students assignments that invite them to confront messy problems for which there are no easy solutions. But since every new text is a dialogue with the texts before it, students need to engage with models and learn how to draw lessons from them, even if the lesson leads them to reject the models and face the rhetorical consequences.

Table 14.1. Analyzing mentor texts

Rhetorical Situation	
Who writes these op-eds? What *kind* of people write them? (*rhetors*)	What provokes someone to write an op-ed? (*exigence*)
How do the writers make their op-eds timely? (*kairos*)	What do op-ed writers want audiences to feel, think, or do? (*purpose*)
What kind of audience reads an op-ed? Be as specific as you can. (*audience*)	What do you think makes an op-ed successful? (*rhetorical situation*)
Rhetorical Strategies	
How is an op-ed organized?	What kind of *style* or *tone* do you notice? Do op-eds use personal experience, humor, metaphor, links to other online sources, etc.?
What seems to be standard across examples? How do they differ from each other?	How do the writers establish credibility or appeal to emotion?
How do the writers support their opinions? What kind of evidence is presented?	What surprised you about the examples you looked at? What did you learn that you didn't know already?

Students can respond creatively to models in rhetorical situations of their own devising. We have yet to exhaust possible responses to even established, conventional rhetorical situations.

We've already talked about using genres as models. Students look at a variety of examples of the target genre and abstract rhetorical principles at play in the sociological system in which that genre circulates. Amy Devitt points out that when we lead students to examples that respond to a cultural exigence in a variety of ways, thereby showing the genre's affordances and constraints, we avoid teaching writing as "a static set of formal rules" (2014, 148). The genre, then, reflects the alive and flowing social milieu in which the recognizable form took, and is taking, shape ("flowing, and flown," as the poet Elizabeth Bishop would have it).

When I have taught the opinion editorial in the past, I've created a genre analysis assignment that asks students to read ten op-eds and respond to the questions in table 14.1. These kinds of questions can be handled in a homework assignment or a class discussion or both. Notice that this assignment assumes that I've covered key terms in rhetoric. The genre analysis should reinforce those concepts.

This exercise leads students to study models not for direct one-to-one imitation but for staking out what Anne Freedman calls the "rules for play" for genres (in Devitt 2014, 148). This method works particularly well for multimodal genres familiar to the students (e.g., product reviews on YouTube). In the planning stage, students can look at models of the target genre, abstract important rhetorical strategies available in the genres, and then set product goals for how they want to create their own genre. Then they write the dang thing.

This pattern of modeling—show examples, have students analyze them for rhetorical principles, ask them to practice—can be used for rhetorical strategies ranging from genres down to punctuation, in every unit and in every day of instruction. It's an old and powerful teaching tool; in the late 1980s, Australian educators developed a model of modeling called the "teaching-learning cycle" to teach genres (Cope and Kalantzis 1993). Devitt suggests that American instructors are not as excited about this direct instruction as are the Australians. We should be. Direct, guided instruction based on clear outcomes is one of the most effective teaching methods we can use (Hattie and Yates 2014, 72–73; Hillocks 1986, 122–23). We do not have to sacrifice engaging discussions with our students to ensure they have practice, in class, playing with the rhetorical strategies we teach.

NOTICE, NAME, NOW YOU

I'd like to share a simple method for teaching almost any rhetorical principle under the sun by using models, analysis, and practice. Let's call it *notice, name, now you.*

I'm stealing this method from a variety of sources who know quite a bit about teaching writing. (I'm particularly indebted to Katie Wood Ray, whose book *Wondrous Words* [1999], for elementary school teachers, is indeed wondrous.) The process is simple: you show students a model text, you guide them to describe what they see, you give what they describe a name (e.g., a key term from rhetoric or writing studies), you discuss what that thing does (rhetorically or linguistically), and then you ask them to practice it in their own writing ("Now, *you*"). Getting the students to use this "inductive" process helps them "derive generalizations" or mental models for themselves, which is an exercise in mindfulness (Weaver 1998, 26). Also, the harder the student works to understand a principle, the better (Brown, Roediger III, and McDaniel 2014, 82–90).

Want to teach students how to write effective introductions? Supported arguments? Descriptive paragraphs? Syntheses of disagreeing sources? Complex, modifying sentences? Close-reading paragraphs? Insightful, mindful reflections? Anything?? Try this in class.

Let's see how the notice, name, now you method might work in a lesson on cohesion, which is how a text "hangs together" at the sentence level to lead readers gently down the path of meaning. Imagine you're watching a teacher in a brick-and-mortar classroom. We'll name the teacher *Dewey* to honor the Grandpappy of progressive education in America, philosopher John Dewey. I'll write the script for Dewey, but I'm shy about writing one for the students because I'm afraid it would sound too corny and contrived (as if I've shown any reluctance so far for being corny). So please imagine how the students might respond; I've included some possibilities in brackets. Imagine, also, that the boxed texts below are presented on slides from a projector. I've labeled the stages of the model in bold all-caps in brackets.

DEWEY: I want you to take a look at this paragraph from MIT professor Sherry Turkle's book *Reclaiming Conversation* (2015, 125). She's interviewing young adults about their social media use. Mari, will you read this for us, please?

> So, Jon's frenetic sharing is part of a larger story. We become accustomed to seeing life as something we can pause in order to document it, get another thread running in it, or hook it up to another feed. We've seen that in all of this activity, we no longer experience interruptions as disruptions. We experience them as connection. We seek them out, and when they're not there, we create them. Interruptions enable us to avoid difficult feelings and awkward moments. They become a convenience. And over time we have trained our brains to crave them. Of course, all of this makes it hard to settle down into conversation.
>
> —Sherry Turkle

[NOTICE]

DEWEY: OK. Interesting topic! We could talk all day about whether or not Turkle's right about interruptions, but I want you to pay attention to how she talks about interruptions throughout the paragraph, so I'm going to highlight a few words, like this:

> So, Jon's frenetic sharing is part of a larger story. We become accustomed to seeing **life as something we can pause** in order to document it, get another thread running in it, or hook it up to another feed. We've seen that in all of this activity, we no longer experience **interruptions** as disruptions. We experience *them* as connection. We seek *them* out, and when *they're* not there, we create *them*. **Interruptions** enable us to avoid difficult feelings and awkward mo-

> ments. *They* become a convenience. And over time we have trained our brains to crave *them*. Of course, all of this makes it hard to settle down into conversation.
>
> —Sherry Turkle

DEWEY: What's going on here? What is Turkle doing with these bolded words and phrases?

[responses from the students, either through full-class volunteer discussion or cold-calling—see next chapter]

DEWEY: Good! Yeah, you can see how she's using *they*, and *them*, and *they're* to refer us back to the central theme of the paragraph: *interruptions*. You can see she's introduced that theme with the cool phrase, "life as something we can pause." By the way, what do we call all those *them*s and *they*s? Where are my grammar nerds?

[NAME]

[a few grammar nerds call out *pronouns*, delighted to be dusting off some grade school knowledge]

DEWEY: You got it. Now, why does Turkle use these pronouns? What is she assuming about us? What do the pronouns *do* for her?

[answers about avoiding repetition, keeping readers focused, etc.]

DEWEY: Yes. When we're talking about the art of a paragraph, we call this little move *cohesion*. It's how writers connect one sentence to another, and then another, and then another, making this nice focused paragraph along the way. Now, in this next example we see a writer using pronouns to create cohesion, but there are other methods. How does Jonathan Safran Foer create cohesion in this paragraph from his book *Eating Animals* (2009, 124)?

> The 1918 pandemic has been remembered as the "Spanish flu" because the Spanish press was the only Western media to adequately cover its massive toll. Despite the name, Spanish flu struck the entire world—that's what made it a *pan*demic instead of simply an

> *epi*demic. It was not the first influenza pandemic, nor the most recent, but it was by far the most deadly. Whereas AIDS took roughly twenty-four years to kill 24 million people, the Spanish flu killed as many in twenty-four weeks.
>
> —Jonathan Safran Foer

[class discussion, or discussion in pairs]

DEWEY: OK, so you see that he's repeating certain key words—and in this case, he's repeating key terms about the flu, which I'll emphasize in bold, and also repeating phrases to dramatize the consequences of the flu, which I've rendered in *italics*:

> The **1918 pandemic** has been remembered as the "**Spanish flu**" because the Spanish press was the only Western media to adequately cover its *massive toll*. Despite the name, **Spanish flu** *struck the entire world*—that's what made it a **pandemic** instead of simply an *epi*demic. It was not the first **influenza pandemic**, nor the most recent, but it was by far the *most deadly*. Whereas AIDS took roughly twenty-four years to kill 24 million people, the **Spanish flu** *killed as many in twenty-four weeks*.
>
> —Jonathan Safran Foer

[NAME, THEN NOTICE AGAIN]

DEWEY: So here we see a second strategy for cohesion—creating consistent topics and topic chains. You see how these topic chains tightens up the focus of his paragraph. Good. Let's look at a third strategy now. The next two are a little tricky. In this example from Malcolm Gladwell (2008, 76), I want you to look carefully at what he's doing at the front of every sentence, which is often (but not always) where cohesion takes place:

> So far in *Outliers,* we've seen that extraordinary achievement is less about talent than it is about opportunity. In this chapter, I want to try to dig deeper into why that's the case by looking at the outlier in its purest and most distilled form—the genius. For years, we've taken our cues from people like Terman when it comes to understanding

> the significance of high intelligence. But, as we shall see, Terman made an error.
>
> —Malcolm Gladwell

[class discussion]

[NAME]

DEWEY: Excellent. We call these cool moves *transitions.* Or if you want to get even fancier, some people call it *metalanguage*—that's language that provides kind of a commentary about how the paragraph is being shaped. Transitions help readers understand how to process the information we're giving them.

> **So far in *Outliers***, we've seen that extraordinary achievement is less about talent than it is about opportunity. **In this chapter**, I want to try to dig deeper into why that's the case by looking at the outlier in its purest and most distilled form—the genius. **For years**, we've taken our cues from people like Terman when it comes to understanding the significance of high intelligence. **But, as we shall see**, Terman made an error.
>
> —Malcolm Gladwell

DEWEY: As a writer, you have several options for creating transitions, and they all help your reader through the reading experience:

> **COOL TRANSITION OPTIONS**
>
> *compare:* also, likewise, similarly
> *contrast:* however, nevertheless, conversely
> *cause and effect:* as a result, consequently, therefore
> *logical relationship:* since, therefore, for this reason
> *sequence of events:* next, and then, first/second/third
> *example:* for example, for instance, for one thing
> *more:* furthermore, additionally, moreover

DEWEY: What questions do you have so far about strategies of cohesion?

[As usual, no questions. They are stunned into silence.]

[NOTICE]

DEWEY: OK, the fourth strategy is the hardest, but you are rhetoric warriors, so I think you can handle it. Let's go back to Sherry Turkle. And I want you to work with someone next to you on this one, because it won't be obvious. How does Turkle (2015, 7) create cohesion here:

> Time with people teaches children how to be in a relationship, beginning with the ability to have a conversation. And this brings me back to the anxieties of the Holbrooke teachers. As the Holbrooke middle schoolers began to spend more time texting, they lost practice in face-to-face talk. That means lost practice in the empathic arts—learning to make eye contact, to listen, and to attend to others. Conversation is on the path toward the experience of intimacy, community, and communion. Reclaiming conversation is a step toward reclaiming our most fundamental human values.
>
> —Sherry Turkle

[discussion, bewilderment, edging toward enlightenment]

[NAME]

DEWEY: Fantastic! I didn't think you'd get it, but you did. You notice how each new sentence starts with some of the themes mentioned in the old sentence. Writing experts call this the "known-new" contract. The writer ends a sentence with a new principle, which is a good idea because closers carry rhetorical emphasis. And then that info, which is now "old," starts off the next sentence, which itself ends with something new. It's magic. Let me show you with bold and italics how Turkle uses the known-new contract:

> **Time with people teaches children how to be in a relationship, beginning with the ability to have a conversation.**
>
> **And this** brings me back to the anxieties of the *Holbrooke teachers.*
>
> As the *Holbrooke middle schoolers* began to spend more time texting, **they lost practice in face-to-face talk.**
>
> **That means lost practice** *in the empathic arts—learning to make eye contact, to listen, and to attend to others.*

> *Conversation is on the path toward the experience of intimacy, community, and communion.*
> *Reclaiming conversation* is a step toward reclaiming **our most fundamental human values.**

DEWEY: OK, so we've reviewed four strategies for creating cohesion in your paragraphs: pronouns, topic chains, transition phrases, and new the known-new contract. Now I want you to practice. Get into pairs. Exchange drafts of your Very Important Current Paper you're working on. Find a paragraph for your peer that you think could use better cohesion. Put a mark next to it and write one or two cohesion strategies he or she might use. Then trade back and rewrite your paragraph. I want to hear from two of you about how your new paragraph is more cohesive than the old one!

[delirious excitement and buzzing conversation ensues—and later discussion reveals, as usual, that some students got it and some didn't]

* * *

This model is a helpful antidote to the most common, and yet least effective, method of college teaching, which is presenting information. It also improves on the already-pretty-great rookie teaching I described at the beginning of the chapter. Students can get excited about a topic (like diction) and then practice on their own writing, when the idea is fresh in their minds.

If you're thinking right now, *Shoot, I'm teaching in twenty minutes and I don't know what to do,* think about this modeling model. If you're teaching students how to write effective research paper introductions, bring in three examples and ask the students what they see. Give what they see a rhetorical term (e.g., many intros have "hooks"). Then ask them to practice, right there in class, writing an introduction, even if they don't feel they are ready yet to write one.

15 CLASS DISCUSSION

In Cicero's *On the Ideal Orator*, the Roman rhetorician's masterwork, Antonius tells his friend Catulus that many of the teachers of rhetoric are "ridiculous" because (a) they have no experience practicing what they preach, (b) they divide rhetoric into tedious categories, and (c) they lecture too much. By contrast, Antonius celebrates the great Greek philosopher Isocrates as "the teacher of all rhetoricians," whose school produced some of the best speakers in town. The classical rhetoric scholar Jeffrey Walker explains that the Latin term that Cicero uses for Isocrates's "school" is not *schola*, which connotes "a place for leisure and learned discussion" but *ludus*, "a place for gaming, exercise, and practice" (2011, 47). Antonius praises Isocrates for creating schools where students can play and practice, rather than receive a lecture or engage in delightful, but ultimately aimless, pupil discussions.

This distinction between practice and discussion is important. Discussion is a fundamental—if not *the* fundamental—class activity in courses in the humanities. You've been there; I've been there. A class discussion imitates the *salon*, the place where brains meet and debate, where taste and critical thinking are sharpened, where public opinion is refined. I once took a graduate course from a man who assigned books he'd never read. He conducted class exactly the same way each time we met: He'd come in moments after the bell buzzed, throw down the text we were reading for the day, and say, "Well, what did you think?" We had great conversations. It was grad school and we were all motivated not only to read and learn and talk, but to *look* smart doing it. This worked.

But let me tell you something. There may not be a lazier, more misused, and overrated and wasteful pedagogical exercise in FYW than class discussion.

I feel like a monster saying that.

If one of the goals of education is to condition us to be lifelong learners, engaged thinkers, inquisitors, and dialogic companions, then surely "learned discussion" is on the menu. Talking to people *feels* good. When

DOI: 10.7330/9781607329374.c015

you respect those people. And you're engaged in a collaborative assaying of art and ideas with those people. And those people honor your right to speak as yourself, but still challenge you. And you are led by a tutor who can model how to read closely, ask important questions, and draw inferences from texts. Good discussions have an emotional ecology conducive to lifelong learning. I'd guess that's why my mother was part of a book club for thirty years.

Remember, though, that learning is to a great degree *goal oriented.* In many respects, you want students to move from A to B; and, ostensibly, B has some kind of advantage over A. While learning can be spontaneous, unpredictable, alive and unwieldy, we craft outcomes to focus our curriculum building on helping students develop rhetorical power. The backward design model I mentioned in chapter 6, sketched by Wiggins and McTighe, is an exacting (and, sure, perhaps overdetermined) standard for classroom practices, including discussions.

Class discussions can be aimless, even while pleasurable. Often discussions project a class energy that only a portion of the class actually feels, because only a portion actually participated (listening included). They can reinforce dynamics of cultural privilege (see Brookfield 2006, 116). They kill time efficiently. They can hide the fact that the instructor did little to prepare to teach beyond assigning some pages of a text. They can reinforce misguided assumptions that go unchallenged. In your average discussion, teachers tend to dominate, even when they think they're sharing the time. The instructors think of their questions as "polite and open-ended" while their students perceive them as "content-directive, authoritative, and middle class" (Haswell 2008, 334). Discussions can turn into a sequence of teacher-student exchanges rather than student-student exchanges. Because students get to participate in their learning, active discussions can make them feel empowered, even if they don't take away any new skill, disposition, or principle.

However, teaching expert Stephen Brookfield just stepped into the room to slap me over the head for being too pessimistic about what discussion can do for students: "Discussion is the jewel in the crown of the engaged classroom. It appears to equalize student-teacher power relationships, to affirm the validity of students' opinions, to get learners used to grappling with diverse (and sometimes contradictory) perspectives, and to encourage students to take responsibility for the development of their own judgments" (2006, 115). Recent research at Northeastern University confirms these positive outcomes, as does (I assume) your experience with class discussions, especially when compared to lectures (Dallimore, Hertenstein, and Platt 2017).

In *The Skillful Teacher*, Brookfield explains that while discussion, obviously, doesn't suit all teaching ends, there are good reasons you'd want to have one. Brookfield breaks these reasons into "intellectual, emotional, and sociopolitical" categories. For example, discussions engage students in diverse and ambiguous perspectives. They push students to test assumptions and refine the way they communicate with others. On the emotional or sociopolitical side, discussion connects students with the material, validates their experience, teaches listening, and teaches habits of "democratic discourse" (2006, 118–24). More important for us, discussion can promote critical thinking about rhetorical concepts or writing topics. It can create an artisan atmosphere: In our writing class, we "talk shop" about writing, as writers. At least, we hope it can do all these things.

Maybe I should amend my surly attitude about discussion. But only if we can all agree on one thing: *class discussions are meant to support student writers.* Before we plan a class discussion, we should ask ourselves, *How is this discussion going to help my students as mindful writers?* If we approach discussion with this somewhat demanding principle in mind, we can use it to light up those students and at the same time support their writing goals. Below I suggest a few practices that might help us have more effective discussions in FYW.

PREPARING FOR DISCUSSION

Syllabus statement. Write a statement on your syllabus describing why you depend on discussion, what you hope discussion does for students, and how you hope discussions will work in class. Since, like other forms of rhetorical practice, discussion norms are culturally contingent, you may want to lay out normative principles for civility and respect. Sometimes universities have ready-made policies on classroom civility. You want to establish early on that every voice in the class matters and everyone should respect everyone else, especially during disagreements. If you feel like everyone should participate in every class discussion, say so. There are some forms of speech (e.g., discrimination) you will want to categorically condemn. I'm writing this chapter in the midst of a national conversation about microaggressions and free speech on cultural (i.e., race, class, gender, sexuality, ability) issues on campus. Give your students your philosophy/policy so they will know what to expect.

Discussion discussion. Have a brief discussion about discussion so your community can co-create some ground rules. Brookfield does this by asking students to reflect on past discussion experiences in small groups ("Think of the best/worst group discussions you've ever been involved in . . .") (Brookfield 2006, 125). This kind of conversation might reveal norms like turn taking or listening or questioning or respecting or signaling the desire to speak that the students themselves can support from their own experiences. In *Tools for Teaching*, Barbara Gross Davis lists a few potential ground rules, such as "keep an open mind" or "stick to the subject" or "avoid long stories or examples" or "give encouragement to others" (Davis 2009, 99). These rules will be more powerful if students come up with them themselves.

Participation points. Be cautious about assigning participation grades or points for discussion in an FYW class. It's hard to quantify a student's participation. (It's easier in an online class when you can capture and count comments.) Did Student A comment each day? How many times? What kind of behavior constitutes "*full* participation"? What about students who are paying attention and writing notes but not speaking during a discussion? B- for them? What about that student who always participates but never says anything worth a tinker's cuss? Tough questions. I've seen teachers who want to use the participation portion of a final grade to penalize a student who is being a pest about grades or policies or whatever. The potential for mischief or miscalculation is high. If you don't keep quantitative track all semester, you may fall prey to a cognitive bias when you sit down to evaluate each students' participation (e.g., the "peak-end bias," in which you judge an experience based on how you felt at its most intense and at its end, rather than as a whole). If discussions serve a purpose (see next note), they are their own reward.

Outcomes. Write down an outcome for the discussion that supports student writers. Discussions can clarify (or complicate) rhetorical principles. They can present multiple perspectives and arguments on an issue. They can tease out multiple readings of a text. They can serve as prewriting or invention activities. Discussions about process can create a community of writers writing. As you create your lesson plan, express what you want your student writers to get out of the discussion. I've often heard my literature colleagues say they want to have a *thesis* for their discussions—a point the discussion is meant to support. Brookfield is against this. He defines discussion as "a free and open conversation in which no end point is specified" (2006, 128). That's interesting. He separates discussion from more guided conversations for which there is some preconceived answer—about a text's purpose, for example. Whether your discussions have a thesis or not, they should have a goal oriented to transformations in the disposition of mindful writers.

Time limit. Set a time limit for the discussion and stick to it, especially if you want students later to write about what they've discussed. Write the time limit on your lesson plan.

Questions. Prepare yourself for the discussion by writing several questions that will bring out the best thinking from the students. List the questions in an order that builds understanding.

Homework. Prepare students for discussion by giving them meaningful homework before class. If you want students to discuss a reading, prepare them for the discussion by asking them questions to consider and write about *before* the discussion. You can also invite them to prepare their own questions. This can happen in class right before a discussion. You may even want to assign a discussion leader or two whom you ask to prepare questions and comments.

DISCUSSION METHODS

Begin with a bang. In the chapter on lesson plans, I suggested starting lessons with some kind of hook to draw students in. The hook doesn't need to be a gimmick; in fact, as I noted, attention grabbers fail when they don't engage students in thinking carefully about the content (Willingham 2009, 80). You can start discussions with messy questions ("Why does the author of our text tell so many stories about himself?"), controversy ("Some people suggest that peer review is the 'blind leading the blind'—where do you stand?"), experience ("When have you been most aware of your identity as writers?"), or a zoom-in on a reading detail ("I noticed that this text does X on page 3; how is that helping the authors achieve their purpose?"). You can use audio or video clips to get students thinking and talking.

Ask good questions. As much as I enjoyed as a grad student being asked, "What did you think?," this kind of question might not help students focus their comments. Good questions take many forms. Often the less effective question is the one that seems too obvious ("Why is it important to have other people give you feedback as a writer?") or the one that merely tests recall ("What does *exigence* mean?"), though there may be moments when you want to test their understanding. Books on teaching lay out a variety of question types that ask students to exercise deep learning: evaluate, apply, connect, interpret, refract, challenge, extend, rebut, predict, imagine. *Why* and *how* questions are gold. Ask only one question at a time (says the guy who can never stick to that rule).

Listen attentively with your whole body. Group expert Daniel Coyle encourages us to "overcommunicate" our listening (2018, 75). I love that idea. Know your students' names, and use them often. When a student speaks, listen carefully with your eyes. Smile and nod your head. Wait for them to finish, unless they're taking too long, and then break eye contact. Thank them for their comment and, if you can, point out what made their comment insightful.

Go deeper. My students are surprised when after making a comment they find themselves still in the hot seat. Asking follow-up questions is a great way to draw more out of student comments: "Say more about that." Or: "Interesting. I'm not sure, though, if I understand X about what you said. Can you give me an example or tell me more about what you're thinking?" Or: "I agree with you, but I wonder, what evidence do we have that supports that conclusion?" Or: "So, what you seem to be saying is X. Am I right about that? What have I left out?" We don't need to be satisfied with weak or surface or confusing comments; we can kindly persist. If we do ask questions that have right answers (a process Brookfield would say isn't exactly discussion), we need to hold students accountable for getting the right answer. Educator Doug Lemov talks about how teachers "round up" when students give us "almost-correct answers," which sends the message that the right answers don't matter (2010, 35). Since you don't want to say "wrong!" and then move on to another student, you can help almost-there students work through an answer by asking them additional questions that might jog their memory or help them stumble into a better answer.

Involve as many students as you can. You'll want to be a mindful discussion leader, paying attention to the discussion as it happens: to the emotional atmosphere, who has spoken and who hasn't, facial expressions, opportunities to put student comments in dialogue with each other, how or whether the discussion is helping student writers based on your outcome. Class discussions can reinforce dynamics of privilege. In other words, white males (like myself) might speak more and with more conviction than other students. Everyone has something to give. We want to engage everyone, every day. Smaller discussion groups can help with this dynamic. To be frank, I have found cold-calling—or calling on students "regardless of whether they have raised their hands" (Lemov 2010, 112)—to be fundamental to the way I teach. In my syllabus and on the first day, I warn students that I will call on them to share without notice. I explain that I do this so we can hear from everyone, and not to test their knowledge of any principle. There's no "gotcha" game here; I'm on their side, and I'll support them as they answer. I tell them that if this method makes them uncomfortable, they should email me and let me know and I'll leave them alone. (There may be student populations, like some English language learners, for which this strategy will be uncomfortable. You'll have to read the room.) Cold-calling is easiest on the students when you know everyone in class has something to say because they've all just written something. ("Student A, what are you planning to write about, and why?" "In two minutes, after you've written your answer to this question, I want to hear from Students B and C.") I sometimes cold-call by region: "Let's hear from someone over in this corner."

Decenter yourself. Find a way to get out of the habit of asking a question, hearing an answer, making a comment yourself, and then moving to another student. Limit your own gilding of student comments. It is a common vice for leaders to "reflexively add value" to everything anyone says, turning discussion into dialogue (Coyle 2018, 163). As Glenn and Goldthwaite put it, "cultivate your own silence" (2014, 64). After asking a question, wait ten whole seconds for students to respond; and don't answer your own question, unless you want to reinforce their silence. Get the students responding to each other. After one comment, nod and then just sit and see what happens. You may want to say, "Who else felt the same way?" or "Who has a different perspective?" In classrooms in which we've been able to sit in a circle, I will tell students to direct their comments—and their heads, eyes, faces, whole bodies—to the group as a whole and not just to me.

Comment randomly to comments. This works nicely in online environments and discussion boards. Often we don't need to comment on every single discussion comment. We can pick a handful and reinforce good discussion behavior or challenge students.

Take notes. While the students are talking, pay attention to the direction of the discussion so you can reflect later and provide more instruction.

Use the front board meaningfully. I've sat in many classes in which the front board (chalkboard or dry-erase board, sometimes even the projector) is used for a mess of notes that seem paradoxically both priceless and worthless. I think the assumption is that if we put a term or idea on the board, the class has somehow cognitively *captured* that concept for future use. Maybe, but probably not. If you do use the board, I recommend reviewing what has been written with the students afterward to see what is most useful. Sometimes I've asked students to come up and write down ideas as the class has discussed something, but of course then the scribe doesn't get to participate in the same way. If you use a shared Google Drive document, which I've done before, students can type notes together in real time on their laptops, and then the document can be archived as class notes.

DISCUSSION VARIETIES

Full-class volunteer. By far, the most common discussion type I see when I observe teachers is the full-class volunteer (FCV) discussion. That's when a teacher asks a question to the whole class, someone raises a hand, and the teacher calls on them. And this goes on for twenty minutes. Sometimes it's necessary, but I'm not a fan, for reasons I've already stated.

Write, then speak. Assign students to write, and then ask them to talk about what they've written. This is a particularly good strategy for shy students. Even better might be . . .

Write-pair-share. Give the students a writing (or thinking) prompt. Then have them pair up (or group up) and talk over their answers to the prompt with a neighbor. I use variations of this method in almost every class. Sometimes after they've paired up and talked, I'll ask, "Who wants to 'out' their partner as having said something cool?"

Circular responses. Brookfield recommends you get students in a circle (or several smaller circles) and ask everyone to share something in a minute or less. However, the second person to speak must "incorporate into her remarks some reference to the preceding speaker's message" to use as a "springboard" for her own (2006, 145). The circular response turns students into listeners, not just talkers.

Class debate. In Richard Light's research, many college students reported that "structured disagreements" bring out some of their best thinking (2001, 48). I've had great success teaching students how to detect claims, reasons, and assumptions or how to restate, as a rhetorical listener, a claim they oppose by dividing the class in half and asking each half to prepare arguments for or against a proposition. Even more productive are those debates for which I schedule time for students to do research and prepare.

Fishbowl. Get all the desks (or chairs) in a circle. Put three to four desks in the middle. That's the fishbowl. No one in the room can talk except the folks in the fishbowl. If you want to get in the fishbowl, you need to tap someone on the shoulder who is already in the fishbowl. Students in the fishbowl discuss planned questions or whatever they want. Students outside the fishbowl take notes, following the conversation to prepare to enter it. You can assign a few points to anyone who gets into the fishbowl.

AFTER DISCUSSION

Summarize. Ask the students to sum up what has been discussed.

Make connections. If the students have had an enjoyable, open-ended, free discussion, they may need you to spend a few minutes explaining how the discussion supports them as writers. You can help them reflect on what they've learned from the discussion and how they can use what they've learned for the current writing task. It is likely that a focused discussion has somehow contributed to the students' ability to monitor and control their writing process.

Practice. If the discussion was about writing strategies, have students practice them.

Make changes. On your own as teacher, reflect on what went well and what needs to change to make discussions more meaningful for writers. Think about what you may need to revisit in a future class, paying particular attention to the emotional ecology of the students. Maybe you detected a student who felt alienated or confused.

DISCUSSION CHALLENGES

Class of the Living Dead. What if no one responds? What if they didn't prepare for the discussion by reading or writing? What if they look at you blankly, sparking a staring contest? Well, it could be *my* fault for asking dumb questions or not preparing them well enough. But it could also be *their* fault for not preparing, and in those instances I want them to know that I'm not pleased. Remind them that they'll get so much more out of class if they come prepared. You may need to ask them to prepare again and require them to turn in their preparation for credit. Otherwise, if you use cold-calling, you won't need to worry about them not responding because you can compel them (yikes!) to respond. Having them write first is another way to bring the energy level up for a discussion. And, heck, silence isn't evil; let them sit and stew a while until they break.

Stump the chump. Sometimes students challenge me or ask me a question I can't answer, because I don't know the answer. "That's a great question!" I say, feigning enthusiasm. "I have no idea. Let me look into it and get back to you." If students disagree with me, more power to them. Disagreement gives me an opportunity to model the kind of intellectual conversation I want them to have. However, I have worked with grad students, many of them women, who have students who decide to take it upon themselves to question the legitimacy of the teacher or the course. This is not appropriate. It can distract the rest of the class and start an ugly foment against the instructor. If you are feeling undermined or harassed or even threatened, please consult with your friendly neighborhood writing program administrator (WPA) on strategies. I've found that in most cases, a private conversation with a student can go a long way in educating audience awareness. Sometimes university policy protects teachers against distracting students.

Battle royale. What if the students get contentious with each other? What if a cultural conversation goes screaming off the rails in a ball of fire? This is my biggest fear. Let me get a bit personal here. When it comes to contention, I become a fragile little snowflake in the sun. I don't like anger, and I don't like fighting. In the presence of contention, I find myself singing The Youngbloods: "C'mon people now, smile on your brother, everybody get together, try to love one another right now!" For a rhetorician, this is embarrassing. And here at the end of the second decade of the twenty-first century, we find ourselves in a festering cauldron of accusation, offense, discrimination, shout-downs, diatribe, trolling, gotcha games, boycotting, misunderstanding, and all kinds of frothy ill will. The 2016 election season was particularly divisive; old fissures yawned, new ones cracked open. And yet, heated debate can be so instructive. The students are engaged. If not exactly mindful, they're awake to the moment and therefore open to learning (Dannels 2015, 159). Dannels suggests that when things get too heated and your outcome is threatened, you can (1) point out how *exciting* it is to engage in this way, (2) remind students of the ground rules you established (listening or turn taking or respect, etc.), and (3) ask students to pause and reflect, either silently or in writing, on the consequences of the discussion's energy, particularly on how their own comments might be perceived by other students (2015, 159). You may need to model the kind of dialogic perspective taking that creates strong deliberative environments. I believe one of the biggest challenges we face as communities right now is learning how to listen and engage with respect with the people around us on heated issues.

The vigilante. Wait—I spoke too soon. My *bigger* fear than the Battle Royale is that one student will say something demeaning, dismissive, racist, sexist, offensive, or caustic, maybe to someone else in class, and I won't know how to respond in the moment. On the first day of the first class I taught in graduate school, one student introduced himself and then accused leaders of a major religious group of being rapists. I had no idea how to respond, and therefore clumsily moved on to the next student, as if the first guy had commented on the weather. (As a freshman, I'd also heard a demeaning comment about my own religious tradition on the first day of a creative writing class.) In her outstanding book *8 Essential Questions Teachers Ask,* Deanna Dannels, professor of communication at North Carolina State University, points out that in her experience, explicit and malicious discriminatory statements are rare. Far more common are comments that are "suggestive, implicit, and coded," for instance, microaggressions or stereotypes. In many cases, we have a liberal graduate instructor teaching conservative students, and such statements can upset the instructor and other students. Dannels suggests a "curious not furious" approach that confronts the thinking without confronting the person: "Can you help me understand how someone's sexual orientation is relevant to the topic we are discussing?" Or: "I'm wondering how those who identify as conservative would feel hearing these comments." Or: "When you say [fill in the blank], my guess is that there are several in the room who feel uncomfortable with that statement" (2015, 161–62). I've often marshaled the rest of the class in responding to a faulty assumption. In a course on rhetoric, it is more than appropriate to point out the consequences of discriminatory language, considering how writing constitutes identities in both writers and their audiences. If the behavior persists, you might need to meet with the student privately and discuss what's happening, or talk to your WPA.

Class clowns and Hermiones. What if one student wants to beta test a stand-up routine? What if a Hermione wannabe dominates the discussion with an anxious raised hand after every question? What if the Hermione type is socially blind and cannot tell that her comments are too long, too self-indulgent, or too off-topic? I've encouraged instructors to meet privately with good-natured but disruptive students to describe the distracting behavior and ask them to help create a strong learning environment in the class. You can follow a script that goes something like this, "I'm so glad you feel free to comment in class. Sometimes, though, I feel like your comments distract us from what we're trying to do. Can you help me keep us more focused without losing that signature energy of yours?" If you use cold-calling instead of volunteer discussion, then you don't need to worry much about the Hermione Granger types, the perpetual hand raisers, the ones who, after a while, spark involuntary eye-rolling in the other students for being a know-it-all.

To conclude, discussion is an effective learning tool if we use it to strengthen student writers' ability to monitor and control their writing practice. That's the main point of discussion, even though there are others. I'm with Isocrates: FYW is not the best place for "leisure and learned discussion" but for "gaming, exercise, and practice." If done well, discussion can lead to more mindful engagement as a community of writers.

16

COLLABORATIVE LEARNING

THE PHILOSOPHY OF COLLABORATION

"I am a rock," sings Paul Simon, "I am an island." No you're not, says the poet John Donne. Everyone is "part of the main," and when the funeral bell tolls, no matter who's dead, "it tolls for thee." Nevertheless, the Western idea of the single learner/reader/writer, striving in solitude to overcome, persists. Perhaps we continue to lionize solitary accomplishment because we want a tidy action-actor association—a doer and her deeds united, and protected by austere intellectual property law. I want to believe that whatever I bring to the table is sufficient alone for the task. Depending on others is needy.

This romantic notion is misguided. Collaboration is fundamental for growth. We construct knowledge in communities that make good use of our interdependence (Bruffee 1999). We grow as individuals in the "contact zones" of social life, starting in our families. When problems arise, we learn quickly that going it alone is not always an option.

The research on collaborative learning is nested in the social psychology of *group processes*, defined by social psychologists as "the behavior of human beings as they work together to make decisions, solve problems, and perform tasks in working groups of between three and twelve members" (Stangor 2017). This research describes how groups work together (or not) to make decisions (or not) that lead to effective solutions (or not!). In general, the research indicates that group outcomes are more accurate, wise, and able than that of individuals working alone. The most effective groups are made up of no more than four or five people. (Common wisdom suggests that groups of four tend to pair up and compete, and groups of three isolate one member, as anyone knows who has witnessed one of their children play with two other kids.) Groups work more effectively when they have a focused goal, when they're well trained, and when they have experience working together (Stangor 2017).

On the other hand, groups can be weak because of our tendency to loaf when others take charge. As you may already know from sad experience, free riding is common in group work, driving overperformers

DOI: 10.7330/9781607329374.c016

almost crazy with resentment. Also common is *groupthink*: that irresistible pressure to conform our judgments with the consensus judgments of others, even when doing so will hurt the group or betray our own inner compass (Aronson 2012). I've met many FYW students who have been poisoned by dysfunctional group work in the past, mostly by loafers content to stand by while others finished that poster collage on *To Kill a Mockingbird.*

In spite of, or maybe even because of, the challenges of group work, almost every massive study on student learning has concluded that peer interactions have a profoundly positive impact on student growth (Barkley, Cross, and Major 2005, 14–16). In one metastudy, collaborative learning improved student outcomes over competitive or individual approaches by at least half (Brame and Biel 2015). In George Kuh's research on "high-impact practices," he describes collaborative learning like this: "Collaborative learning combines two key goals: learning to work and solve problems in the company of others, and sharpening one's own understanding by listening seriously to the insights of others, especially those with different backgrounds and life experiences. Approaches range from study groups within a course, to team-based assignments and writing, to cooperative projects and research" (2008). The research synthesized in *Collaborative Learning Techniques* shows time and again that students who engage in collaborative learning learn more, enjoy school more, feel more motivated to work and learn more, transfer what they learn more, and (yay!) even *like* us, their teachers, more (Barkley, Cross, and Major 2005, 18–20). Collaborative learning decenters the class and drives students to construct their own learning.

I find this evidence convincing. In every class I teach up and down the curriculum, I use collaboration more than almost any other teaching strategy. I want my students talking and working together as much as possible. I like the phenomenon that Kenneth Bruffee describes: effective student collaboration can break "the chain of hierarchical institutional authority" and give students the freedom to "reacculturate" into a working community that is somewhat independent from the teacher (1999, 20). Collaborative work can help students build metacognitive skills as they learn to depend on others as part of the workflow of a writing task. Collaborative learning can go anywhere in the task model, but I put it here in part III because of the pervasive role it can play in the day-to-day learning of the students.

For this chapter, I adopt the distinction presented by Elizabeth Barkley, Patricia Cross, and Claire Major in *Collaborative Learning Techniques* between informal groups and formal groups. Informal groups are thrown together for only a single discussion or class period. Formal groups stay together until a major task is completed. Because peer review—an essentially collaborative learning experience—is such an important part of the revision stage, I'll wait to talk about that till part IV.

INFORMAL COLLABORATIONS

Buzz groups. Barkley, Cross, and Major suggest an easy way to get students working in groups. Combine students into groups of four to six students and ask them to talk about a question in any way they see fit. Buzz groups can help prepare class for full-class discussions (Barkley, Cross, and Major 2005, 112–16). For this, and for all the other activities, you can decide to form the groups yourself, using what you understand about your students and their skill levels, or have students form their own groups of (usually) peers sitting closest to them. The challenge—for buzz groups and all the others I mention below—is to get everyone to participate, and participate well. I wish I had a clear solution to this challenge. In your instructions, you can always explain that you do not want them to finish their group discussion until everyone in the group has spoken.

Write-pair-share. One of the easiest ways to get students engaged in class is to invite them to think or write about a question and then pair (or group) up and share what they thought or wrote about. I may begin class with a video or a rushwrite (projected on the screen: "What from last night's reading reminded you of experiences you've had in your own life?"). After three to four minutes of writing, I ask students to share with other students what they wrote about. I can then call on pairs to report what they discussed or move on to other things. This short exercise works well with mindful writing prompts related to goals, drafting, and reflection.

Consensus. This comes from Bruffee (1999): In groups of three or four, students work together to come up with a definition to a key term that they can all agree on (e.g., "Writing is *good* when it . . ." or "In research writing, persuasive evidence is . . ."). This exercise falls into Bruffee's social epistemology—specifically, that individuals working in communities of practice co-construct their world and its meanings. Bruffee suggests we ask groups to keep track of any disagreement that emerges in the group as they work to define the term.

Read-around groups (RAGS). I can't find the original source of this practice. I first heard of read-around groups as a graduate student in 2001. Give a writing prompt to the students. Put them in groups of three to four. Have them each read to each other what they've written. Optional next step: ask the groups to select one of their members to read what they've written to the rest of the class. Use RAGS as part of the scaffolded writing process: have students complete an introduction to their research paper and then share in groups.

Summary/analysis/synthesis/application. Ask students to work in groups to engage in a deep learning activity to summarize, analyze, synthesize, or apply class content, including reading homework. This is one of my favorite activities, but you need pretty good connectivity to pull it off, unless you want to go old school and use paper, which works just fine. Form groups of three to four, with each group having at least one person with a laptop. (I've had groups work on phones before, but it's much harder.) Give students a link to a Google Document everyone can edit. (I create the document on Google Drive and then project on the screen a shortened URL.) Ask them to select one scribe, one spokesperson, and maybe one timekeeper/discussion leader. Before class, I create a "graphic organizer" on the Doc, which is a table with three columns: one for "team name" (students go nuts with goofy names), one for a summary question ("What is the main point Ta-Nehisi Coates was making in this *Atlantic* article we read?"), and one for synthesis or analysis or application ("How does this article relate this other article we read?" or "What rhetorical strategies does Coates use?"). Give students five to ten minutes to discuss the prompts and write notes directly on the Google Doc in the separate cells. It's a blast watching all their thinking magically appear on the Google Doc as the groups simultaneously compose answers. (Warning: You will have jokesters that vandalize the Doc by changing fonts or inserting pictures—of kittens, or Batman. It's all part of the magic.)

Teaching each other. Assign homework that teaches a writing principle. The next day, ask students to pair up and teach each other that principle to demonstrate they understand it. Sometimes I'll make this a role play in which each student teaches the other about an important rhetorical principle assuming that the other is a "ten-year-old child" or "your great-aunt sitting next to you at a family dinner." Related to this exercise, I've seen many classes that assign students to teach the class a writing principle, either individually or in pairs/groups. If good teaching isn't modeled—and here I'd suggest teaching students the *notice, name, now you* method, described in chapter 14—these teaching moments might fall flat. I see students resorting to the "monologue through the handbook unidirectionally" method of teaching.

Jigsaw. Another method I learned way back in grad school. Divide the class into four or five groups. Ask each group to become an "expert" on a specific aspect of the course (e.g., various methods for proofreading or editing). Ask each group to work together in "expert groups" to master the material. *Then* create "new jigsaw groups" composed of one expert from each field of expertise who teach each other what they've learned (Barkley, Cross, and Major 2005, 157).

Circulate. If your room allows it, circulate among the groups and listen to their conversations *without intervening* unless students are way off course. I know this sounds like the panopticon. I suppose you could just sit up front and play Fruit Ninja on your phone or step out for a little stroll while they work. In an attempt to give students autonomy,

I've left the classroom once or twice during group work. Usually when my students get into groups, I'll walk around the class and crouch next to a group and just listen, not even making eye contact. It makes students crazy self-conscious at first, but when they see I'm not going to correct them or pass judgment, they get used to it. Circulating helps students stay focused, and it gives you power to add direction when you sense students aren't getting the most out of group work or one of its members. Doug Lemov talks about how circulating breaks the "plane" or that "imaginary line that runs the length of the room" between you and your students (Lemov 2010, 85).

Online groups. Form groups for online discussions using the course management software or other social media. You'll have to reinforce online group chats with some kind of point system if you want the students to talk to each other (e.g., five points for one post and two responses to others' posts).

Talking shop. As students are struggling with a writing task, pair or group them up and invite them to talk about their challenges. What are they struggling with *right now* in the midst of a mindful writing task? What did the just-now completed writing task teach them as writers? Talking shop is a great way to teach students how to be mindful writers who engage others in the writing process. You can use this method in peer review groups.

FORMAL COLLABORATIONS

When I say "formal collaborations," I'm talking about when we assign students to complete major projects together—as in, all their names are going on this thing. Coauthoring may seem bizarre to folks in the humanities. When my department gets together to discuss a candidate for promotion who has listed coauthored work, inevitably someone asks, "Yeah, but can So-and-So stand on his/her own two feet?" Sometimes we fixate on the ostensibly quantifiable amount of work the candidate has done on the coauthored project, as if a 50 percent effort could never be worth more than 50 percent of a single-authored work. It's hard for me to explain to my colleagues that a single article I wrote over four years with two rhetoric scholars and a statistician—with data from 1,000 students from surveys, writing assessments, and interviews—took more effort out of me than any single-authored article I've written. By my calculations, 25 percent = 135 percent.

Outside the humanities, in most other disciplines, and in the workplace, coauthoring is the way the work gets done. Scientists don't talk about the merits of coauthorship; they talk, and talk heatedly, about the order in which the authors' names appear up top (Venkatraman 2010). (Fun fact: There are over 130 names on the 2017 Nobel Prize–winning article about gravitational waves.) In a study reported in 1990 of around 500 professionals in mental health, engineering, chemistry, public management, and technical communication, 87 percent of respondents said they wrote in teams or groups during the 50 percent (!!) of their career they spent writing (Lunsford and Ede 2012, 73–74). In *The Rise of Writing*, Deborah Brandt, after interviewing sixty professionals who write "as a routine part of their work," concluded that most workaday writing is collaborative: team-written, corporate-authored, anonymous, transactional, and hierarchical (2015). No writing alone in a cork-lined Paris apartment for us!

And so: We should not be afraid of assigning collaborative writing. In fact, teaching students to be effective collaborative writers might prepare them for mindful team writing in their careers. Surely digital writing (web-based writing, social media, multimodal composing) has made collaboration not only easy but necessary—a global economy, accelerating technology, expanding networks, location-variant employment, radical interdependence, and so on.

We can approach collaborative pedagogy purposefully. Andrea Lunsford and Lisa Ede, longtime writing collaborators and scholars of collaboration, point out that professionals who write in teams express the same challenges we see in any group project: speaking with one voice/style, extra time required for coordinating, emotional dynamics, "equitable division of tasks" (writing is painful; there will be loafers), and a general sense that energy has been diffused in sharing the task (Lunsford and Ede 2012, 127–29). This is why Lunsford and Ede are cautious about all of us running around setting up cool collaborative projects without teaching students to "negotiate" the "conditions of collaboration" in a meaningful way (199).

In his research on group dynamics, Daniel Coyle discovered that successful groups, whether groups in business or education or sports or the military, interacted in very similar styles to create the overall feeling that "we are safe and connected" (2018, 15). This feeling was far more important to the outcome of the group than whether team members were smart or experienced. In the strong teams, Coyle found the following attributes:

- close physical proximity, often in circles;
- profuse amounts of eye contact;
- physical touch (handshakes, fist bumps, hugs);
- lots of short, energetic exchanges (no long speeches);
- high levels of mixing; everyone talks to everyone;

- few interruptions;
- lots of questions;
- intensive, active listening;
- humor, laughter;
- small, attentive courtesies (thank-yous, opening doors, etc.). (8)

In successful groups, everyone talks and everyone listens—in and with their bodies.

The following are some practices that might make formal collaborative writing work more effectively:

Sell collaboration. The students will need to be convinced that collaborative writing will help them learn to work in teams, develop collaborative dispositions, and teach them something about the social nature of writing. (WPA Outcome: "Experience the collaborative and social aspects of writing process.") Describe the learning goal for formal writing. You will also need to convince them that you will hold them accountable, separately, for their contribution to the group.

Set up the groups yourself. I know of no research confirming this method empirically; you could have students select groups themselves. Some students like to pick their own teams, while others feel left out, maybe even ostracized by this method. You know your students. You know their strengths and weaknesses as writers. Select teams you think will provide a healthy balance of motivation and skill. You could also make random selections or ask students to sign up in groups based on topic interests. Since formal collaboration is more difficult than informal, I make formal groups smaller—three is my ideal number, even considering the risk of a 2-against-1 dynamic.

Ask groups to talk about working in groups. After students have been grouped up, they should introduce themselves to each other and exchange contact information. Then, as with class discussions, students can work together to reflect on the potentials and challenges for working in groups. Lunsford and Ede encourage us to ask students "to examine how authority is negotiated, shared, distributed" in collaborative writing (2012, 161). Share with them a few principles of effective groups, and maybe even a few from ineffective groups. Virginia Satir, a family therapist, developed categories of behavior that create group conflict. My colleague Liz Dixon has repurposed them for team writing: the controller (wants to take charge of everything), blamer (blames others for failures), pleaser (wants to keep the peace, often at the cost of quality), distracter (group goof-off), and ghost (stops showing up). Students can talk together and establish norms that maximize group success.

Ask groups to establish rules, roles, and workflow. Once they've talked together about the norms of group work, they can establish some rules for their group (e.g., "Consensus will always be the goal, but majority rule if not" or "We will respond to texts or emails of other team members within twenty-four hours"). Barkley, Cross, and Major suggest a "Group Learning Contract" with lists of commitments the students come up with themselves ("I will come to every meeting prepared to share," "If I am unable to prepare for a group assignment, I will make up for it by doing an additional proportional share of the work on the next assignment") (Barkley, Cross, and Major 2005, 37). Joanna Wolfe calls this document a "team charter" (Wolfe 2010, 28–29). You might want them to discuss group roles: Who will do what? Options for roles might include project manager, researcher, editor, document manager, note taker, and so on. On workflow, the group should talk about how and when they want to meet. In my experience, students' schedules are so skeewompus that sometimes a team can't find *any* time, from dawn to dusk, to meet physically. If so, they should establish an online working space, like Google Docs, and set up a schedule for what gets done and when.

Lead groups through the mindful writing process. Invite them together to assess the task (including analyzing the genre), set goals, draft together, seek feedback (from the writing center or other groups), make revision plans, and then reflect on what they've learned. I reserve two to three entire class periods for students to come in and work together or meet with me as a group to discuss concerns or show work in progress for my feedback.

Help with group difficulties. There will be static, I assure you. I work at a religious institution with a strong sense of shared values. Some of our students can see conflict, even mild disagreement, as a sign that Paradise is compromised and disaster is around the corner. It takes some experience to learn that problems get resolved, that disagreement, as uncomfortable as it may be, is a tool for wisdom. Every group on earth is made up of silly humans who can be selfish, lazy, dismissive, or disagreeable. Lunsford and Ede found in their research that several factors influence the success of groups, such as "the degree to which goals are clearly articulated and shared" or "the way credit (direct or indirect) is realized" or, maybe most important, "the degree of openness and mutual respect characteristic of group members" (2012, 159). Some teammates will miss deadlines, turn in shoddy work, or dismiss the good work of others (Wolfe 2010, 104–23). Encourage your students to speak frankly and respectfully to each other when disagreements arise. Encourage them to be flexible, adopting the greater good of the group. You may have to speak to students individually if they are not working well with other group members. Sometimes students just fall off the edge of the earth during a semester. You may have to ask the surviving members of a group to go on without that person.

Set up a fair evaluation system. Shoot, this is tough. Let us admit that in general grades kill the learning vibe. No way around that. Yet here we are, being paid to distribute them. For formal group writing, you want to set up a grading system that balances individual and group effort. If

> you assign a single grade for the group, someone might get rewarded even though they were a terror as a teammate. A hardworking, conscientious student could take a hit in the grade book because other group members didn't pull their load. You can strike a balance by assigning a grade with a rubric, as you'd normally do, and then requiring students to fill out self- and peer-evaluation forms. (Mine has a 1–5 rating scale for subjective impressions about cooperation, quantity, and quality for each person.) I wish I could tell you I've figured out concretely what to do when peers blast each other on these evaluation forms. If students score low on an evaluation, do they get penalized? Or do the other students get a bump if the group grade was low to correct for dysfunction? If two students say the same thing about one student, and they provide specific details, is that sufficient grounds for an adjustment? (I say "yes.") And how much adjustment should be made? Because of these difficulties, I keep formal group writing's percent of the final grade low (say, no more than 10 percent). You will need to take all these data into consideration as you make a subjective, but not arbitrary, grading decision.

* * *

In my experience, students underestimate significantly the amount of time they'll spend in their lives working with other people to accomplish things. Seems like we struggle merely getting along without killing each other, let alone writing a paper together. Students can learn mindful techniques for collaboration right here in our FYW classrooms. Maybe it can dawn on them, right here, that collaboration is a powerful engine of creativity and productivity, that knowledge-making and accomplishment are rarely solo performances.

17
TEACHING READING

EPIC FAILS IN TEACHING READING

One semester as a grad student, I . . .

Hang on. Let's try something a little unorthodox. Before you fling your eyeballs on this chapter, I want you to

1. decide whether or not you're ready to give this chapter your undivided attention (are you sitting somewhere comfortable? is your cell phone silenced and hidden from view? do you have enough time—say, an hour—to commit to it? are you ready to focus?); if so, then
2. look up from the book right now and predict what this chapter is about (i.e., what it will cover, what it won't, what it will argue, etc.);
3. ask yourself one of the following three questions: "What are my own reading strategies? What do I know about teaching reading? What have I learned about good and bad practices from being a student?";
4. preview the chapter by flipping through it quickly, looking for key terms or concepts (in headings, e.g.) or conclusions; and, finally,
5. decide what you hope to get out of this chapter (perhaps "I hope as a teacher that by reading this chapter I learn to do Y because Z").

While you read this chapter, I may interrupt you from time to time and ask you to do stuff. By doing so I hope not to insult your intelligence. What I'll ask you to do will help you think more about effective practices for teaching mindful reading.

Okay, let's go back to the beginning.

EPIC FAILS IN TEACHING READING

One semester as a grad student I taught a Developmental Writing course for the first time. My students had been corralled into the course by a combination of transcript data and a placement exam. Needless to say, they were ambivalent about a course the institution was requiring them to take before they could take the two-course "mainstream" FYW sequence and get the whole mess over with forever. They were great students—so fun, and so insecure.

DOI: 10.7330/9781607329374.c017

Early in the semester I assigned an excerpt from Annie Dillard's book *Pilgrim at Tinker Creek.* "They say of nature that it conceals with a grand nonchalance," writes Dillard, "and they say of vision that it is a deliberate gift, the revelation of a dancer who for my eyes only flings away her seven veils" (Dillard 2000, 18). Swoony! Who wouldn't love this stuff? I prepared for a vigorous class discussion. The next day during class, I began by asking the students what they had noticed about the essay. No hands. I asked a second question, assuming I hadn't been specific enough. Crickets chirped, and eyes darted away from mine. After one or two more dead-on-arrival questions, I asked in exasperation how many students had read the essay. Two hands went up, out of twenty. My whole lesson plan was rendered worthless.

I can't remember how I expressed my frustration, but I should have saved it for the mirror. Looking back with piercing 20/20, I see several problems with my approach . . .

Let's stop again. Can you predict what I'm about to say, based on your own experience with effective reading pedagogy? What do you think I did wrong? This reading process I'm forcing you to go through is called "priming" or "generating" by instructional psychologists. By asking readers to predict future content or puzzle out a problem before hearing the solution, the principle will be "better learned and more durably remembered" (Brown, Roediger III, and McDaniel 2014, 86). It also creates anticipation for the discussion to follow.

I'm not sure what your Bad Brian list looks like—and I'm not sure I *want* to know—but I see several problems with my approach. First, I had assigned students to read something *I* liked, that *I* found valuable, without asking myself whether the students—likely reluctant readers—would find it valuable. Second, I assigned the reading without introducing it. The students went home from class one day and saw "'Seeing,' pp. 16–36" on the schedule and a link to a PDF. And that was it. They had no idea who Annie Dillard was or what "Seeing" was or why they had to read this woman's musings about the dance of amoebae in a white china bowl. Third, I hadn't asked students to do anything with the text. *Just read it,* was the assumed command. They had no idea how to prepare for class. Even if they had read it, as those two star students had, they might not have been able to recall details from the twenty pages of scintillating prose, because they likely read it the way a farmer plants an acre of potatoes: one row at a time. Maybe some of them bet that there would be no penalty if they didn't read it, and they were right.

Finally (in probably an inexhaustible list of failures), and most significant, I had not at any point in the semester taught my students why and how we would read in class. I hadn't given them strategies, nor told them why I assigned reading or how reading might help them as writers. Perhaps I assumed that reading was a straightforward schoolish routine. I hadn't taught them to be mindful readers, or any kind of readers for that matter. And they gave me back what I had given them.

WHY WE MUST TEACH READING

It may seem overkill to task FYW teachers with teaching reading, in addition to all those other things we have only one semester (or, if we're lucky, two) to teach. Like writing, reading is thought of as a remedial skill of cognitive decoding—learned once at a young age and then taken for granted. However, reading is a complex activity that requires a person to master language use embedded in complex social practices. In *Social Linguistics and Literacies,* James Paul Gee explains that "literacy" is best understood not as an isolated cognitive practice but as the mastery of "ways of using language and other symbolic expressions" in a specific "socially meaningful group" to "signal (that one is playing) a socially meaningful 'role'" (2012, 159).

Since there are different socially meaningful groups (called "discourse communities" in our scholarship), there are different *literacies.* (It is fascinating, though, that neurological studies have revealed that every reader ever studied—even readers who read in languages from right to left or in languages that use characters instead of letters—experiences the first moments of reading in the same back lower-left area of the brain. After that, the signals move up and out from the back parts of the brain, and each reading culture has slightly different pathways [see Dehaene 2009, 68–71].) We read texts as members of communities that read certain texts for certain reasons and talk about them and value them and adopt attitudes about them in certain ways (Gee 2012, 41).

While for some it may seem that reading pedagogy is extraneous to what we do in a writing class, it turns out to be intimately woven into it. If reading is a sociocultural way of knowing and doing in a community, then it is inherently a rhetorical activity, just like writing. Research into the relationship between the two has revealed an *interactive configuration,* a term Nancy Nelson uses to describe the way writing influences reading and reading writing (2007, 437). We learn to write various text forms by reading them; we learn to read texts rhetorically by becoming writers ourselves. "Both practices," writes Ellen Carillo, "involve the construction—or *composition*—of meaning" to achieve social purposes (2015, 5, emphasis Carillo's). Both practices, though technically done in isolation, are meant to have us reach across the social divide to make contact with each other through text. Textual intercourse, if you will.

In addition, since almost every writing class for the last 100 years has had some kind of assigned text—a reader, rhetoric, and/or handbook—we might as well teach students how to engage with texts more effectively. Luckily, we're in a golden age of reading pedagogy for FYW.

WHY READING IS A CHALLENGE

I remember as an undergraduate buying used textbooks for required courses and finding that after a first chapter bombed up with a yellow highlighter, the rest of the text was unscathed. Students have a hard time reading, and there are several reasons why. John Bean lists eleven:

> Schools reward "surface reading."
> Students resist the "time-on-task required for deep reading."
> Teachers lecture over the reading, or don't address it in class.
> Students don't adjust reading strategies for different purposes.
> Or different genres.
> Students cannot parse, chunk, or dissect a reading/argument into constituent parts.
> They have a hard time reconstructing the original context.
> Or imagining themselves "in conversation" with the text's author.
> Or assimilating unfamiliar material.
> They lack cultural literacy assumed by the author.
> Or specialized vocabulary. (Bean 2014, 162–67)

Additionally, many of our students are in the middle of learning English as a second or foreign language. Bean does not include in this list the challenges imposed on our students by digital writing, social media, and mobile technology. You don't need to be a tech curmudgeon, like Mark Bauerlein, author of *The Dumbest Generation*, to believe that accelerating technologies make our jobs more complicated. However, there is reason to be optimistic: In 2016, the Pew Research Center revealed that of all demographic groups, eighteen- to twenty-nine-year-olds were more likely than any other group to have read a book in the last year. They are also the group most likely to have read an e-book, listened to an audiobook, read for work or school or pleasure or to keep up with current events, or read to research a topic of interest (Perrin 2016). The rumors of reading's death have been greatly exaggerated.

However (what an emotional seesaw!), every year since 1994, about 63 percent our nation's twelfth graders score at or below a basic reading level, defined by the National Assessment of Educational Progress as "partial mastery of fundamental skills" ("Reading Performance" 2017). A variety of other assessments show that only half or fewer of our students are meeting reading benchmarks for college readiness (Horning "Enhancing"). Add to that problem the practice of *readicide*, Kelly Gallagher's not-so-hyperbolic term to describe how testing culture and teaching malpractice kill reading interest in adolescents (Gallagher 2004), and, well, we have a problem.

WHAT ARE OUR GOALS FOR READING PEDAGOGY?

Alice Horning, one of the rock stars of reading pedagogy, has argued that our ultimate goal as FYW teachers is to help students develop "academic critical literacy." She defines academic critical literacy as the "psycholinguistic processes of getting meaning from or putting meaning into print and/or sound, images, and movement, on a page or screen, used for the purposes of analysis, synthesis, evaluation, and application; these processes develop through formal schooling and beyond it, at home and at work, in childhood and across the lifespan and are essential to human functioning in a democratic society" (2011, 4). The goal of any undergraduate education is to build in our students "the ability to read [mostly] extended informational prose texts in a college course" for the purposes described above (4). Horning makes clear that FYW cannot do this on its own; teaching reading is every faculty member's responsibility across the disciplines. Students come to us as learners who lack the "meta-reading" dispositions we find in expert readers—specifically, "meta-textual awareness" (of the shape of genres), "meta-contextual awareness" (of audience, writer, purpose, and conversation), and "meta-linguistic awareness" (of grammatical and lexical aspects) (5). Experts apply these meta-reading dispositions most often unconsciously and only after years of deliberate practice.

The Council of Writing Program Administrators provide another layer of reading outcomes under the category "Critical Thinking, Reading, and Composing" (2014):

- Use composing and reading for inquiry, learning, critical thinking, and communicating in various rhetorical contexts.
- Read a diverse range of texts, attending especially to relationships between assertion and evidence, to patterns of organization, to the interplay between verbal and nonverbal elements, and to how these features function for different audiences and situations.

- Locate and evaluate (for credibility, sufficiency, accuracy, timeliness, bias and so on) primary and secondary research materials, including journal articles and essays, books, scholarly and professionally established and maintained databases or archives, and informal electronic networks and internet sources.
- Use strategies—such as interpretation, synthesis, response, critique, and design/redesign—to compose texts that integrate the writer's ideas with those from appropriate sources.

This is an ambitious list of outcomes for a single course many students take before their frontal brainware has been assembled. While we cannot prepare students completely for the reading that will be required of them as students and employees and citizens, we can teach reading as a mindful practice that strengthens students' disposition to monitor and control reading strategies to serve writing.

WHEN WE GO DIGITAL

Before I describe a few reading pedagogies, a word on digital text. Textbooks can be expensive. If you assign an all-in-one, they can run to over $100 to the student, and you may end up using only 10 percent of the text. Sometimes costly textbooks are the tail wagging the curricular dog. Digital texts can be cheaper and more accessible to students, but they can also challenge our students' self-regulating strategies.

In February 2018, *New York Times* columnist Farhad Manjoo prophesied of the posttext future. "We have only just begun," he wrote, "to glimpse the deeper, more kinetic possibilities of an online culture in which text recedes to the background, and sounds and images become the universal language" (2018). While we're still awash in words—the fundamental building blocks of the front *and* back of the internet—our machines are making it easier to communicate through speech and image. There are smart people right now trying to make it easier to speak to digital assistants, archive and navigate the nonalphabetic semiotic web, and share user-generated multimedia. Manjoo could be wrong, folks, but are you willing to bet against him?

Yes, moving from print culture to digital culture has required some adjustments, to put it lightly. As many a hyperventilating teacher or parent has feared, the research on mobile technology use has shown significant drains to our attention, memory, and daily cognitive functioning (Wilmer, Sherman, and Chein 2017). Our students are most likely doing work for our classes, including reading, with their cell phones nearby—most likely lying on the table next to their textbooks like a malignant mind-sucking noise-making slab. Various controlled research studies have shown that students perform better (i.e., recall better, process better, synthesize better, focus better) when reading paper texts when compared to digital texts on e-readers, tablets, phones, or computers (Jabr 2013; Keim 2014; O'Malley 2017; Subrahmanyam et al. 2013). Surprisingly, 92 percent of so-called digital natives, worldwide, prefer print texts to digital texts such as e-readers, *if* the cost is comparable, even though that number is bound to decline (Schaub 2016). Maybe there are still tactile rewards for holding a book in your hands. Maybe students know intuitively that digital reading opens them up to the continuous partial attention and multitasking, two separate cognitive activities that do not bode well for deep reading.

Then again, maybe we are in a literacy revolution for which our brains have not yet made the necessary adjustments. Our technology innovates faster than our ability to reflect on it for optimal human flourishing. Reading expert Maryanne Wolf is concerned that "deep reading" will take a significant hit in the digital age if we do not prepare students to be mindful readers. Wolf defines deep reading as the kind of reading we use to "find, reflect, and potentially expand upon *what matters*" from our texts (2016, 112). Therefore, and finally coming to the point, when it comes to teaching reading in the digital age, we must teach students to "tack to and fro," like a sailor tacks in uncertain waters, between kinds of texts and the media through which they are presented (157). We should be aware of the difficulties students face when reading digital texts and prepare them to do their best in a variety of reading environments, including environments full of moving ads for H & M, Spotify, and Mountain Dew. In other words, we should teach students to be mindful readers as well as writers.

STRATEGIES FOR TEACHING READING

OK, pause again for a moment. You know what's coming next based on the previous chapters of this book: I'm going to dump on you a bunch of teaching strategies, some of which will be useful to you, some not. Ask yourself, How can I make the following list useful to me as a teacher? How will I capture the ideas that seem useful to me? How can I *transform* what Brian says here so I can apply it to my unique teaching setting? If you're feeling really ambitious, get out a piece of paper and draw two columns, one labeled "my uses" and one "my questions/push-backs." In the "uses" column, write down all the ideas you want to try in your class; in the "questions" column, pick fights with me or ask questions provoked by the advice.

Unpause. The following is an exhausting list but far from exhaustive. I don't see how any teacher can use all of them, even though I think all of them are pretty darn good. Pick and choose.

Keep the class about writing. Just a reminder. I recommend we never frame our courses by special topic readings (immigration, sexuality, food) unless the special topic is *writing*. Reading, for FYW, is in the service of learning a mindful writing process. Remember that designing meaningful writing tasks requires us first to articulate the ways we imagine student empowerment. We begin at the end, which is a writing end, not with the textbook we want to assign.

Talk about reading. This suggestion is intentionally vague, but you get the spirit of it: Talk to your students specifically and reflectively about reading. Ellen Carillo assigns her students texts about reading, for example, Mariolina Salvatori's *College English* article titled "Reading and Writing a Text" (cited in Carillo 2015, 141). This "reading about reading" method is similar to Wardle and Downs's Writing about Writing approach; in fact, in their textbook they have a few fantastic readings on literacy. I was so particular about what I wanted students to learn related to reading that I wrote my own write-up on reading. You learn quite a bit by asking students about past reading habits or interests. You learn that students' reading habits generally are not similar to yours. I've had many students who tell me they do not read—a fascinating claim from people who read on their phones all the time. (When it comes to the words *reading* and *writing*, our students can take a narrow, school-ish perspective. They need us to validate their everyday literacy practices as legit reading and writing.) At any rate, engage your students in a conversation about reading early in the semester. Ask them about their reading practices—what they like, what they hate, what they do, how (or whether) it influences them.

Have an outcome or purpose. When I assigned Dillard, I did not have a clear outcome other than some vague goofy humanistic sense that reading something beautiful would lead to rapture and therefore eager writers. We assign reading for a purpose; be clear about that purpose. Sometimes we assign texts because we want students to master the content, which is the most common reason texts are thrown at college students. Some texts are meant to kickstart enjoyable conversations, others to dramatize situational dynamics. Other texts are meant to function as models to be emulated by students (Adler-Kassner and Estrem 2007). The best way to orient students to these various purposes is to provide a reading guide that explains this frame and/or an informal W2L assignment that will require students to read for that purpose. For example, if you assign a text as a model, you can ask students as homework to write down what they notice about a text's strategies—say, its use of a specific term or metaphor.

Frame texts. It is all too common for students to encounter a reading "cold"—that is, knowing nothing about the text before casting their eyes on it. We can frame readings for students before they read them so their reading will be focused. In the last five minutes of class, get them excited about the reading they'll do that night in their dorms. Let's say you're assigning Helen Garner's delightful little essay "The Insults of Age." Before students read the text, I'd tell them the following: "Tonight we're going to read a short essay by novelist Helen Garner titled 'The Insults of Age.' I want you to think about what it might be like being in the body of a seventy-year-old but feeling mentally like you're still twenty-one. How would you respond when people in public treat you as fragile or dim-witted?" Then I'd read them the two paragraphs in which Garner describes yanking the ponytail of an insolent schoolgirl. "As you read, I want you to pay particular attention to how Garner uses personal experience to build her *ethos*. Write 200 words describing how she does that, pointing to specific moments in the text." This framing tells them a little about the writer, the genre, and the purpose for reading. Share with them background knowledge (e.g., if the content is about a topic they may know little about) or tricky vocabulary. Consider creating a reading guide, with information about the author, topic, cultural issues and understandings, and structure; include discussion questions. James Lang suggests inviting students at the end of class to predict aspects of that night's reading assignment based on their current understanding (e.g., what they know about "reparations" before reading Ta-Nehisi Coates' article about it) (see Lang 2016, 58).

Talk about the reading. A companion to that last point, this principle is simple: If you assign reading, talk about that reading in class, using what you learned about discussion a few chapters back. Reward students for the pains they took to prepare. Assume they've read the text; ask questions and lead discussions that will communicate that you expect them to read. Engage the class in the kinds of discussions that make reading a rewarding social activity. Get them talking to each other.

Teach reading as a mindful and flexible process. Teach students that reading, like writing, can be enhanced by a mindful process that includes monitoring and controlling habits similar to writing. Ellen Carillo describes mindful reading as a stance "characterized by intentional awareness of and attention to the present moment, its context, and one's perspective" (2015, 118). Model for the students how they can assess a reading task by confirming their own purpose for reading (e.g., "To prepare for class discussion") and setting a few goals for self-regulation (e.g., "I'm going to turn off my phone and place it out of view in my backpack while I read, and I'm not going to listen to music with lyrics till I'm done"). Model for them how you vary reading strategies based on your own purposes for reading (Bean 2011, 169). For example, some texts should be read closely, and some skimmed. Daniel Keller explains that when reading in digital environments, "readers oscillate between hyper and deep modes of attention and faster and slower speeds of reading" (2014, 120). For more important texts, teach students to preread the text using what Kelly Gallagher calls "first-draft reading" (2004)—studying the rhetorical situation (see next point), thumbing through the content, looking at design features such as headings, and, most important, predicting what they will learn from reading the text ("What do I know about X? What will I learn about it from this text?").

Teach texts as rhetorical artifacts. After introducing students to the concept of *rhetorical situation*, assign a variety of (short) texts one day: a poem, a Wikipedia article, a social media post, a science article, some instructions for putting furniture together. Ask the students to reconstruct the rhetorical situation in which those texts function. Specifically, discuss genre, audience, and purpose. Discuss the discourse communities that want/need/use these kinds of texts. Ask students to analyze the purpose of the text—how the writers want to influence readers' judgments, attitudes, and behaviors. In *Reading Rhetorically*, John Bean, Virginia Chappell, and Alice Gillam list a variety of "rhetorical aims" students should understand, like express, explore, inform, interpret, persuade, propose, and evaluate (2014, 19–20). Ask students to analyze the writers—what is known about them, how they command attention and credibility, what their values or identities say about their motives. Show students how genres influence the way we read and the why.

Teach them slow, close reading. These two adjectives can connote different aspects of how students exercise a particular kind of attention to a text. Slow reading requires a high-quality level of attention to a text. When we read closely, we analyze how the text works on a microlevel—its various rhetorical strategies down to the word. To teach close reading, assign students to track their reading in some kind of graphic organizer. I've assigned students to take an "analytic snapshot" in which they identify a dozen or so rhetorical strategies in a text by writing quotes from the text that demonstrate (e.g.) metaphorical language or sarcasm or an emotional appeal. Kelly Gallagher and other reading experts talk about graphic organizers that ask students to divide writing tasks into double and sometimes triple cognitive tasks. Gallagher uses T-charts for this purpose. Students make columns and write observations based on "what a text says" and then "what it does" or "why it matters." When studying persuasive texts, I ask students to describe the main claim and then the reasons/evidence. This reading supports course outcomes related to critical thinking. A rhetorical analysis writing task requires students to do this kind of reading.

And therefore assign less reading. If we want students to read slowly or closely, we should assign less of it. Keller is just one of many scholars who finds that students "shirk school reading" because of the volume assigned to them. Keller suggests "fewer readings and more support with strategies" (2014, 82). Large expensive anthologies bias us toward the coverage model of teaching, which, remember, is one of the great teaching sins of our age. If we're willing to let students read online, we can find plenty of free stuff there at any length we want. I have found that students grow significantly as readers when I assign a short text (fewer than 1,000 words) but ask them to move deeply through it, writing summaries and analyses and responses that make the text meaningful to them as writers.

Avoid quizzing. There is no better way to encourage surface reading than giving multiple choice quizzes on readings. While it is good practice to get students to recall from memory what they've read, especially if they are reading for class content, quizzes turn students into "gist" hunters, searching a text only for what they think will help them on the quiz. Critical thinking goes out the window (Bean 2011, 168).

But hold students accountable for reading. Reserve a portion of the class grade for assignments students complete based on their reading experience. Ask them to keep a reading journal, write a response, make a T-chart (see a few points above), write questions or applications, or complete summaries. If you use learning management software, you can ask students to respond to reading and then respond to each other's reading of a text.

Teach omnivorous reading. For a long while, FYW, housed in English departments, was dominated by reading practices informed by literary study (Carillo 2015; Keller 2014). That still seems to be the case in secondary language arts in the United States. Your institution may couple imaginative literature (fiction, drama, poetry) with FYW. But if FYW habits of mind are meant to transfer to other settings, then we must assign a variety of genres from various discourse communities, such as science or journalism or personal essay. Assign texts from writers representing a variety of backgrounds and identities.

Teach "dangerous" openness, as well as critical thinking. Carl Rogers, the famous psychotherapist, writes that "our first reaction to most of the statements which we hear from other people is an immediate evaluation, or judgment, rather than an understanding of it." Critical reading puts us in a critical stance; evaluation and analysis often precede, even supersede, understanding. Rogers continues: "Very rarely do we permit ourselves to *understand* precisely what the meaning" of a statement is. "Understanding is risky" because, as he puts it, "if I let myself really understand another person, I might be changed by that understanding" (1961, 18, Rogers's emphasis). We can encourage students to listen first before they make judgments, to let themselves be open to the argument presented to them. When your students encounter a persuasive text, ask them to write a summary before casting judgment on it. Even twenty-five-word summaries nutshelling an argument can help students delay critical analysis until they understand the essence of an argument (Horning 2017, 64).

(And related to that last point,) Teach personal connection. School reading keeps students from intimacy with texts. They (texts, I mean) can be friends, after all, as Wayne Booth and Marcel Proust argued. American students are growing up in a system of Common Core standards that ask them to "cite, determine, summarize, analyze, interpret, assess," but not to "respond, react, connect," let alone *enjoy* (Jolliffe 2017, 9). And then, as Rita Felski recently wrote, students are compelled to adopt a critical mood, a "stance of againstness" (2015, 189), that turns them into vigilant enemies of texts: ever hunting for hidden cultural agendas, logical fallacies, institutional malevolence, power flexing, and persuasive tricks that must be unmasked. Sure, that's part of reading like a smart person. But what about *pleasure*? What about openness, receptivity, connection—heck, joy? Before you jump into a critical reading, ask students how they *felt* as they read the text. Ask questions such as "How did this text remind you of your own observations and experience?" "Where in the text did you feel most/least engaged?" "If the author is right, what do *you/we* need to change?" "What in this text filled you with what theologian Krister Stendahl calls *holy envy*—an appreciation bordering on jealousy for the writer's rhetorical attributes, attributes you yourself want to develop?" If students are offended by a text, treat the moment with curiosity instead of condemnation. We read texts in our bodies, and our bodies often endure intense affective states, especially if we feel like our culture is threatened by a text. Invite students to share their affective experiences reading.

Teach synthesis. Graff and Birkenstein's blockbuster textbook *They Say/I Say* is a brilliant little work, and I'm madly jealous of its success even as I worry about the death-by-template approach it advocates. In an immediately accessible way, it shows students that when they write, they write in a conversation with other texts. And they need to learn the rhetorical moves of inhabiting these conversations, for instance, "disagreeing without being disagreeable" and "agreeing—with a difference." Such moves can get tricky when students are required to introduce three or four other voices to their conversation, showing how one voice reflects or refracts or rejects another. This is the kind of deep reading and writing we want students to engage in. At their best, research papers can teach students how to do this. But students have a difficult time processing a single text, let alone several, as research from the Citation Project has shown. This is why Sandra Jamieson, co-investigator on the Citation Project with Rebecca Moore Howard, argues that if we want students to engage meaningfully with other texts when writing with sources, "there is no real reason for that process to include more than three or four sources" (2013). That's a provocative statement I'm not sure I agree with, but there is so much wisdom behind it. Effective synthesis reading can be modeled by showing the work of students past and pointing out the textual moves that demonstrate effective reading-for-writing strategies, such as introducing other writers' writing and then reacting to that writing.

SET GOALS (I MEAN *YOU*—RIGHT NOW)

Now that we've finished a conversation about reading and reading strategies, take a few moments and write down *three specific strategies* you will use in your class the next time you teach a text.

PART IV

Revise

18
REVISION AS MINDFUL WRITING

As we move into part IV of the learning cycle (figure 18.1) for mindful writers, I want to offer a refresher. I've argued in this book, echoing a chorus of excellent scholars and teachers and thinkers, that the ultimate goal of FYW is for students to develop a self-regulated disposition toward writing tasks. Self-regulated (or self-directed) learners use metacognitive practices to help them monitor (assess, evaluate, reflect on) and control (act, apply, adjust, revise) their learning to maximize their awesomeness. They are motivated by the sweet complexity of a writing task, and they approach it with what John Dewey called "intelligent action" and "reflective thinking," which is the "active, persistent, and careful" analysis of what they're doing and how they can do it better (1986, 113, 118, 125).

If your students have gone this far with you, they've

- received a meaningful writing task;
- assessed that task;
- set goals;
- drafted a theory of writing;
- learned rhetorical principles (including genre, audience, purpose, and strategies);
- reviewed models—of genres and other microstrategies (like paragraphing);
- practiced invention and drafting methods;
- worked in groups to learn and apply principles;
- practiced mindful reading strategies;
- adjusted their goals and approaches while drafting;
- accepted the grim reality that they are writers for life.

With any luck, they have been practicing metacognitive processes along the way, including adjusting earlier approaches, even if only in their heads. Likely they have already received feedback from you or peers on early ideas, introductions, or paragraphs—all opportunities to monitor and control their process. In part IV, we'll focus on how we can continue to build writing mindfulness as students complete full drafts and get feedback. Feedback is at the core of mindful learning.

DOI: 10.7330/9781607329374.c018

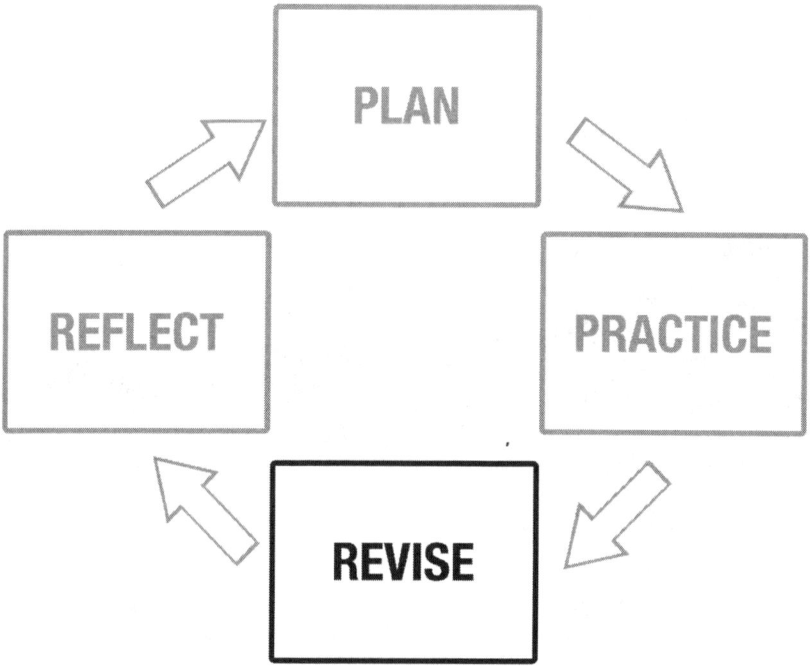

Figure 18.1. The revision stage

WHAT IS REVISION?

This morning as I was thinking about this chapter, I thought I would tell you a story about how in one of the first academic papers I wrote in college I made a reference to the 1984 movie *The Terminator* and got criticized for being too informal. But then I changed my mind without having written a single word of the story and went with this paragraph instead. Is that revision? When I wrote "word" in that last sentence, I first wrote "world" automatically and had to delete the "l." Is that revision? In the first go at this paragraph, I had a different ending to the first sentence (more colloquial: "got thumped by my teacher for it"), used the word "page" instead of "single word" in the second sentence, and just now thought that "just a moment ago," which was once the first phrase of the paragraph, did not accurately reflect my cognitive process, so I changed it. I also moved the "in one of the first . . ." phrases so that it follows the word "how." Revision?

Yes. And not entirely.

I've placed *revision* as a mindful activity after *practice* in order to isolate the important work of assessing full drafts. In reality, we revise the moment we commit mentally to one possibility but then adjust it. We're revising the moment we start thinking of writing, and therefore in a real sense we cannot step in the same writing project twice. While there are a variety of ways we could define revision, Jill Fitzgerald provides what I think is the definitive one: "Revision means making changes at any point in the writing process. It involves identifying discrepancies between intended and instantiated text, deciding what could or should be changed in the text and how to make desired changes and operating, that is, making the desired changes. Changes may or may not affect meaning of the text, and they may be major or minor. Also, changes may be made in the writer's mind before being instantiated in written text, at the time text is first written, and/or after text is first written" (1987, 484). Research on cognition and writing shows that we make these changes as our working memory detects dissonance between what we intend (amazing, life-changing prose) and what we produce (fetid garbage). Revision, then, is the essence of writing mindfulness. Revision is the iterative, ongoing instantiation of the metacognitive process (Harris, Santangelo, and Graham 2010). Revision helps us do a number of things as writers, not just make corrections. Through it we discover and create new knowledge, shape discourse effectively, overcome egocentrism, achieve rhetorical goals, perform our identities, polish and prune, expand ideas, change course, and otherwise improve our work (Harr 2006; Murray 2001).

Our students may not be in the mood to do much or any of that stuff, perhaps because *no* writer is overjoyed at the thought of taking a sledgehammer to the edifice. For more than forty years now, our research has been showing us the revision limitations of novice writers. In 1980, Nancy Sommers showed how novice (i.e., student) writers understood revision as a "rewording activity" to "clean up speech" rather than an opportunity to refine meaning or connect better with readers (1980, 381). One study showed that over 80 percent of revisions made by twelfth graders were minor stylistic changes or surface corrections (Beach and Friedrich 2006; see also Fitzgerald 1987; MacArthur 2013). Students are afraid to lose what they've paid so dearly to put on the page. Unsurprisingly, they cannot detect problems of meaning, syntax, grammar, or punctuation as consistently as experts (Hayes 2012). They lack revision task schema (e.g., genre knowledge) or the critical reading skills necessary to understand how even their own work is working (MacArthur 2013; McCutchen, Teske, and Bankston 2008). They also struggle keeping their audience in mind while writing, which is a developmental challenge for all novice writers from childhood into early adulthood (Kellogg 2008). They stick with what they've learned, and sometimes what they've learned isn't helpful.

How do mature or professional writers revise, then? It's hard to say. Experts demonstrate a variety of strategies for revision, some of which may look a heckuva lot like what inexperienced writers do: after-draft cosmetics (Faigley et al. 1985). However, experienced writers have dramatically different dispositions from the very beginning of a writing task. Experienced writers approach revision with the metacognitive mindset we are seeking to instill in FYW students.

In her research on expert revision, Nancy Sommers showed that experienced writers talk about revision in terms of the rhetorical situation: finding the shape of the argument, connecting with readers and their needs, discovering what they mean in connection with their purpose (1980). More recently, Alice Horning has confirmed these findings. Expert writers, like expert readers, have several different kinds of meta-awareness—about their readers, about their own strategies, about the way language works, about writing technologies, about collaborative work (2006). Expert writers revise with significant advantages over novices because their long-term memory is stocked with subject matter knowledge, genre awareness, and process schemata that have been refined over the years (McCutchen, Teske, and Bankston 2008). They've also been typing for longer; sometimes we overlook the fact that students' typing skills influence their working memory capacity.

The road to this kind of expertise runs right through our classrooms. We have to convince students that revision will be rewarding. We have to convince them, in the words of our threshold concepts, that "a text is an object outside oneself that can be improved and developed" (Bazerman and Tinberg 2015) and that "failure can be an important part of writing development" (Brooke and Carr 2015). We have to convince them that their first attempts likely are inadequate to the demands of the situation. We have to help them catch the vision that *re*vision is a vital tool for the self-directed writer.

TEACHING REVISION

Teaching revision is challenging in no small part because revision strategies can be wildly idiosyncratic. Think about your own revision strategy. Would you recommend it to your students? I find after all these years that as a professional academic writer, I spend significantly more time planning my writing than I do revising it. Before I commit anything to paper, I let a project colonize my mind, thinking and reading and neglecting people I love while in a nerdy reverie at the dinner table. By the time I start writing, I've written a draft of the thing in my mind. As a result, I'm (over?) confident in the shape it takes. In fact, research suggests that students benefit more from a plan-heavy process than they do a "throw everything up there and then change it all" approach, even though the findings are not entirely conclusive (Galbraith and Torrance 2004). While writers will have their own ways of approaching revision, there are more or less mindful ways of going about it, and the following ideas will help students engage in revision in a more mindful way.

Share tales of revision. Show students your own work you've had to revise significantly. Or you can borrow from professional writers. I know Ernest Hemingway rewrote the end of *A Farewell to Arms* approximately 1,347,563 times. Or something like that. Find some artifacts showing students how much professional writers revise. Tales of revision lend credence to the idea that all writers can improve—specifically, they can improve what Anne Lamott has called so memorably "shitty first drafts" (1995). It helps students adopt the growth mindset promoted by Carol Dweck.

Teach discovery drafting. I know I just said that planning in some ways works against thorough revision, but there is something to be said about encouraging students to "outrace the censor," as Donald Murray put it, and draft without worrying too much about policing first sentences (2001, 10). I don't think discovery drafting and planning are opposed to each other. Planning, after all, is about self-regulating and rhetorical architecture (i.e., genre, audience, purpose), and many kinds of sentences can dress a rhetorical frame. Once those first things are established, your students should let out the Wild Thing and leave the fine tuning for later. I feel this is especially true for sentence-level issues. Novices can paralyze themselves when the Revision Police crack down on every sentence (Perl 1979).

Teach revision in stages. Since mindfulness works most effectively throughout a process, not just at the beginning or end, give students opportunities to test ideas and get feedback on work at various stages: first ideas, theses, introductions, first paragraphs, and the like. If you cut back on the assigned readings, you can use class time for workshopping writing at different stages. I've found it helpful to teach students to revise for surface-level concerns—stylistic changes, editing, and error correcting—*after* they have revised for global concerns related to genre, audience, and purpose.

Teach scales of concern. Related to this last point, teach students—by modeling or by rubrics or through peer review or your comments—to recognize what is most important to work on when revising (Breidenbach 2006). It may surprise students to find that their instructor is not particularly concerned about grammar, punctuation, or mechanics in an early draft. I can't tell you how many times I've surprised friends and family members when I've commented mostly on genre issues on their personal statements for law school or medical school, ignoring (with *great personal anguish!*) their misuse of the comma. I separate out my scale of concern like this: rhetorical situation (genre, audience, purpose), rhetorical strategies (argument, character, emotional appeal, style, design, maybe organization if that isn't clear in genre), and then sentence-level stylistics (grammar, spelling, punctuation, mechanics). Your scale will communicate what you value most. It can also help students organize the sequence I mentioned in the last point.

Use models as revision tools. You can tell I'm big on models. You can use them as revision tools. Ask students to write an intro and bring it to class. Then show them an effective intro, analyze it with them, and then give them time to revise their work in imitation of the model.

Give sufficient time to revise. If you teach FYW in one semester, you're already stuffed to the rafters with things to cover. When I review syllabi, I often see a prolonged drafting process, a day for feedback, and then maybe a day for revision practices. Now, the last point about revision in stages may mitigate this problem, but students need time—a few days, at least—to get feedback and practice revision strategies.

Teach revision as reader centered. Mature writers keep in mind the needs of their audiences. Maybe we can, in fact, draft "with our eyes closed" to audience needs, as Peter Elbow teaches us, but even Elbow has argued that "the most trustworthy motive for revising is the desire to make things work on readers" (1987; 1981, 122). Once students have completed a draft, ask them to consider some of the following questions: "Who is your audience, and what are their needs?" "How/where in your text have you considered the needs of your audience?" "How have you used the conventions of the genre effectively, considering the discourse community in/for which you write?" "How/where have you provided support that your audience will accept?" "How will someone who disagrees with you respond to your argument?" "How have you used the conventions of the genre to guide readers from one point to the next?" "How/where have you used rhetorical strategies to *delight* your readership?" "What in your draft needs to change, considering the needs of your audience?" Since you, dear teacher, are an important reader and grader, you should consider prompting them to review the rubric you've provided and ask, "How does your draft respond to the exigence of the assignment?" Here's some bitter medicine for us all: These questions are much more motivating, more alive and generative, when students write to real audiences for their own purposes. I don't know how we get around that problem completely in a school setting, with required assignments and grades.

Teach revision as collaboration. In the next few chapters, I will talk more about how to set up peer review and respond to student writing. Both activities communicate to students that writing is a sociocognitive exercise attempting to cross the divide of our cultures, boundaries, and bodies to make connections and influence judgments. Peers and teachers can reinforce the social purpose of writing by helping writers beta-test ideas.

Use the rubric to cue students to genre needs. Donald Murray's fantastic book *The Craft of Revision* walks students through a variety of revision exercises for a variety of writing traits, including accuracy or focus or detail or coherence or form or design or a magical mysterious trait called "voice." While these traits may be to some degree universal in all good writing, they sound more to me like genre questions. For example, to what extent does *this genre*, the one students are writing at the moment, require accuracy or detail? What voice is appropriate or typical for this genre? If you've articulated levels of quality in an analytic rubric with separate descriptors of traits, you can ask students to review the rubric while revising. This kind of self-evaluation using established criteria has led to measurable improvements to student writing (MacArthur 2013). You can turn rubric traits into genre questions such as "How/where have you synthesized more than one credible source to support your position?" You could have students use the rubric to rate themselves—that is, circle or mark or score their draft on a rubric—as an exercise in self-evaluation.

Ask students to write a "Dear Reader" letter. In *Responding to Student Writers,* Nancy Sommers suggests that we ask students to write a Dear Reader letter once they've completed a draft or even when they turn in a final draft (see also Elena Shvidko's work on "Letter to the Reviewer" [Shvidko 2015] and Jeff Sommers's work on "The Writer's Memo" [Sommers 2012]). The Dear Reader letter represents the best of metacognition. Students can use it to reflect on their process and ask specific questions related to concerns about the draft. Sommers lists the following questions as prompts for a Dear Reader letter: "What are the strengths of your rough draft? What are the problems of the draft?" "What were the challenges you encountered writing your draft?" "What is your thesis?" "If you had two more days to write this draft, where would you focus your attention?" "What questions are you asking about your draft that you want to make sure your readers answer?" (N. Sommers 2013, 12–13). The writers themselves should ask questions in the Dear Reader letter. Their questions should not be yes/no questions ("~~Are my ideas clear?~~") but questions like "Where do I lose you?" or "How have I provided evidence to support my thesis?" Because the Dear Reader letter asks students to monitor their practice, it works as an assessment tool to help you determine the quality of their metacognitions. However, in a recent article Jeff Sommers wisely cautions that these letters may have conflicting purposes if we intend them to be used both, and equally, for student reflection and teacher/peer response. Work-in-progress reflection is a different kind of reflection than the kind a student might do as a culminating experience at the end of a task or semester (J. Sommers 2016).

Teach revision beyond the grade. If our goal is to help students become better writers, then we can invite students to revise their work even after we've graded it. I include in my syllabus the following revision policy:

> **My Revision Policy.** I want you all to succeed as writers. And since the only way you succeed is by *deliberate practice* from feedback, I accept revisions if you receive a B+ or lower on the first three major assignments. Since I want you to get the most from these revisions, I do require you to do the following:
>
> 1. Read carefully my comments on your paper.
> 2. Visit with me in my office to discuss a revision strategy.
> 3. Ask at least one other person (a roommate, a peer tutor, a parent, or a friend) to read and comment on your paper.
> 4. Rewrite the paper *with significant revisions highlighted* (with a highlighter or using markup on a word processor).
> 5. Write a reflection (between 300 and 500 words) describing (1) the changes you made; (2) how the changes make the paper more effective, considering your genre, audience, and purpose; and (3) how revising the paper will help you in future writing tasks, in this class or other classes. Please be specific in your reflection by providing details, referring to specific page numbers, and using language from class instruction. (And tell me who you asked to read the paper, from no. 3.)
> 6. Turn it in *with the graded draft* and reflection included. I won't accept the revisions without all three parts—the graded draft with my comments, the new highlighted draft, and the reflection.
>
> All six of these tasks must be completed before I will grade your revision. I will treat your revision as if it were the paper you turned in in the first place. (In other words, if your paper received a C, but the revision makes it an A–, then you get an A– on the paper. I don't average the scores.)

Expect drafts to get worse after revision. Students don't always improve incrementally upward (Christiansen and Bloch 2016). Our best longitudinal studies demonstrate this. When we ask students to do things they haven't done, say, consider audience needs through genre composing, their working memory takes on extra freight and has to work harder. Expect that sometimes iteration will not lead to obvious improvement in the quality of their work. I once worked with a student who revised two paragraphs at least four times in consultation with me, and each draft made the writing more obtuse. There is no happy ending to this anecdote. Cathleen Breidenbach teaches us that if we want students to take risks, do new and unexpected things, "depart from formulas and conventional protocol," then we need to make revision to some degree "risk free," by which she means that we shouldn't penalize students with lower grades for taking seriously the wrecking-ball approach to revision (Breidenbach 2006, 207).

Teach portfolio thinking. A portfolio is a curated collection of artifacts, either in hard-copy or digital folder, showcasing work across time. Programs that use portfolios may ask students to compile a portfolio near the end of the semester that will include work across drafts and writing tasks and may include a critical reflection that refers specifically to places in the work that show writing growth. Portfolios are powerful metacognitive tools because they demonstrate student growth—or, they ask students themselves to track their growth as writers across drafts (Belanoff and Dickson 1991). Revision is made more powerful for students when they can see how much their revisions have transformed their writing. (Kind of like the odd satisfaction people get watching pressure-washing videos on YouTube.) I ask students to keep shared folders in Google Drive with multiple documents for each writing task: drafts (and yes, they have to duplicate drafts to preserve them in Drive) and reflection essays. I've also asked students to use "track changes" so they can see their own growth as writers across a draft.

Use a revision checklist. Before students turn in a final draft of a writing project, ask them to review a series of questions related to their work. A checklist gives students one more opportunity to step back from the project and ask themselves whether or not they've done their best work. The following list, which I composed with the help of other instructors in our program, is likely way too thorough for any human writer to account for, but it may inspire some reflective self-assessment before the work comes due:

Review

I have used an effective writing process that includes goal setting.
I have been willing to cut, rewrite, and rework my writing so I can resee.
I have saved editing and proofreading till the end (as much as I can).
I have read my writing out loud.
I have revised the sentences that don't sound good to my ear.
I have proofread it—closely, in hard copy if necessary.
I have asked peers, the Writing Center, and my instructor for feedback.
I have incorporated their feedback through multiple drafts.
I have consulted a handbook or reliable online source to understand conventions.
I have done my best—or, the best I could do within the time constraints.

Rhetorical Situation

I have written in the genre appropriate for the rhetorical situation.
I have studied a variety of examples of the genre.
I considered my audience carefully—their needs, their values, their time.
My purpose is clear.
I have used the conventions my instructor expects.
I establish my credibility by showing I understand the topic (i.e., I've done my research).
I establish my goodwill with my audience.
I treat rhetorical adversaries fairly.
I present alternative opinions accurately.
I have shown balance by anticipating and respecting alternative viewpoints.
I considered the assumptions I'm making.
I have provided sufficient credible evidence to support my point.
I make emotional appeals fitting for the situation.
I have tried to give readers a good reading experience.

Flow

In my introduction, I capture my readers' attention.

My introduction is relevant, specific, and compelling.

When appropriate, I forecast the organization of the rest of the paper.

I transition between paragraphs using signals/transitional words.

My paragraphs develop single ideas.

My paragraphs roll out in a sequence that makes sense.

I use cohesive strategies (e.g., transitional phrases) to connect sentences together.

My conclusion does not merely reiterate the introduction.

My conclusion ties together the writing and gives readers something to think about.

I have checked for topics/ideas that don't apply to my main thesis and taken them out.

I have checked my paper for balance. I don't spend too much time on trivial information.

My tone is consistent.

Style

I used an editing/proofreading process only after I wrote a rough draft.

My sentence types vary.

My sentence lengths vary.

I've considered carefully my word choice.

I've cut back all the dead wood (wordiness).

I use concrete words.

I use powerful words for imagery or compelling connotations.

I avoid sexist or demeaning language.

I avoid clichés.

I use "to be" verbs sparingly and purposefully.

I write in active voice most of the time, with clear subjects and verbs.

My sentence fragments are intentional.

I've read my paper out loud and revised for rhythm, flow, voice, mood.

I use metaphors to argue, delight.

I use rhetorical schemes (e.g., balance or repetition).

I use commas purposefully (as in, I understand where to put them).

I use other punctuation appropriately, and for variety and emphasis.

Formatting

I have given my writing a catchy and descriptive title that will draw in readers.

I have proofread my paper! Get off my case now!

My paper is in the documentation style (MLA or Turabian or other) the genre demands.

My sources are cited appropriately (for the documentation style).

If I cite sources, I have a works cited page in the proper format.

I summarize sources in my own language.

I use block quotes sparingly, if at all, and I contextualize them.

My sources are cited ethically (to distinguish my writing from the writing of others).

I have consciously selected a font and format to maximize my rhetorical effect.

19
RESPONDING TO MINDFUL WRITERS

"I think you are actually quite prejudicial," my teacher said at the bottom of the analysis I wrote for an undergraduate literature course. "I'd really like to see you recast this without the soapboxing." Five years after that, as a graduate student I received a rejection from an academic journal: "I found the style of the paper smug." Three years after that, now safely in an assistant professorship, I got bounced at another journal with the following judgment: "This essay is clear to specialists and nonspecialists alike because it is essentially shallow."

Ouch. Prejudicial, smug, shallow. They forgot ugly, lazy, and disrespectful.

When you give your writing to other people, you lay bare your soul. You get up on the examination table with a breezy hospital gown that doesn't cover all your weaknesses. When I give my writing to someone else, I am at that moment most vulnerable to the desire to be *liked*—even more than understood, which is anti-intellectual and vain. I'm embarrassed at how acutely my long-term memory has stored these comments. I'm equally sheepish of the fact that at this late stage in my career, I still commit the "fundamental attribution error" by thinking that my writing is an extension of my identity, rather than just one situationally bound symbolic expression of it (Aronson 2012, 162). Unless our students are cyborgs, they, too, will have emotional experiences reading what we and others have to say about their work. (That was unfair to cyborgs.)

There is no learning without feedback. Chris Anson said it succinctly enough: "Writers improve by *being read*" (1999, 302, Anson's emphasis). Several years ago I had an argument with an instructor who insisted her students, if left alone to do their work all semester without anyone commenting on it, would grow in their knowledge as writers through radical self-actualization. I didn't believe it then, and I don't believe it now. And yet, as I've said from the beginning of this book, there are better and worse ways to provide feedback to students. This chapter is about how we can respond to the major writing tasks of mindful writers consistently, effectively, ethically, and efficiently.

DOI: 10.7330/9781607329374.c019

RESPONDING AS A KIND OF ASSESSMENT

A note on terms. In writing studies, we distinguish responding to writing, which is any effort we make to give feedback on student work in progress or completion (including grading—more on that in the next chapter), from assessing writing, even though responding is a kind of assessment. Assessment is the intelligent design of learning based on careful judgments about student performance. It is the process of establishing measurable outcomes, deciding on acceptable evidence that students have achieved those outcomes, planning and executing curriculum, analyzing evidence of learning, and then doing the whole dang thing all over again with informed revisions to outcomes or curriculum (Suskie 2009; Wiggins and McTighe 2005).

Since writing assessment, as Brian Huot describes it, "consists of the judgments we make about student writing ability, the form these judgments can take, and the context within which these judgments are made," it can include classroom practices such as responding and grading (2002, 7). Assessment is the larger professional project of curricular evolution, both in our own teaching and as communities working in writing programs. Programs can assess student learning directly by evaluating a random sample of FYW papers and making program changes as a result. If we're not reflective enough, assessment is also the means by which institutions continue to sort and punish nondominant identities (Inoue 2015). I hope you are invited to participate in program assessment at some point in your careers for what it will teach you about your institution.

This chapter is about the assessment we do at the individual level, specifically how we, as mentor writers, *respond* to student writers in marginal notes, end comments, student conferences, and grades. Responding can take a significant amount of our time and energy. And it's time and energy well spent, if we can learn how to do it without wearing ourselves out. Our program routinely surveys thousands of our FYW students to know how useful various teaching strategies are for them as writers. Time and again, over 90 percent of the respondents label teacher comments and conferences "useful" or (around twice as often) "very useful." Don't ask me what they say about the textbooks, including the one *I* wrote. (I'm sure they find it prejudicial, smug, and shallow.)

WHAT DO WE KNOW ABOUT RESPONDING?

As with many other principles we've talked about in this book, teacher response is a much-discussed, much-researched aspect of what we do.

There are research findings. There is also a significant amount of *lore*, which is the word Stephen North used to describe the "accumulated body of traditions, practices, and beliefs" built up by the many years of teachers experiencing their own teaching (1987, 22). Both can be useful. Here I review the research findings that I think are most helpful for beginning teachers to understand about responding to student writers.

First, and somewhat depressing, it has been difficult for researchers to demonstrate significant improvements in *quality* within and across drafts based on teacher comments (Haswell 2008; Hillocks 1986; Knoblauch and Brannon 2006). Let that sink in a moment. No, let Cy Knoblauch and Lil Brannon sink it into us like a hatchet: Controlled research experiments have shown that teacher commenting "has limited meaningful impact on draft-to-draft revision and virtually no demonstrable effect on performance from assignment to assignment" (2006, 14). Now, I'm convinced—and I think Knoblauch and Brannon are convinced, too—that evaluating changes in writing quality in controlled studies based on short-term curricular treatments is a sucker's game. Writing development is a multidecade journey that takes almost as long as it takes to watch the *Lord of the Rings* trilogy, director's cut. Yet it does seem to be the case that aside from the changes students make as a result of a directive ("Change this comma to a period" or "Cut this sentence"), we are unsure (empirically) to what extent students improve the quality of their work as a result of what we write on it.

However, there is convincing evidence indicating that students will not engage with revision meaningfully, or at all, without feedback (Beach and Friedrich 2006). Our responses cue students to the social nature of writing by dramatizing a reader reading. We show respect for writers by taking interest in what they are trying to do. Moreover, it is evident that teacher commenting influences significantly the quality of the writing experience for students. For example, studies show that students who receive negative feedback write less and think less of themselves as writers and of writing generally (Hillocks 1986). *Negative* here can connote comments directed only at what students have done wrong *or* comments that sound impatient, demeaning, or angry. Such comments hurt students emotionally, which, as biologist James Zull makes clear, hurts them sociocognitively. In other words, positive emotions prime learning; negative ones do the opposite (Bean 2011, 319–20; see also Bain 2012).

And even if we jump the low hurdle of "just not being jerks" in our responses, research shows that we teachers leave a bewildering array of idiosyncratic responses, often misunderstood by students, that tend to be influenced by our own pet peeves or unreflective prejudices. In several studies, teachers routinely ignored or misdiagnosed student errors, perhaps because they were themselves unclear about the rules (Beach and Friedrich 2006; Haswell 1983; Lunsford and Lunsford 2008). Unsurprisingly, we have found that students respond more warmly to comments that are positive, specific, improvement directed, criteria backed, and aimed at engaging them in a conversation about their writing. Our comments can help students step away from the writing task and make adjustments that will reinforce their mindful habits.

RESPONDING TO DRAFTS

My publisher has warned me that it would violate copyright law to open up Nancy Sommers's *Responding to Student Writers* and copy it all down here. So, short of that, I'll have to synthesize what I've learned from amazing mentors (including Sommers and other scholars) and seventeen years of teaching. Pick and choose what works best for you. You'll notice that some of these suggestions have advice that will help you reduce the dreaded "paper load," a phrase that almost every teaching textbook uses to describe what it's like to wade into a pile of student work. (By "paper" I'm referring also to digital writing.)

Use response to extend teaching. Our responses to student drafts should reinforce what we've been teaching, in class or in online lessons. Our responses should use "the familiar language of classroom instruction," including key terms we've discussed in class, in readings, on assignment sheets and rubrics (N. Sommers 2013, 7). Specifically, our comments should help students think mindfully about the genre they have spent time analyzing in the planning part of the learning cycle.

Respond as a reader. As a specific form of reading set in a learning context, responding to student writing is not necessarily inauthentic, but it is quite funky. We're sure as heck not reading these things for pleasure in our spare time. We're reading work in progress intended (ostensibly) for readers other than ourselves. Louise Wetherbee Phelps uses the term *pedagogical hermeneutics* to describe the "interpretive frameworks" we use as teachers when we read and respond (1989, 47). Often writing teachers read with a hypersensitivity no everyday reader would exhibit. Our vigilance pays off; students make plenty of errors upon which we can practice our editing marks. It would be better if we tried to see a student text as an attempt to engage with a readership in a rich social context of genre, audience, and purpose. "As responders, we dramatize the presence of a reader," writes Nancy Sommers (2013, xi). In our response, we can approximate rhetorical reception and thereby reinforce a fundamental dimension of mindful writing—rhetorical awareness. We can respond as a reader by pointing out places where we get lost, where we expect one thing and get another, where things get tedious, where we might take issue with what is being said. Often I write things like, "Your intended audience might respond by thinking X" or "What can you do here to make your meaning more clear for readers?" or "Seems like we need more background before we understand Y."

Be selective. As with revision strategies, in our responding we should have an order of concern that demonstrates what we value most. Stay focused on those global issues that professional writers, as mindful practitioners, attend to. Consider performing triage; ignore minor problems in a paper to focus on such global aspects as genre, evidence, and coherence. We don't have time to point out everything that could change in a paper, and doing so would paralyze the student writer anyway. Being selective also helps us keep the balance of responsibility for revision with the students. N. Sommers suggests we ask, "What *single* lesson do I want to convey to students" in our comments (2013, 18, Sommers's emphasis)? Instead of "marking" all over a paper, look for specific patterns of concern and make a single comment that can influence the whole text.

Praise. As we've seen, student writers, especially struggling writers, need encouragement (Daiker 1989). They need to feel supported. I'm not saying this because I think college students should be coddled or have spaces free from criticism. Specific, sincere praise is just good psychological motivation. It helps students feel less apprehensive about the writing process, thus freeing them up to write with less hesitation, less inhibition. One way we can do this is to begin comments with "I like the way you . . ." to show that writing can actually *please* readers—imagine! (Daiker 1989, 111). We should never respond to student work without pointing out the good things we're seeing in the draft, the things we hope to see in subsequent drafts.

But maintain high standards. In one research study, students revised more and improved more when they received feedback—called by the researchers "magic feedback"—that could be summarized like this: "I'm giving you these comments because I have very high expectations and I know that you can reach them" (Coyle 2018, 56). I care about you, says this kind of comment, and while I have high standards, I want you to succeed and I'm giving you this moment to practice.

Be kind. You may not be a fan of emojis, but you have to admit that they help fill in the affective gaps in written communication. I am not one bit ashamed of the fact that I draw smiley faces when I comment on student work. I'm also more, uh, *chatty*, if that makes any sense, when I comment. ("Hmm . . . A lovely description, Kayla, but you seem to have gone on a tangent here!" Notice the playful exclamation point!) Writing devoid of affective meaning can be misconstrued as being abrupt or more impatient or grouchy than we intend. I think we should overcorrect for this challenge when we comment on student writing by overcommunicating our nurturing rigor.

But be specific. Our praise should be specific—specifics in the text, specific key terms, specific challenges. "Good job" is about the worst thing you can write on student work, second only to "bad job," I guess. Vague, positive comments tend to reinforce a fixed mindset about their identities as writers rather than their efforts as writers. Along these lines, recent research into parenting shows that praise along the lines of "You're so smart" or "You're a great writer" tends to transform children into anxious quitters who think success is largely out of their control (Bronson and Merryman 2009). Specific praise reinforces good writing decisions and encourages more. Constructive comments for change should be specific as well. Think of writing comments a la "On p. 5 I see where you have effectively quoted a scientist, but I don't see how that quote relates to the rest of that paragraph. How can you write a sentence or two after the quote to incorporate it more effectively?"

Be directive with care. Telling students directly to make specific changes takes all the thinking away from them. What often happens is that students read the directives as a summative list of everything they've done wrong, and they change only those things that we've "marked" (White and Wright 2016, 54). Then after we give them a C+, they'll ask, "Why did I get such a bad grade when I made all the changes you asked for?" As White and Wright have rightly written, "We must convey to student writers that responsibility and control remain with them and that they need to do more than merely respond to our comments" (55). On the other hand, if we can explain, briefly, why they may want to consider a change as it relates to audience, we can continue to reinforce a reader-centered disposition. If you're anything like me, this advice will be difficult to follow. If your students are like mine, they will want oodles of directive comments to serve as convenient checklists for surface revision. Deny them the satisfaction.

Wait. If you're responding to hard-copy papers, write with a pencil. Because chances are you're gonna write something dumb and then have to erase it. Wait to respond till you've read most of the paper. I can't tell you how many times I've written, "You haven't done X here" and then three paragraphs later wrote "Oh! *Here's* where you do X!" Give students time to lay out an argument before jumping in. I'm a much better commenter if I've read the entire draft once without making any comments. I have a felt sense of the entire project.

Be marginal. Marginal comments—meaning, comments at specific points in the margins (or word-processing comment boxes) of a text—work nicely to draw students' attention to specific issues where they occur in a text. They can also start to look like a crime scene if we get too crazy with them. Questions work nicely as marginal comments; editing marks do not, in no small part because students likely won't understand them. Several writing scholars suggest that we use marginal comments sparingly and deliberately.

Use end comments as part of the dialogue. I've found it useful to read an entire draft making no comments and then write a longer end comment that I hope helps students think mindfully about revision. Nancy Sommers suggests a six-part format to the genre of the end comment: (1) salute the student ("Dear Sonia"), (2) highlight strengths, (3) highlight weaknesses, (4) provide "guidance across the drafts" ("In your next paper . . ."), (5) "reinforce the writer-reader relationship," and (6) sign off with your name (2013, 24). If we use the end comment effectively, we will have responded to their "Dear Reader" letter with a reader's perspective on how the text could be improved in light of the writer's purpose and audience needs.

Ask students to write a revision plan. Also an idea I've taken from Sommers. A revision plan is now the student's response to your response to their Dear Reader letter. Once they get their feedback from you and their peers, ask them to write a brief informal revision plan describing what they're going to change and how those changes will strengthen the text. This is yet another moment for mindful writing—they are setting new product goals based on the beta test of their writing task.

Focus on the student writer. It's easy to get caught up in the topic of a student paper, especially if the topic is political. It is likely that not all your students will share your political views, and if you give them the option, they *will* write about, and defend, political views you find repugnant. Such moments can extend teaching if we can learn how to take on the role of rhetorical listener and not pick fights about political issues. On the other hand, students will be excited to see that we are engaging with them about ideas and not just grammary stuff.

Treat error lightly, deliberately, and systematically. To be frank, I do not spend a significant amount of my teaching energy worrying about, or teaching about, or drawing attention to, or mitigating error. (I first typed "mitigating *against* error," technically a usage error.) There is almost universal agreement on this point: We should not mark every error in a student text. It is a waste of our time; it inordinately hurts nondominant students; and it will not teach students how to understand error, correct them in the text, and avoid them in the future, which is not a worthy goal in the first place. When we go error marking, we commit our own unforced errors. When we mark errors, we end up mismarking aspects of the text as "errors" when they reflect usage or style issues instead. Sometimes we mark errors that are not really errors. Or we mark some errors and not others, but students don't know that. Or we mark things as errors that will likely go unnoticed by readers. Or we mark as errors what linguists would recognize as acceptable usage in a student's cultural context. Or we mark more errors when the content displeases us, or the student. Or we mark errors on drafts that will be significantly rewritten, so why bother when those sentences will no longer exist? (There are some classic academic texts on this problem. E.g., see Haswell 1983; Lunsford and Lunsford 2008; Wall and Hull 1989; Williams 1981.) All that said, it feels like malpractice to ignore errors that likely will impede the reading experience, even though (again) our unnatural hypervigilance as teachers makes me wonder what kind of "reading experience" we're imagining. Ideally students will learn to proofread their own late-stage drafts, if the rhetorical situation demands that kind of polishing. So, Richard Haswell has suggested a compromise between doing nothing and draining an entire ink chamber on a student text: He proposes a method he calls "minimal marking." With minimal marking, we put checks or *X*s in the right-hand margins by lines that contain "*unquestionable* errors in spelling, punctuation, capitalization, and grammar" (Haswell 1983, 601, my emphasis). In a short study, he found that with minimal marking students corrected on their own around 61 percent of the errors they committed, with no explanation needed from him. Look for patterns of error, not isolated single errors. An alternative is to use a "find and fix" method: At the bottom of the text, write something to the effect of, "I notice you've made a few comma errors. Check our handbook p. XX for a discussion about this principle, and then see if you can find and fix all the times when you do that." It is particularly important to discuss with students how such language standards are rhetorically situated. (It is likely, at least I hope it's likely, that we will be the most understanding, forgiving, celebratory of language difference and/or error of any professional audience our writers might encounter in college and in their careers.)

What if your students are L2 students—English-language learners, international students, immigrants, refugees, or Generation 1.5 learners (children born in the United States whose parents immigrated and whose language-at-home is not English)? What if their cultural language practices deviate from the rigorous publishing qualifications of standard written English (SWE), the language of privilege? Will they be able to detect "unquestionable" errors or "find and fix" them? Some L2 students will know more about the terms of English grammar than you; others will have what a hypervigilant error-hunter will consider errors in nearly every sentence of a draft. To ignore entirely syntactic, lexical, or morphological errors does them no service. Research in Second Language Acquisition (SLC) suggests that giving limited corrective feedback does in fact improve L2 students' writing over time, if we give feedback on serious, frequent, and "stigmatizing" errors (Ferris and Hedgcock 2014, 282, 286). According to Ferris and Hedgcock, L2 students benefit from direct, "point-of-error" feedback (i.e., label the error where it appears with language terms they've learned). They also benefit from advanced editing training. In short, if you teach an L2 writing class, you should receive training on L2 pedagogical approaches, and some of the critical theory that comes with it.

Aggregate feedback. I should get stamps made with phrases such as "This sentence does not seem to be connected with the rest of the paragraph" or "What evidence do you have that this is the case?" My high school calculus teacher had a stamp that had on it the words "Get off your" and then the back end of a donkey. Often you'll see the same problems in several students' drafts. Take note of that. Instead of writing the same thing on everyone's draft, make a handout or LMS post of the seven to eight challenges you see many students having.

Massacre one paragraph. Related to this last point, you may decide to give students significant stylistic feedback in a single paragraph of their work to show the extensive, detailed revision they can perform in later stages of the drafting process. I take a twisted enjoyment out of going "*New Yorker* editor" on a paragraph of student writing, cutting out all the clichés and dead wood and replacing bloated subjects, just to show them options for careful stylistic revisions in late-stage drafts.

Have an editing party. Related to the last two points, once students have done the revisions and they are preparing to turn in a "polished" draft, ask them to bring it to class and exchange papers for one last proofreading party before turning it in. Such an activity could be preceded by instruction on punctuation and other horrible, confusing, joy-killing rule systems.

Use tech to comment. We have a part-time instructor named Lisa who has for over thirty years given her students audio feedback on their papers in the form of cassette tapes. From what I've heard, the students loved listening to this gifted teacher praise their work and offer specific feedback for future drafts. But at some point, Lisa's students started complaining that they'd been forced to borrow a grandmother's Oldsmobile to play the cassette tapes, since cassette players hadn't been sold in stores for twenty years. (By the way, I love the idea of students driving around in old cars listening to their teacher praise their writing, windows [manually] rolled down, tears of joy streaming down their faces.) With learning management software, digital recording, screencasting, voice memos, and other tools, audio responses to students have never been easier. Research on this topic shows that with audio and/or video comments (or screencasting comments) we can say more in less time and create powerful affective experiences that reinforce our relationship with our students (Anson et al. 2016; Grigoryan 2017; J. Sommers 2012). In our program, we've experimented with both audio and video feedback, and we've found that both students and teachers enjoy the experience, but it's easier on the teachers if the software lets you stop and start rather than requiring one take, like our LMS does.

Blow it up and start again. Occasionally, in my experience *rarely*, students give you a turd sandwich swaddled in rank seaweed sprayed with toxic chemicals and drizzled with wastewater. In such instances when you can tell students have spent very little time on a draft, you can kindly ask them to start over. There is no reason to spend much time on a draft if there's no "there there," so to speak—no material in the draft worth salvaging. Once I had a student copy the blurb on the back of *The Autobiography of Benjamin Franklin* and turn it in as a draft of a rhetorical analysis. Not her best moment. I did not comment on the draft but asked to see her in my office. Through a tearful conference, I found out that she was struggling with college life, both the culture and the academic side of things. The sloppy work was symptomatic of a bigger problem. I extended due dates and we worked on a new draft. That was labor intensive. There are other times when I've written on a draft, "Dear Friend, this is not a rhetorical analysis. This is a summary of the article. Please review the assignment sheet and examples we read in class and try again. Let me know if you have questions."

Conference with students. After students turn in a draft, cancel a class or two and meet with students one on one in your office to talk about their drafts. (Some teachers meet with more than one student at a time for these conferences.) This method can replace written comments, or, if you want your teaching to control every moment of your waking life, you can give students both written comments before and oral comments during a conference. The agenda for such a conference varies, depending on the student's agenda. I often begin by asking how the semester is going for them—their other classes, social lives, and so forth. Every once in a while students will start crying at this point, which is probably good for them. Richard Beach suggests that if we want students to learn metacognitive dispositions, we can use conferences to get students to *describe* their rhetorical goals ("What are you trying to do in this section?" "What are you trying to get your audience to do or think?"), *judge* how the current text achieves those rhetorical goals, and then *select appropriate revision strategies* that will lead to improvements in the text (Beach 1989, 133). Conferences are so much easier for me if I've reviewed their draft beforehand and made a few notes, but I've found I can give them substantive genre-level feedback after reading the first few paragraphs quickly while they look aimlessly at all the books on my shelf. ("Have you read all these books?" they ask. "Yes," I lie.) The big danger of the conference for me is the Hostile Brian Take-Over, when I end up talking more than the students, telling them what to do and where and how and how much. Beach's method mitigates this by asking students to set the agenda themselves by explaining what they tried to do and how it might have gone awry. Sometimes I'll ask students to describe the overall argument they want to make; then we go hunting in the first few paragraphs for how they've oriented readers to this purpose. The most important aspect of the conference for me is the wrap-up at the end. If you've had a free-flowing conversation, much of what was said has now disappeared in the air molecules, and students will have only a faulty memory of what they decided to do to revise their text. I end every conference by asking, "So, what are the two to three specific revision strategies we discussed today?" I ask them to write down the answers. Recently I started sitting side by side with students during conferences, both our laptops open, and both of us typing on a shared document, both writing notes and reminders and suggestions. I'll ask, "What are you trying to say here?" and as they talk through it, I transcribe their words in brackets so they can review them later as they revise.

Be transparent. Describe in your syllabus or in a handout how, when, and why you respond. Here's what I've settled on:

How I Respond to Writing. Responding to student writing is a labor-intensive exercise, but it's one of the best ways I can teach you to write more powerfully. While I want to help you become a better writer, I can't attend to every single issue you should address in your paper. Often when I respond to your writing (with my own writing), I will focus on what is most important or pressing or "global" in the text, hoping that you will be critical and attentive enough to discover other spots for potential revision. Below I describe four of my practices that will help you understand better how I respond as a writing teacher:

Informal writing. Throughout the semester you will turn in rushwrites or response papers or other assignments that I call *informal* because they don't need to be polished (i.e., revised and proofread). Sometimes I'll respond to these papers, and sometimes I won't. Sometimes I'll just highlight parts I like or ask questions. Sometimes I'll just put a check at the top indicating I have scored the paper. These activities are more for practice than evaluation, but please give them some time and thought. If they're not done well, I'll ask you to do them again.

Marking error. Research tells us that marking up all the errors in a student's paper doesn't do much to help students avoid those errors in the future. We'll have more important things to occupy us than worrying inordinately about all the possible ways we make mistakes in writing. However, since errors produce *static*—in other words, they get in the way of the message you're trying to convey and damage your *ethos*—you'll need to practice proofreading your writing carefully before sending it out to the world. While I'm not your editor/proofreader/error hunter, I will draw your attention to error by highlighting sentences or putting checks in the margins of your paper where there are errors in grammar, punctuation, or mechanics. Sometimes I will take one paragraph and go "editor" on it, just to show you how you can read your work carefully while revising. I'll also point out *patterns of error* in the end comment. Please get in the habit of consulting the web, the Purdue Online Writing Lab, or our handbook for questions related to style, grammar, punctuation, and mechanics.

Marginal comments. I tend to make few marginal comments in the middle of the paper. When I do, I try to use them to dramatize the reading experience you've provided. Think of me as a representative of other interested readers out there who want a good experience reading your stuff. Occasionally I'll use marginal comments to dramatize that representation. On final drafts, I may not put marginal comments at all.

End comments. The end comment is the teaching moment. Its purpose is threefold: (1) to point out the strengths and weaknesses of the paper—we find both in every piece of writing, (2) to help you think forward to the next draft or writing task and how you'll continue effective strategies and/or work on less effective ones, and (3) to evaluate your work by assigning it a grade, if it's a final draft. The end comment represents our conversation about your writing.

How we respond to students will compose in part the emotional ecology of writing—that full-self attunement that leads a writer to write, to persist in writing, to enjoy the process. Our response can break students out of their writing-centered reverie and get them thinking metacognitively about their work. We can encourage them to see writing not as perfectable but certainly improve-able.

20
GRADING MINDFUL WRITERS

If we're not mindful about it, grading can strangle the spirit of writing. Students fret about grades. When we return student texts with grades, the students stand there in front of you and turn quickly to that big letter and then react emotionally, as we did as students (or as we do now when we get our student ratings), and then the learning is over. Anecdotally, students tend to look at the grade and ignore any comments we made on the draft. Why read the autopsy report? The paper is *dead.* Move on, or fight the teacher.

For most of us, grading is not an option; our institutions require it. So we might as well do our best to recover grading for the mindful writer. Ideally, grading is yet another intervention into metacognitive development. Grades can present another reflective moment in a student's self-directed learning process. If students trust our judgment, they will be able to see grades as a fair and accurate assessment of what they have accomplished in relation to a desired outcome and a transparent benchmark of quality. At my most cynical, I have seen grades as a motivation-crushing summation that hijacks the dialogue I want to have with students about their writing. Actually, grades can support intrinsic motivation if they (a) give students an assessment of their skills and dispositions, (b) convey specific and constructive feedback, and (c) celebrate, in some way, what the student has accomplished (Walvoord and Anderson 2010, 26).

At least, that's what I tell myself while drinking the Kool-Aid of metacognition. In reality, a few of the most frustrating experiences I've had as a teacher have come from haggling with students about a minus or plus that may or may not ruin a student's chances of getting into medical school. Such conversations are almost always irrelevant to the writing process. They have all the charm of a disgruntled consumer spat. And even without haggling students (which, cheer up, are the exception and not the rule), I struggle assigning grades. I'm a wimp, as you already know, and therefore grading rigorously is an emotionally fraught experience. While I hate the idea of giving high grades to mediocre work,

DOI: 10.7330/9781607329374.c020

I don't like to make people sad. When I'm writing the grade on the paper—in the dark of my office with the door locked like I'm up to something illicit like trading cryptocurrency on the Dark Web—I find I have to stay focused intensely on my standards. And even then, as I see what the students have accomplished, both their limitations and strengths, how they've surprised and delighted and disappointed me, I notice how the grades I assign cannot fully be justified by objective standards, how the difference between a B and a B– is driven by an impulse, an often-vaporous professional intuition, rather than a measurable gradation reflective of values that exist Out There in tidy increments.

Well. We must be vigilant. As Daniel Kahneman, the Nobel Prize–winning behavioral economist, has taught us, we tend to exercise judgment at two different levels he calls System 1 and System 2. (They do not map onto any neurological model.) System 1 has been conditioned by evolution to make quick, effortless, and automatic judgments about similarities, difference, threats, causes, intuitions, emotional states, and patterns. From System 1 we get all kinds of useful mental activities (e.g., reading street signs), and some really bad ones (racial stereotyping). System 2 is an "effortful system" that kicks into gear when we need to calculate, analyze, evaluate, and focus. Because such activities are effortful, they cause "cognitive strain," which in turn makes us not always enthusiastic to engage in them (2012, 59). So, we end up depending on a variety of judgment heuristics—tools for evaluating our surroundings—that often turn out to be cognitive biases that keep us from making good decisions. Check out Wikipedia's long list of cognitive biases to see the scope of the problem.

All this is to say that we may end up grading students more harshly if we are tired and hungry or if they are student athletes. Writing teachers are not robots, even though college bureaucrats may see them that way. We are prone to a variety of cognitive biases that Linda Suskie calls "evaluation errors." To set up this mine field, she lists ten possibilities, including too lenient, too generous, too harsh, too medium (i.e., avoiding the extremes of the grading scale), too contaminated (with irrelevant student attributes like ethnicity), too anchored in first impressions, too biased toward students we like, too adrift on a sea of shifting standards (2009, 44). Even if we use detailed rubrics to grade, we may find that we come to the grading process with a constellation of unspoken values that make objectivity in writing assessment a chimera (Broad 2003). Because of these biases, I know some teachers who require students to remove names from papers before grading them. (How does that fool you if you've read early drafts and conferenced with students?)

Let us admit these challenges and thereby transcend them. We'll just have to do our best. Knowing that these biases exist in us may help us be more mindful graders. I explain to my students that grading writing is a somewhat subjective enterprise, but it is hardly arbitrary. By presenting students with outcomes and showing them models of success, I am constituting, in discourse, the standards of rhetorical excellence to which I want them to aspire. I have to construct these standards into a mental model up to which I hold my students' work. I hope when I grade their work that I give them a useful assessment of how they're doing on their quest to build rhetorical habits they can draw from in the future.

Here, then, are a few tips about grading:

Establish clear criteria for success. Remember way back in the chapter on organizing writing tasks that we design our FYW courses by first determining outcomes and then establishing benchmarks for success *before* we begin to organize our course schedules. Grading is made easier and more transparent if students have been brought into this conversation from the beginning. Ideally, by the time you sit down to grade their work, they have read the outcomes, seen a rubric, studied previous student work, and received task-specific feedback. Grading, then, should reinforce this trajectory. When you use models, show students what constitutes an A paper in your class, and show them the specific attributes of the paper that make it excellent.

Refresh your memory about that criteria before grading. As you sit down with your fat stack of glory, look over your rubric and remind yourself what you're hoping to see as evidence that students have learned what you want them to learn.

Use analytic rubrics (but not with points). In his chapter on rubrics in *Engaging Ideas* (run—do not walk—to your local online mega-retailer and purchase this book!), Bean explains that rubrics come in "many different sizes, shapes, and flavors" (2011, 269). Rubrics can be analytic—separating out criteria or scores by writing trait, like "organization" or "conventions" ("this paper gets a 7 on 'organization' and a 4 on 'conventions'")—or holistic—conferring the overall attributes of the paper in performance categories ("the 'A' paper has this and that and the other thing; the 'B' paper . . .").

Bean suggests—and I agree with him—that the best rubrics are analytic rubrics that do three things: (a) separate writing criteria into traits; (b) use a "step-down approach" describing multiple levels of performance, like "developing towards / meeting / exceeding expectations" or "meets most / some / few criteria" (2011, 276); and (c) help us "coach student writers" more effectively (288).

I admit here, with a concession to rubrics' enemies, that when I talk too much about rubrics, I sound like a bureaucrat from a for-profit "learning solutions" company. There's something tedious and overdetermined about rubrics. On the other hand, since I believe strongly that we need to make our evaluation system as transparent and useful to students as possible, I can't see carrying on without them. I'm recommending here that when you grade student work, use an analytic rubric (a rubric with textual and rhetorical categories separated and described on a sliding scale of accomplishment) but *do not* assign points to the various categories. In other words, I would advise against separating out 100 points for a literacy narrative by making "style" worth 15 and "organization" 20 and so on. I've seen how this kind of system causes mischief in myself and other instructors when it comes time to grade. When we read a paper, we have a holistic gut impression. We say, "This is a 'B' paper." Then, if we have a points-based rubric we may start monkeying with the numbers to get them to match our gut. I've seen instructors assign "style" a 5/15 to get the numbers right, which means they've given style a score in the low F range.

Because of this problem, some folks use holistic rubrics that describe the attributes of an A paper, a B paper, and down the line. When I've used holistic rubrics in the past, I then underline the attributes on the rubric that I see in the student text. But for the past five years I've been using non-quantitative analytic rubrics so I can give students specific feedback in a few rhetorical categories (like "rhetorical strategies") we've worked on in class. For each rhetorical category, I create four levels of accomplishment, with a descriptive paragraph in each indicating "exceeding expectations," "meeting expectations," "developing towards expectations," and then "oops!" (Trying to be nice and chatty about their failures!) I underline attributes in the rubric describing what I see in the text. If I'm working in hard copy, I'll staple the rubric (and a typed end comment) to their draft.

A wild idea: after your students have analyzed the genre of your writing tasks, the students themselves could articulate their own performance indicators and help you draft your rubric, which is not an uncommon strategy in FYW teaching (Walvoord and Anderson 2010, 51).

Then, how the heck do you assign specific grades? Heck, I don't know. I rarely give Fs to completed work in the ballpark of the genre. In my reckoning, a D represents a failed attempt that should be rewritten. Cs I hope signal that a student is on the right track but needs to put more work into it. The letter B denotes for me the average good-faith student effort. The A is reserved for exceptional work. Pluses and minuses represent *leaning* trends toward exceptional or average or whatever. To score the papers, I use the highest score a student can get for that letter grade's range (e.g., an 82 for a B–), though I admit I hesitate to assign any paper 100 percent, as if nothing, absolutely nothing, could be improved. John Bean uses a double-check method for assigning letter grades. He jots down a gut-feeling holistic letter grade at the top of the paper, but then he uses an analytic rubric with analytic scores meant *only* to check his holistic impression (i.e., he does not add up the scores) (Bean 2011, 279–82).

Relax, eat, drink. As you sit down to grade, make sure you're relaxed and well fed, with your favorite beverage at your side (if that beverage will impair your judgment, save it for a reward when you finish!). Try grading in the morning, if you can, and I'd suggest grading only five to six texts in a single session; then get up and take a walk, at least.

Read a bunch first. Before committing to a grade, I'll read through about five of them to get a sense of the range.

Time yourself. I was appalled to find out that a colleague of mine spends over an hour on each student text—appalled and humbled at the same time. Our students deserve heroes like this. Unfortunately, my students are stuck with me, and there is no way I'm going to spend over an hour grading every student text. When I teach advanced writing, I have around fifty students in two sections. I have colleagues who teach four courses a semester; they have *eighty-plus* students. And let's not forget our secondary ed comrades who teach writing to ~200 students at a time. Life is too short, and I don't think there's much evidence that spending more time on grading leads to more student gains. Once I get into the groove of grading, I can grade and comment on a final draft of an eight-page text in around twenty minutes—shorter if the text is excellent. (Haswell [2008] reports that the average time-on-task per page for college writing is longer than mine: seven minutes.) Set a timer for the amount of time you want to spend per text and try to stick to it. It's funny, again, how artificial this "reading" of student writing can be, this zipping through someone's sweat-and-tears prose at full speed. In a recent semester, when students came to my office to revise graded work, I noticed how their papers got worse the closer I looked at them. When I grade, I'm grading at the speed of mercy.

Avoid marking. Often when we mark infelicities, errors, stylistic changes, and other surface issues on final drafts, we're merely justifying a grade at that point. Call it the CYA method of response. If the writing task is officially over, the students will not learn much from editorial markup. As with response on drafts, you can point out patterns of concern in an end comment or encourage students to proofread.

Use end comments to reinforce metacognition. When I grade student writing, I do not make any in-text comments, if I can help it. I write a generous end comment that does two things specifically. First, I will praise the student for specific attributes of the text. Next, I will encourage the student *moving forward* to think about adjusting their writing process in this or that direction for this or that outcome. I want them to see the grading process for a single paper as one moment in a recursive model of writing development. I want students to be able to set new goals or make process adjustments for the next writing task based on how I responded to this last one. Nancy Sommers' "single lesson" principle helps significantly with end comments: What single lesson do I want students to learn from me when I grade their work? After all, grading should be about learning.

Ask students to read your comments. When I return student papers, I ask the students to take the time to read over the rubric and my comments before they come talk to me about the paper. They should use these comments in their future planning and reflections. Grades represent one more opportunity to monitor and control a writing process. At some point, ask students to use your final-draft comments to describe changes they will make to their writing process for the next project.

Reflect on what *you've* learned as a teacher. After grading the bunch, I take a moment to think about what I've learned about my teaching based on the student papers. If I see that the bulk of the students did not learn X, then I know I need to spend more time talking about X in the next writing task.

Follow FERPA regulations. Since I teach in a paperless class, I read digital final drafts. Unless I'm safely behind the sign-in firewall of our learning management software, I will likely violate federal law if I leave digital grades on student work—say, in email or on Google Docs. If I'm reading student work on Google Docs, I will write comments and grades on a separate document and print them out to give to students in class. It's so easy to be FERPA compliant, though. Give your students a piece of paper that says, "I give [Your Name] permission to leave comments and grades on Google Docs" and have them sign and date it. As far as I know, there are no FERPA foot soldiers waiting to break into your carrel and cart you away for minor infractions of FERPA.

Use a grade contract. I saved this one for last because it's such a promising method for taking the cuss out of the grading process. Grade contracts are meant to give students power over their own learning by encouraging them to do all that they can regardless of how well they end up writing. It's a way to reward effort—the best a student can do, under their circumstances—while reserving the A for exceptional work. Jane Danielewicz and Peter Elbow have a grade contract that looks like this:

> You are guaranteed a B if you:
>
> 1. attend class regularly—not missing more than a week's worth of classes;
> 2. meet due dates and writing criteria for all major assignments;
> 3. participate in all in-class exercises and activities;
> 4. complete all informal, low stakes writing assignments (e.g., journal writing or discussion-board writing);
> 5. give thoughtful peer feedback during class workshops and work faithfully with your group on other collaborative tasks (e.g., sharing papers, commenting on drafts, peer editing, on-line discussion boards, answering peer questions);
> 6. sustain effort and investment on each draft of all papers;
> 7. make substantive revisions when the assignment is to revise—extending or changing the thinking or organization—not just editing or touching up;
> 8. copy-edit all final revisions of main assignments until they conform to the conventions of edited, revised English;
> 9. attend conferences with the teacher to discuss drafts;
> 10. submit your mid-term and final portfolio.

> Thus you earn the grade of B entirely on the basis of what you do—on your conscientious effort and participation. The grade of B does not derive from my judgment about the quality of your writing. Grades higher than B, however, do rest on my judgment of writing quality. To earn higher grades you must produce writing—particularly for your final portfolio—that I judge to be of exceptionally high quality. (Danielewicz and Elbow 2009, 246)

Contract grading is meant to keep students focused on the processes that lead to mindful writing instead of the grade. Hardworking students who may be developmentally behind other students will benefit significantly from going through this rigorous checklist. And they will gain confidence as writers, knowing that their diligence paid off. Asao Inoue has argued that grade contracts validate the labor of struggling students. He tells his students, "How much *labor* you do is more important to your learning and growth as a reader and writer than the quality of your writing" (2014, 105). This is an ethical stance to take with students who are disadvantaged by the disciplining power of standard written English.

GRADE DISPUTES

Occasionally you will have students who want to dispute their grades. Their value system is not matching up with yours. Or maybe they feel like their hard work somehow should have "earned" a higher grade. Or maybe you misjudged their work because Brian told you to read like lightning. Rubrics and models and checklists and revision policies and B contracts can mitigate disputes, but you might still get them. Here are a few principles to consider when you do get into a grade dispute:

- Listen carefully to the student with an open mind. Repeat back to the student his/her concern to make sure you understand it.
- Keep the conversation focused on writing and writing principles. Steer away from personal issues or issues related to your teaching or the students' effort. If the student goes there, politely tell them that you are here to talk about what you both see on the page or screen.
- Avoid getting defensive about your teaching. Keep the conversation on student learning and writing. Focus the student's interests on future developments as a writer.
- Admit when you're wrong, but otherwise hold your ground. I have found that looking more closely at an essay reveals sloppiness on both our parts. Unlike whisky or cheddar cheese or cast-iron skillets, completed student essays tend not to improve with the passing of time.
- If you feel threatened by the energy of the student, say so and end the conversation. Students do not have the right to be belligerent or threatening. If you know you are meeting with a student who tends

to get worked up, ask a colleague to be close to you to listen to the conversation.

- Be cautious about bringing in external readers. I've had instructors in my program ask me to step in and grade a student paper as an "impartial" observer. Often this happens after the instructor has been badgered to the point of caving. The few times I've given in to the request, I've found myself descending on the student text with vengeance in my heart. In every instance, my grades were worse than the instructor's. The result is that the instructor's authority has been compromised, and the student is still upset.

21
PEER FEEDBACK

Peer review is an example of the "problem-centered small group" pedagogy that has a significant impact on student learning (Hillocks 1996, 66). Various studies, including reviews of research, have shown that peer feedback, *when we set it up effectively*, helps student writers become more audience aware, develop revision strategies, and engage in revision activities more than if they get feedback only from us (Bishop 2014; Dochy, Segers, Sluijsmans 1999; Hoogeveen and Gelderen 2013; McCutchen, Teske, and Bankston 2008, 455; Nystrand and Brandt 1989; Zhang, Schunn, and Baikadi 2017).

These findings tend to be consistent across disciplinary courses and in writing courses for English-language learners (Atkinson and Connor 2008). In other studies, peer review or peer response (PR) has been shown to benefit the reviewer even more than the receiver of the feedback (Cho and MacArthur 2011). Even in a more mixed review of the research, the scholars conclude that effective PR creates an interactive class environment, with peer-to-peer shop talk reinforcing the fact that writing is a "deeply social, necessarily flexible act" (DiPardo and Freedman 1988, 143). The research on PR shows that this practice supports mindful writing as students help their colleagues evaluate work in progress and make useful changes. It invokes a different "evaluative community" outside the teacher-as-evaluator rhetorical situation (M. Harris 1995; Newkirk 1984). It magnifies and distributes the feedback each student writer receives.

Although we have strong research on the results of peer review, it's a challenge coming up with a convenient "best practices" list to draw from. Over the years, I've struggled to find workable answers to questions to these and other questions: How do we train students to be effective peer respondents? How should peer groups be, uh, grouped? What specific reading strategies should peers use when responding? How do we help students overcome timidity when giving feedback to peers? How much time should we set up for peer groups? How as teachers should we monitor the groups to make sure writers are getting feedback that will

DOI: 10.7330/9781607329374.c021

help and not hurt their revision process? How can we demonstrate to skeptics that peers are better respondents than robots?

While we may not have a definitive list of evidence-based practices, we have a significant body of practitioner wisdom to draw from here. (Isn't "practitioner wisdom" *evidence based,* for goodness sakes?) What I share with you below comes in part from the scholarship but more from practical experiences teaching and observing teaching. I do know quite confidently that if we do not prepare students for PR—specifically, to attend to higher-order rhetorical needs rather than surface issues—then PR sessions will fall short of our expectations. We can't just have students exchange papers and then say, "Have at it" and walk out the room to check our phones, as appealing as that sounds some days. We want peer review to *habituate* students to seeking, receiving, and then synthesizing feedback as a metacognitive practice embedded in a community of practice. Peer response helps students "experience the collaborative and social aspects of writing processes," as our WPA Outcomes statement puts it. It creates, and enriches, the affective dimension of writing.

Below I've aggregated suggestions for PR into generic time-sequenced categories: before, during, and after. I hope some of what I'm about to say will trigger memories of what we talked about in chapter 16.

BEFORE PR

Acclimate students to standards of success. If you've followed the learning cycle for mindful writers, by the time students are ready for PR they will have read an assignment sheet with outcomes, analyzed the genre, learned writing and rhetorical strategies, reviewed a rubric, and looked at student models. This method will acclimate the students to your high standards of success for the writing project. It will also give them a sense of the range of successful responses to the rhetorical situation of the writing task.

Create a collaborative class culture. In a handout or class conversation, teach the students why collaborative writing, including PR, is important to them as learners. Discuss how knowledge is constructed in communities of practice and how they will learn to write by being read and by critically reading other members of a writing community. Share with them the dispositions they can expect by practicing PR, as articulated by Fiona Paton: "Peer review fosters important interpersonal skills: the ability to listen respectfully, to voice opinions openly, to offer advice tactfully, and to negotiate between different points of view" (2002, 291). Explain to them that PR will help them monitor and control their writing process.

Practice informal PR early and often. You can continue to foster a collaborative class culture by asking students to do informal PR often—weekly, or even daily. When students write early brainstorms or thesis statements or intros, pair (or group) them up and ask them to read each other's work and make brief comments. This practice will help them prepare for more formal peer review by getting them used to sending out their work and commenting on the work of others.

Decide on a medium for formal PR. For me, formal PR happens only when students have completed a full draft of a writing task. I've done formal PR with hard-copy and with digital copies and completely online. There are benefits and drawbacks of every kind. Recently I've preferred using Google Docs for all my group work. Students share project-specific writing folders with me and their peer group. (For my purposes, *share* in Google Docs means granting editing privileges to all your reviewers.) Peers can access the document anywhere, and they can make comments right on the draft without having to save and upload and send as an attachment. In fact, anyone at any time can make simultaneous comments on the draft. When I review drafts afterward, I can see what the peer groups had to say about the text (as long as the writer does not "resolve" the comments while revising), and I can adjudicate if comments conflict or mislead. Of course, you can have students print out papers and hand them out. You can also use learning management software for the arena of PR, which is what online writing courses do.

Divide students into peer groups. As we learned in chapter 16, high-functioning groups are usually small enough to engage everyone and hold participants accountable for their contribution. How small is small? I think three is a good number for peer groups, considering the time constraint of the class period. Should they form their own groups? I'm not sure. Obviously self-selected groups are self-directed, but maybe I don't want the two good-natured knuckleheads who always sit next to each other in the back and talk about video games to team up. I always feel like people get left out when I let students form their own groups, and regrettably those left-out students are often already marginalized. Therefore, I form groups randomly. Other instructors balance writing strengths; I admit that I make subtle un-randomy adjustments after forming the groups. Some teachers keep students in their peer groups all semester. In industry, successful groups cohere for long periods of time. But since my students aren't in careers at Pixar together, I have no problem breaking them up and reforming groups after every PR session (Paton 2002, 295). During one recent semester, I let the students tell me in a private post-PR assessment whether they wanted to stay together or not. Groups that voted unanimously to keep the band together stayed together for the next writing task.

Use a task-specific PR process. I suggest you not make a single PR process for all writing tasks. I don't know how you'd do that anyway if you buy into the rhetorical power of genre pedagogy. Each genre takes its own shape and purposes. Each PR session should be genre specific, with language discussed in that unit.

Model PR. Shelley Reid has made this point quite profoundly: "Anything you *really* want students to do on their own at a critically engaged college-student level, and that you suspect they might not have done before, you need to do together—in class—at least once—for 20 minutes" (2008). Amen to this. Model the kind of PR you want to see from your students. With one student's permission, give everyone in class a copy of a student's draft or put it up on the projector. Lead the class in the kind of response you want to see from them in their peer groups. Show them how to praise sincerely and read critically, how to apply criteria from the rubric, how to use class key terms from rhetoric and writing studies. You could even make a video of an effective peer review session. (I'm partial to the YouTube video made by Tim Bedley's fifth graders about "Peer Review Bozos," e.g., "Jean the Generalizer," "Pushy Paula" and "Off-Task Oliver.") Modeling effective PR mitigates against some of the common problems associated with PR: unclear goals or procedures, expertise problem, inadequate vocabulary, discomfort giving criticism, and the like. (Bishop 2014, 313).

Prepare writers. Each student should come into the PR having written a full draft and a "Dear Reader" letter (see chapter 18). Not to sound grouchy, but there should be consequences for students who don't do these things. Peer groups fall apart if there are no drafts to read. If you ask students to print out copies of their writing for other students, every printer on campus will get possessed by the devil five minutes before your class. Plan accordingly with clear expectations. I've experimented with "bring what you have at this point" PR, and it flopped. My students told me later they'd rather I give hard deadlines and penalize them if they don't meet them. (Isn't that interesting? And that was from an overwhelming majority, across two courses.)

Assign roles. Wendy Bishop suggests assigning students roles for PR: "group secretary," "group historian," and so on (2014). Maybe. In the past, but not always, I've asked one student to serve as a "primary" respondent to provide more thorough feedback and lead the small group's discussion about a student's writing. This works particularly well in full-class workshops. The "secondary" respondent can keep time and take notes for the writer on what the group discusses. In a fifty-minute class session reserved completely for PR, students will have around fifteen minutes to talk about each paper.

Prepare a PR response sheet. The word *sheet* makes me cringe. It reminds me of the "Law and Courts" class I took as a senior in high school. The teacher would hand out a worksheet on, I guess, Law and Courts, and then she'd go over to her desk and stare out the window. Educator Marcia Tate has written a marvelous book called *Worksheets Don't Grow Dendrites* (2010) to warn school teachers against handing out worksheets that turn students into brainless fill-out zombies. (Dendrites are the branches of a brain cell that stretch out to connect to other cells when we're thinking.) Point taken. Yet, students still need an effective *protocol* for peer review. As you know from your extensive experience as a reader, reading carefully takes a significant chunk of your working memory. And reading someone else's work is like trying to pay attention to one thing while walking through Times Square—there's too much to take in. Students need an order of operation. You can make a sheet for this with the usual blank spaces for their answers, or you can have them read online instructions. They should have access to a protocol that you've constructed beforehand.

Minimize response duties. I'm tempted to give responding students eighty-seven things to think about while reading their peers' work. This is a mistake. You should have a minimal protocol that reflects the order of concern you've established in your outcomes, rubric, and class instruction. Minimal might mean no more than five questions/ tasks. Particularly, I urge my students on the PR sheet I give them to *ignore as much as possible* surface-level errors and issues related to grammar, punctuation, and design. We're after transferrable writing dispositions, and debates about commas (e.g., to shove them in whenever you take a breath) do not build dispositions any more than worksheets build dendrites. If proofreading is important to you—it is to me—we can get them to regroup and do some peer editing on the day before they turn in the final draft.

I should say more about what I mean by *protocol.* I have found it useful to give peer reviewers specific reading protocols for their PR so they can read and respond mindfully. In table 21.1 I list five potential protocols you can ask your students to use when reviewing each other's work. As you can see, Protocol 1 is the least desirable of the bunch.

DURING PR

Have them read, then talk. Some instructors encourage peer groups to meet face to face and read their texts aloud one at a time. Since I can't stand that practice, I don't have my students do it. When a writer reads aloud a text we're both looking at, I'm forced into a linear form of reading that requires both listening and reading at the same time, which are activities activated in different parts of the brain. While I'm a big fan of requiring student writers to read drafts out loud for revision purposes, my preference for PR is to let students read each other's texts as homework and then show up the next day for a face-to-face conversation. While they read alone and silently, they can respond to the student writer directly on the text. These responses work as primers for the conversation they'll have when they are sitting next to each other looking at the draft together (on laptops on Google Docs, in my class).

Teach writers to listen. It is customary in PR or full-class workshops to ask the writer to listen carefully to feedback, taking notes and asking one to two questions only after the peers have made their comments. Once writers hear feedback, they will want to jump in and justify everything

Table 21.1. Protocols your students can use when reviewing each other's work

Protocol I: Directive response	Shelley Reid suggests that peer responders have a hard time evaluating the overall quality of a text or making accurate suggestions about how to improve a text (2008). Directive responses look like change this, fix that, add this, rearrange that, scratch this, do more of that. Peer responders often feel pressure to be directive, as if they are imitating what they think a teacher does when responding. Directive responses tend to close, rather than open, discussions about writing. Student writers like directive feedback because it presents checklist-able actions for them that often do not require much thinking. Peer tutors are trained not to give directive feedback, because it takes away the agency of writers to solve their own problems. We know from learning research that when the learner exerts effort to understand, the learner grows (Doyle and Zakrajsek 2013). But this is a hard principle to teach to peer responders in a few short weeks. Perhaps it would help to show students how reader response statements (e.g., "You say in your Dear Reader letter that your purpose is X, but my reading of your text is Y") rather than directive statements (e.g., "Cut this paragraph—it doesn't add") can help writers think for themselves how to engage with audiences more effectively in the next draft.
Protocol II: Praise	Ask students to describe specific strengths they see in the text. Praise reinforces desirable strategies. It inspires students' hope and confidence. It strengthens the affective orientation to writing. It'll need to be modeled, especially the specific part. "Good job, Leah!" is not what we're looking for. More like "I really like how you added personal experience to this opinion editorial. I didn't expect it!" Praise is just one of several "motivational scaffolding" strategies—along with "showing concern" or "giving sympathy"—peers can use when responding to each other (Mackiewicz and Thompson 2015, 43).
Protocol III: Descriptive response	Descriptive responses ask peers to identify various aspects of the text as they see them. Such responses can be descriptive or evaluative. For example, you can ask peers to make simple markings next to the text: "underline the thesis"; "put brackets around at least two sentences you really liked/caught your attention"; "put a wavy vertical line next to the most coherent paragraph." Descriptive responses can also answer questions: "What is the writer's purpose?"; "What does the writer assume about the audience?"; "What is the writer's main point?"; "How did the author use/misuse conventions of the genre?"; "How is the argument organized?"
Protocol IV: Questions	In my own peer writing groups with colleagues, I end up asking a series of "why?" questions on drafts. Like, "Why have you separated this principle from that one in the organization of the paper?" or "Why is this paragraph necessary if you've already established X?" or "Why is this source important for your overall argument about X?" Encourage peer responders to ask 2–3 what, how, or why questions about the text.
Protocol V: Reader response	We can prompt peers to be attentive to their own experience as trained readers reading the text. We can ask questions like "Where did you, the reader, feel most connected or confused?" or "Why were you convinced/not convinced of the writer's argument?" The best peer tutor research we have insists, quite rightly, that the best thing any responder can do is provoke writers to think critically on their own and solve their own writing problems. In her research on peer tutoring, Muriel Harris notes that students who had positive experiences with peer tutors used language along the lines of "she helped me by making me do the work," "she got me thinking," and "she didn't just tell me what to do to make it right" (1995, 30). Peer responders can facilitate this ownership if they make readerly comments: "You're trying to do X, but I'm reading this like Y" or "If I were your audience, I would need to see more X here" or "At this point, I'm expecting X to happen in the rest of the text." Harris describes this activity as "helping writers match intention or plan with the written result" (1995, 35). One way to encourage peers to respond this way is to ask them to review how the writer describes what he/she intended to do in the Dear Reader letter.

they've done. I ask writers to listen, take notes, thank respondents, then ask no more than two clarifying questions at the end.

Circulate, or don't. What am *I* supposed to do while the students peer review? Butt out. You'll probably want to stay in the room (reading student drafts, maybe) to answer questions that arise and keep students in your vigilant panopticon. Maybe you want to walk the room and listen to how the groups are doing. I've learned, though, that sitting down to listen to a group has the same effect as when I sit down next to my teenage son and his friends while they're playing *Overwatch*. Vibe-killing. Party's over. Power's in the house. Time to perform the dutiful student. If we want to give students autonomy to work and create their own drive as self-directed learners, then we should let them know we trust them by leaving them alone. We can monitor the groups' success by looking at the feedback and asking for reflections on peer work afterward.

Try full-class workshops. For several years I used full-class workshops (FCW) exclusively for PR in FYW. Full-class workshops are old hat for creative writing classes. Here's how I set them up: Each student would have the opportunity once in the semester to be read by the entire class. We would have enough time in the schedule to read three student essays a day for two to three days. I'd assign one student as the primary respondent tasked to read the essay, write a page-long response, and lead the rest of the class in discussing it for fifteen minutes. The rest of the class posed as secondary respondents who filled out a three-question sheet and brought it to class to give to the writer. I ended up ditching FCWs because (a) students wanted feedback on *all* their major writing tasks, not just the one for which they got workshopped, and (b) receiving twenty secondary responses, though theoretically satisfying, paralyzed the writer with too much to think about. If you are a creative writer, you may know how to mitigate (a) and (b), but I've moved back to small-group PR.

AFTER PR

Open up class for questions. During PR, specific questions about the assignment may have come up that the peer groups couldn't answer—for example, questions about grammar, punctuation, usage, formatting, or editing. I hold a brief Q & A about issues for which the whole class might benefit from hearing answers.

Ask students to write a revision plan. After students get feedback from you and peers, ask them to think critically about that feedback, remembering their own agency to incorporate all or some or none of it, and write a revision plan describing what they'll do to reimagine their text. Revision plans continue a student's dialogue about their writing and promote metacognitive habituation.

Review the reviews. You likely do not have time to look at every comment every student made on a peer's text. When I use Google Docs to read student drafts, I can see the peers' marginal and end comments, and I can get a sense of their quality. Peer responses in my class count as informal writing assignments, and I grade them swiftly with no, partial, or full credit. Partial credit is reserved for students who responded but did not follow instructions or use key terms.

Share exemplary reviews. As you read the student responses, collect two to three exemplary ones and share them with the class with the peer responder's permission.

Ask students to reflect on PR. In a two-minute end-of-class response, ask students to answer a few questions about the PR experience, like, How did this work? What was most helpful to you as a writer? What did you learn about yourself as a writer? What can we change about the process to make it more effective? How do *you* need to change as a writer as a result of this process? I've also asked students to rate the quality and participation of their peer reviewers. If two students complain about a student's participation in peer review, then I don't grant that student full credit for the PR.

Encourage students to go to the writing center. Why not? If your institution has a writing center, get your students over there. Writing tutors are often well trained, with a significant degree of experience helping student writers work out their own writing needs. Writing center director Muriel Harris argues that writing tutors can strengthen "the writer's skills in ways that will carry over to future writing" by "offering reader response, leading the student toward finding her own answers, suggesting strategies to try, diagnosing possible underlying problems, listening while the student articulates her message, and offering needed support during the composing struggle" (Harris 1992, 371). Tutoring sessions can, and should, reinforce a dispositional stance to writing. In other words, tutoring sessions can help build in students a transfer-, rhetorical-, and process-oriented disposition to writing by instigating informed writing *talk* with novice writers (Nowacek and Hughes 2015; see also Mackiewicz and Thompson 2015).

WE GET BY WITH A LITTLE HELP FROM OUR FRIENDS

Sharing your work with someone else can make you feel emotionally vulnerable. If students get into the peer review habit, they can discover, as I have discovered, how important it is to check your reading of your own text against the readings of others. While writing this book, I farmed out nearly every chapter to an unlucky but willing soul who showed me instances in which I'd missed the mark, and I've been so grateful for the reviewers' insights and encouragement. If we prepare them, our students will see peer review as yet another support for building mindful writing strategies, another check on the default egoism that so often takes over the writing process.

22
MINDFUL STYLE

In his masterwork on rhetorical education in first century Rome, Quintilian imagines new parents leaning over the crib (or whatever Roman babies were put in), planning out how they will teach the baby to speak with power. "Before all things," he writes, "let not the talk of the child's nurses be ungrammatical" (1987, 11). By the time a baby becomes a youth in such a language-mindful environment, he (yes, alas, in Rome always a *he*) has the *hexis*, the habit, of eloquence from "great practice in writing," reading, and speaking (125).

When I leaned over the crib as a new parent, I was less focused on language education and more focused on how, in this age of advanced technology, diapers can fail so exquisitely. Quintilian imagined a far more rigorous habituation to style than most American children, including my own, receive.

We have at most sixteen weeks with these students, some of which are second-language learners with impressive but still developing experience with English. Students can come into our classes with a storehouse of animate and alive language buzzing in their minds—and then write zombie sentences. Considering all the other things we're trying to do, to what extent can we cultivate a disposition for style under the limitations we face?

At my most optimistic, I'm convinced we can make significant strides in cultivating an orientation to style that will stick with students after they've moved on. From my perspective, a mindful style habit includes mastery of key terms, opportunities to play, and meaningful reflection about rhetorical choices. I hope I can cover that ground in this chapter. What I *can't* promise in this chapter is a logical, scaffolded, semester-long style curriculum that starts here and ends there and makes sequential sense for your students. In my view, what we get from research on style is *bricolage*, the practice of assembling a curriculum from a diverse array of available stuff. I'm hoping here to add some of that good stuff to all your available stuff.

DOI: 10.7330/9781607329374.c022

MANNER AND MOXIE

Style is a *manner* of doing. Our dictionary definitions talk about style as a particular way of doing something, a manner or characteristic habit or practice, which places style at the center of dispositional pedagogy. Style, then, is in this sense unavoidable. We express a style by walking, talking, dressing, dancing, playing sports, eating, or brushing our teeth—even if we're not trying to. When I walk, I choose, consciously or not, how to put one foot in front of the other and how to swing my arms or hold my head. Springing from a lifetime of embodied habituation to walking, these decisions constitute a style of walking.

However, we all know someone with a *distinguished* walk, a walk that really sticks out in your mind. Compared to other walks it has its own special step, swing, or swagger. In this sense, then, style is more than manner: it's moxie. It's about distinct individual expression—it's about grace, purposeful self-assertion, elegance, flamboyance, skill, confidence, pluck, a unique voice.

When I think about style as a quality of writing, I like to think of it in both these ways. Every time you write, you write with style. Each sentence you write reflects a series of rhetorical practices, even if the writing seems straightforward and unadorned. Paul Butler defines style in this way as "the deployment of rhetorical resources, in written discourse, to create and express meaning" (2008, 3). But writing with style also means writing with a distinct voice that conveys a distinct personality to the reader, a personality that seeks to make an impression, that seeks to make the reading experience pleasurable. Novelist Mary McCarthy defines style more in this second sense as voice: as "the irreducible and always recognizable and alive thing" (cited in Yagoda 2004, 23). Style is *ethos.*

I want my students to understand style in both these ways—as manner and moxie. In both perspectives, style represents rhetorical choices students learn to make, even if they've never consciously made them before. Style can manifest itself at all levels of discourse, from genre on down. However, in this chapter I will focus on sentence-level stylistics, or *microstylistics,* following a useful tradition in the literature (Enkvist 1969, 132; see also Connors 2000).

When should you talk with students about style? I introduce the term informally in the first major writing task when we do genre analysis, back in the planning stage of the learning cycle. Students pay attention to how writers convey ethos, use analogical or idiomatic language, or get to the point. In the practice stage, students depend on their storehouse of genre knowledge as they draft as quickly as they can, with audience top of mind. As they are completing a full draft, I may spend half a day introducing students to rhetorical concepts related to style (see the terms I've described later in this chapter). I will also introduce them to sentence-combining and imitation exercises while they practice.

Then why are we talking about style here in the revision stage of the learning cycle? While style and stylistic play are very much a part of the entire writing process, I've placed this chapter under revision to suggest that style activities, including editing, are imagined as conscious—nay, *mindful*—interventions students can apply effectively when they have a completed draft. We make so many of our stylistic decisions unconsciously in the mysterious language generator behind our eyes (Milic 1971). Richard Lanham has argued that "Americans use their language, spoken as well as written, in a chronic absence of mind" (2007, 14). Perhaps we can combat this absence of mind with mindful style instruction to build "an acute self-consciousness about style" in our students (21). You may find that style instruction works better for you in earlier stages of the writing process.

THE VIRTUES OF RHETORICAL STYLE

What kind of style should our students write in? What makes a style *good*? Crassus, who is Cicero's "ideal orator" in the dialogue of that name, contends that eloquence has four virtues: It is correct (as in, error-free), clear, distinguished (or compelling), and appropriate (Cicero 2001, 234). Well, maybe. All four imply relational dynamics between writers and readers, ascribing a rhetoricality for style that can be useful. As individual virtues with different goals, they pound and pull against each other like nucleons in an unstable atom. The first two virtues—correct and clear—suggest to me a charitable stance toward the reader: *I'm going to make this as easy for you as I can.* Errors, insofar as they are perceived, are, in Mina Shaughnessy's words, "unintentional and unprofitable intrusions upon the consciousness of the reader"—again, insofar as they are perceived (1997, 12). While correctness surely is overemphasized in language arts, it plays an important role in the sociocultural exchange of writing.

How much of a role? This is a controversial question. There are many people in our profession who see the idea of correctness as code for whiteness—in other words, for a racist disciplining language system applied in order to "remake those on the margins in the image of the patriarch," as Geneva Smitherman put it (2015, 146). In 1974, the Conference on College Composition and Communication issued the Students' Right to Their Own Language Resolution, which affirmed "students' right to their own patterns and varieties of language—the dialects of their nurture or whatever dialects in which they find their own identity and style" ("Students' Right" 2015, 19). Not everyone in the field was in love with the resolution, as you can see in Bedford's critical sourcebook on the subject. This resolution and the decades-old debate that followed it have done much to open opportunities for students of color, international students, second-language learners, and students with alternative English dialects to participate in writing more fully. However, enduring attitudes about language practice—in schooling, publishing, and professional and public discourse—continue to exert pressures on writers to conform to prevailing conventions of English, the "language of wider communication" (Smitherman 2015, 147). What we mean by "correct," as an attribute of style, must be informed by sociolinguistics and rhetorical theory (correct to/for whom? and why?).

As for clarity, its most ardent advocates claim that we process sentences more easily when agents and their actions are lined up nicely on the left side of clauses (Williams 2010). Clarity, then, is primarily a clear actor-action relationship between subject and predicate in short-ish sentences, with few nominalizations and prepositions and a no-nonsense attitude. The late Joseph Williams made a killing on this pedagogy from his book *Style*, now in its twelfth edition, retailing for sixty bucks. The approach is not universally praised (see Howard 2005). Yet academics and language nerds everywhere continue to celebrate clarity with a zeal that surely would make both Strunk and White applaud from their graves. They assume that an uncluttered mind will write uncluttered sentences that readers will process with the least amount of fuss. Communion reached. Hey, if clarity leads to understanding and communion, why knock it? For its celebrants, clarity is a "convention of readability" that exhibits five attributes: it is active (meaning, subjects and verbs are clear and close), it flows, it's organized for emphasis, it uses familiar language (instead of the hoity-toity), and it is concise (Holcomb and Killingsworth 2010, 41–48). In a time when TL;DR is a popular acronym (too long; didn't read), we need writers who strive for this clarity.

Appropriate seems obvious. We want to write in a style our readers expect, a style fitting for our purpose and their needs. In their excellent book on style, *Performing Prose*, Chris Holcomb and M. Jimmie Killingsworth explain that as "a powerful medium of social interaction," style establishes, even invents, productive "relationships among writers, readers, subject matter, and the relative positions of all these elements within a broader situation" (2010, 7). The Greeks called this principle *prepon*, the Romans *decorum*. I'd say that decorum is the fundamental principle of all rhetorical striving: make your genre, argument, evidence, arrangement, paragraphs, sentences, and design fit your purpose and intended audience! The end. That's a whole semester of instruction in a Tweet. Style fashions itself for the occasion, whether that calls for austere plainness or emotional excess.

Nevertheless, decorum is quite a complicated virtue. How does one land on a fitting style? What do writers need to do to acclimate ourselves, to attune ourselves, to a discourse community's manners? First-year students struggle to find the right level of formality when writing in an academic community for the first time. Guessing that they can't write in a more relaxed, personable prose, they write overly formal, wordy sentences. Credit students for giving us what they think we want. It's a start.

In our efforts to find something fitting to say, we writers are disciplined by the power dynamics of our rhetorical situations. Even people who write professionally can write inappropriately—make mistakes, violate conventions, bewilder, or offend readers. (I'm sure in this book I've done all four.) Experts on a given subject have the "curse of knowledge" and therefore write specialized, jargony, needlessly complicated prose because they can't imagine "what it is like for someone else not to know" what they know (Pinker 2014, 59). Celebrities and other popular folk can step in the stew on social media by posting language they may or may not have understood to be offensive.

Many of our students know very well the disciplining power of a concept like decorum. For students of color, language arts classes have often been sites where the language they speak at home—whether it's a foreign language or a dialect of English—is disciplined out of them by standard American English. Decorum, then, can reflect oppressive cultural attitudes (Anzaldua 2001; Young 2009).

Sometimes a writer intentionally chooses what could be considered a non-decorous rhetorical stance as a way to reject a dominant discourse or celebrate a nonconformist identity or shake up an audience. John Schilb calls such moments "rhetorical refusals" (2007). Is it possible for an inappropriate response to be the most appropriate response of all? Could there be power in deviations from convention, as well as risk? In sum, when we tell students to fit their style to their audience's needs, we are telling them to do a hard, somewhat vague thing.

What about *compelling*, the fourth of Cicero's traits, as a virtue of style? To answer that question, let's look at two separate paragraphs about termites:

> #1: Termites are eusocial insects in the cockroach order Blattodea. Like ants, termites live in colonies where labor is divided in castes. Termites feed mostly on dead plant material, mostly in the form of wood, leaf litter, soil, or animal dung. As pests, they can cause serious structural damage to buildings, crops, or forests. Termites are major detritivores, particularly in the subtropical and tropical regions. Their recycling of wood and other plant matter is of considerable ecological importance.
>
> #2: Or consider termites, the primary groundskeepers of tropical rainforests. They gnaw through dead or rotting trees and return much of the woody wealth back to the forest floor. What is a termite but a set of jaws joined to a petri dish, its gut a dense microecosystem of many hundreds of strains of microbes. Bacteria allow termites to wrest sustenance from sawdust and, like Geppetto, give dead wood a voice.

The sentences in the first paragraph are just fine. Nothing much to complain about here, aside from the obvious concern that this reads like a data-dump, which, coming from Wikipedia, it is. If my students wrote like that consistently, I'd be happy enough. We can work with that. (Making the sentences *cohere*, well, that's a different story.) After all, isn't it appropriate, and therefore effective, for the style of encyclopedia writing?

By contrast, the sentences in the second paragraph buzz with life. Nearly every sentence of *The Cannon*, Natalie Angier's book on science from whence these words come, buzzes with life. In the first paragraph, termites are "eusocial insects in the cockroach order"; for Angier, they're "groundskeepers," a term personifying termites, making them sound like little squishy helpers taking care of business. Whereas the first example talks of "their recycling of wood," Angier uses her *W*s and *F*s in the sonorous "woody wealth back to the forest floor." She also plays with sound when she says "wrest sustenance from sawdust," an unusual phrase. She exaggerates the termite's anatomy, or maybe she underplays it: a "set of jaws joined to a petri dish." That's a fascinating and funny image. Notice, too, the Pinocchio allusion at the end: comparing termites to Geppetto, creator and father of the magical wooden boy, is both weird and wonderful. It surprises and delights. It's playful. It's compelling.

Both excerpts demonstrate rhetorical choices that seem appropriate for their situation. The second one shows how writing can be that "always recognizable and alive thing"—a distinguished and unique voice meant to create a pleasurable reading experience. Writing can be, and should be more often, compelling in this sense. In the words of Aristotle, compelling prose makes "language unfamiliar" (2007, 198). As pattern seekers, we pay attention to variations, surprises, and delights. Classical rhetoricians often called this virtue *ornamentation*, but that word implies cosmetic frippery, making style seem like gilding the lily. Instead, I like the word *compelling* for the power it invokes. Readers admire a compelling prose style almost in spite of themselves. It invites attention, interest, admiration, joy. It breaks the boring plane of row upon row of words and says, "Hey! I want you to enjoy what I'm telling you!" Compelling prose is *pathos* as much as *ethos*.

I know we can't write every sentence like we're plugged into the universe; writing like Angier in your business finance class might not be effective. *Compelling* and *appropriate* are dynamically entangled, and I'm guessing that Angier's style if applied to a manual on thermodynamics would drive an engineer insane. But aren't we all just a little bored? Can't we think of language boredom as a preventable condition? Couldn't even the most banal corporate document use some splash—humor, a story, a metaphor, some repetition, a pop culture reference? What's stopping us from encouraging reckless play in FYW as a way to limber up the language machine in preparation for the heavy lifting of the writing life? I'm convinced that as writers we are more free than we think—and readers of all kinds are eager for us—to write not just clearly but compellingly. Surely social media writing has shown us how creative we can get with our language. We need to give students writing tasks, both informal and formal, that let writers experiment with style so they can find their place in the discourse.

THE LANGUAGE OF STYLE

Way the heck back in part I, we talked about how the content of writing is writing—meaning, we should teach specific principles of writing that will help students learn to be more mindful writers. Content knowledge boosts confidence as students understand principles and apply them and reflect on their merits. But absent application, these principles just clog students' working memory, like paper towels in the plumbing. That's why writing experts have almost completely shunned explicit grammar instruction (definition, then drill/quiz). A 2007 metastudy confirmed previous research showing that traditional grammar instruction has a statistically significant *negative* effect on student writers, including low achievers (Graham and Perin 2007, 21).

As a profession, we've responded to this research in large part by rejecting language instruction altogether. Sentence-level instruction is perceived as formalist, behaviorist, anticontextualist, anti-students'-own-languagist (Connors 2000). For the past twenty years, English departments across the country have been dropping grammar, language history, and linguistics courses from their major requirements (MacDonald

2007). It seems to me, though, that we don't need to retreat from language instruction; we need to integrate it into our students' writing experience. I agree with Francis Christensen's assessment that there are conversations we can't have with students if we do not have a shared language about language (Christensen 1963, 157).

Key terms strengthen mindfulness. If students have declarative knowledge about important concepts, they will be able to think more purposefully about how and when to apply rhetorical strategies. Below I provide definitions for key terms we can use with our students when teaching style as part of a mindful process, from planning through revision. This list is in no way definitive; there is so much more we could say here. We can expand our style vocab in excellent sources such as Jeanne Fahnestock's *Rhetorical Style* or Richard Lanham's *Handlist of Rhetorical Terms.* If we and our students master a handful of useful terms and identify them in writing, we can have more meaningful conversations about style. After defining style itself, I've put these terms in alphabetical order for easier referencing.

Style is the manner in which a writer writes, the voice you hear on the page or screen, the sum total of decisions, conscious or not, writers make at the sentence level. Style also refers to the *distinguished* or *unique* use of language that makes writing an art, appropriate and compelling for its rhetorical situation.

Convention, near-synonymous (in my mind, at least) with *usage*, is "an agreement among the members of a community to abide by a single way of doing things" (Pinker 2014, 190). I prefer the word *convention* over *usage* because it brings us back to the Old French terms *convene* or *convent* or *covenant*—a community committed to some shared language practices. Sometimes we call conventions *rules* of language, because it seems someone from On High has ordered it to be just so. Some conventions are quite rigid—readers may show an empirically measurable high degree of intolerance to variations. Some conventions are about diction or word choice (e.g., When is it okay to use slang or jargon or idioms?), others about syntax (Can I put the adverb *boldly* between the words *to* and *go*?), others spelling (catsup? ketchup?), others punctuation, others readability or genre (Holcomb and Killingsworth 2010). So, conventions are readerly expectations for the way language should work, and expectations create affordances and constraints with varying degrees of freedom. Conventions/usage make comprehension possible. When pressed with puritanical zeal by writing instructors, they constitute the "overwhelmingly negative and arbitrary attitudes of the tradition" (Schuster 2003, 66).

Design is the intentional arrangement of elements in an artifact, for instance, a document, brochure (if there are such things anymore), poster, podcast, or YouTube video. It includes visual cues easily distinguished by a reader: contrast, repetition, alignment, proximity, color, line, sequence, weight, navigation, interface, emphasis, and so on.

Deviation is the freedom to break the perceived rules—to flout the conventions, misuse the usage. Sentence fragments, for example. Like that last sentence, and this one. Sometimes you can get away with writing them. In science writing, it is customary to avoid the first person. Customary but not ironclad. Students should understand that conventions and deviations are rhetorical concepts that help us set up relationships with readers. Edgar Schuster's 2003 book *Breaking the Rules* shows us how our students' mindful deviations against often erroneous conventions ("avoid 'to be' verbs") gives them rhetorical power. It's hard, though. As a writer you get a sense of appropriate deviations by immersing yourself in the discourse community you want to join and its genres. That kind of attunement takes time.

Diction is the word choice of the writer, the range of the lexicon. Much of our word choice happens unconsciously as we work to put words on the page. Yet there are a variety of rhetorical strategies for diction. You can choose words based on denotation or connotation, level of generality (abstract/concrete; I would include conversations about imagery and embodiment in this category), level of formality (colloquialism, idiolect, jargon, spoken language forms, slang, etc.), culture and/or origin, popular circulation (think clichés), or lexical (or semantic) field, which Fahnestock defines as the "patterns in word associations" a writer uses across a text (2011, 62). *Concision*, or the art of reducing the deadwood of our writing, is also part of diction.

Errors are perceived *unintended* deviations from conventions of language accepted by a discourse community, particularly in grammar, diction, spelling, punctuation, or mechanics. You can also make errors of fact or reasoning. Some errors are more obvious than others. Some people call some things "errors" because they don't like seeing those things. Perceived errors create intrusions in the minds of readers and, fairly or not, can send the message that the writer is uneducated or careless, even if the error isn't really an error, or even if such an attitude is unjust. Some communities see error as sloppiness, others as waste. Error is a rhetorical problem. It's also a pedagogical problem. Fixating on error has given us a bad reputation with the public. Sometimes when I tell strangers I'm a writing teacher, they inadvertently cover their mouths with their hands. In chapter 19 we talked about how you can use a light, or more purposeful, hand with student error. As for a philosophical stance, I like what William James wrote: "Our errors are surely not such awfully solemn things. In a world where we are so certain to incur them, in spite of all our caution, a certain lightness of heart seems healthier than this excessive nervousness on their behalf" (1984, 470). A nice sentiment. Yet in many situations, both professional and public, perceived errors send signals writers prefer not to send.

Flow is the feeling that one sentence leads into another or that a new idea builds on an old one. When talking about this connectedness in writing, we often distinguish between *cohesion*—the way a new sentence connects linguistically and conceptually with the previous sentence—and *coherence*—how each sentence or paragraph builds on a single focused idea. Every handbook out there will have instruction on strategies of cohesion (pronouns, key terms, the known/new contract, etc.).

Grammar is often the catch-all term for all the language stuff, even though it shouldn't be. In *Understanding English Grammar*, Martha Kolln and Robert Funk describe three different kinds of "grammars": (1) the language in your head: If you grew up in an English-speaking household, you've known for a long time how to speak English sentences without thinking much about it; (2) a linguist's description of how language works, mostly referring to syntax (including issues related to agreement, say the relationship between subjects and verbs or pronouns and antecedents) and morphology (the forms words can take—past tense, prefixes, suffixes, pluralizing, and things like that); and, (3) "linguistic etiquette"—all those *do*'s and *don't*'s of English usage (Kolln and Funk 2009, 5). Grammar has come to mean any or all of those things.

Mechanics is closely related to convention or usage, but it's also related to design. You use mechanics to capitalize, put certain words in italics, use headings, write or use numbers, or cite and list sources in a specific style (e.g., Turabian, MLA, or APA).

Metaphors are comparisons that fall under a larger rhetorical category we often call figurative (i.e., nonliteral) language. Metaphors tell us how one thing is like something else, even though it is not like that thing at all. One term (our love, The Vietnam War, papa) borrows attributes from another (a red rose, a quagmire, a rolling stone). As creative pattern-seekers, we make meaning through these associative leaps that then influence our worldview. I use metaphor as a master term for similes, personification, synecdoche, metonymy, analogy, and allegory. Metaphors come in varying degrees of rhetorical freshness. Sometimes writers mix metaphors, which seems gauche. Here's a favorite from the comment section of my local newspaper: "Where there's smoke there's fire . . . could this be just the tip of the iceberg???" James Geary describes how some overused metaphors become clichés and others become dead metaphors, so invisible in the language we don't detect them ("I *see* what you mean"). Metaphors evoke and influence, and they can be used skillfully or not (Geary 2011).

Punctuation is what we use to link, separate, enclose, omit, emphasize, and finalize various parts of a sentence with commas, apostrophes, colons, semicolons, parentheses, hyphens, dashes, ellipses, periods, question marks, quotation marks, and exclamation marks (and hashtags?). Some punctuation rules have rigid conventions (you can't omit the apostrophe in the contraction *can't*—unless [!] you're doing it for effect in creative writing, as Cormac McCarthy does), while others don't have such strong restrictions (using a comma after a two- to three-word sentence opener is optional). My experience with teaching punctuation is twofold: (1) I notice that students, if you let them, can really nerd out about the so-called rules; there must be something comforting in the idea that punctuation is governed by straightforward laws, which is a fair but somewhat iffy assumption, and (2) Punctuation is best taught with (a) many examples that show variety, (b) some knowledge of phrases and clauses and how those elements can be separated more or less forcefully, and (c) opportunities to practice.

Schemes are out-of-the-ordinary syntactic structures we use intentionally for rhetorical effect. The two most popular are *repetition* and *balance*. We can repeat sounds, words, phrases, clauses, or ideas. For example, anaphora is the repeating of a word or phrase across successive sentences. Balance is the art of making elements of sentences not only grammatically parallel but rhetorically parallel. In *A Handlist of Rhetorical Terms*, Richard Lanham lists thirty-four different strategies for balance, including *dirimens copulatio*, "a series of not-only/but-also comparisons" (1991, 184). The following brilliant sentence by humor writer Dave Barry shows how balancing clauses can make a strong contrastive statement (he's talking about a group of guys from his hometown who like to ride on sit-down lawnmowers in parades): "My feeling is that if more guys would join mellow, purposeless, and semi-dysfunctional organizations such as the Lawn Rangers, then there would be a lot fewer guys getting involved in aggressive, venal, destructive, and frequently criminal organizations such as the U.S. Congress" (1996, 103).

Spelling is saying or writing in order the letters of a word. With spell-checking programs, the amount of spelling errors in student writing has declined. But "wrong word" problems have increased (Lunsford and Lunsford 2008).

Syntax is the order in which phrases and clauses appear in a sentence. (If you're a bit wobbly on what phrases and clauses are, as I was when I first started teaching, do some googling for a moment before proceeding.) We do not need to get too technical to get at the core and promise of syntax, but it does get a little complicated. Here goes: Sentences present sequences of meaning. The heart of the sentence is its main clause almost always made up of a noun phrase and a verb phrase. There are only a handful of main clause types in English—one expert source lists six (Morenberg 2010), another ten (Kolln and Funk 2009)—and they are defined by the types of verbs used (transitive, intransitive, linking, *be*). Miraculously, we can write an infinite number of unique sentences by building on main clauses with other clauses and phrases, fitting them into various slots to do various things such as modify nouns or verbs. Writers learn about syntax to write clear sentences in a variety of constructions using punctuation to separate the slots.

Many of our students will have heard that there are four sentence types: simple (one independent clause), compound (two independent clauses joined by a conjunction or punctuation), complex (a sentence

> with one dependent clause), or compound-complex (at least two IC and at least one DC). That covers the clause situation. If we want to add phrases into the syntactic mix, then I've found it useful to borrow language from Virginia Tufte from her book *Artful Sentences* and the similarly useful sentence-composing books by Don Killgallon. When we build on the main clause with other phrases and clauses, we put them in two or three common slots. Sometimes phrases or clauses come *before* the main clause ("**In the afternoon**, Kayla plays volleyball"). Let's call those elements *openers*. Sometimes we add material smack in the middle of the main clause either between the noun phrase and verb phrase ("Kayla, **a local high school senior**, plays volleyball") or, much less often, between the verb and its object. These phrases are *interruptors*. Finally, we can build to the right of the main clause with a *closer* ("Kayla plays volleyball, **a sport that requires significant team communication**").
>
> Why is syntax a useful concept for students to understand? Sentence variety has been a key to a compelling style for ages. Through syntactic analysis and exercises, students can learn how to create complex, artful, and varied sentences that together construct the person behind the words. In the next section I'll talk about some of the strategies you can use to introduce students to syntactic options.

How do we teach students key terms without merely requiring them to memorize definitions? For the record, I don't think it's always a bad idea to require students to memorize terms. Some of these terms *as terms* will require very little instructional time—for example, *mechanics*, *punctuation*, and *spelling*. Other terms will be best learned with a text in front of you and your students. When you analyze genres with them, you can point out strategies of convention, diction, flow, metaphor, and syntax. The goal is twofold: (1) to be able to give students a text and say, "Tell me everything you can about the *diction* of this text," and (2) to see students using these key terms when they reflect on their own style.

ORIENTING STUDENTS TO STYLE

We've laid out the key terms. How then do we get our students into the habit of writing with mindful style? From my (admittedly limited) reading of our field's research, it seems to me that we have abandoned the idea that research will tell us anything definitive about teaching style. We've lost interest in studying whether there are semester-long interventions that have a demonstrable, statistically significant effect on the sentence-level stylistics of students (Connors 2000; L2 scholars have been much more productive on this front in the last two decades). As a result, style is a teaching topic about which we can confirm less than perhaps we'd like.

At the same time, our theoretical orientation to style is robust as ever. If you look into recent academic treatments of style pedagogy—for one, Brian Ray's 2015 *Style: An Introduction to History, Theory, Research, and Pedagogy*—you'll see how our conversations about teaching style draw from sociolinguistics, stylistics, classical rhetoric, multiliteracies and world Englishes, multimodality, and rhetorical theory. On this last category, I've been excited about recent work on attunement (Rickert 2013) and embodiment and what these terms might mean for style instruction. Can we teach students to treat sentences as "an embodied, performative, mediated rhetorical act," as Peter Moe hopes we can (2018, 73)? How do we invite them to experience language "through visual, spatial, motor, affective, and other sensory modalities," as Hannah Rule encourages (2017, 21)?

As you gain experience as a teacher, you may decide to drink greedily from these theoretical springs. I've been struggling through them myself since I first taught FYW in 2001. Below is the best I have so far. To habituate students to style and encourage mindfulness, I ask my students to play with, revise, and reflect on style. I offer a few ideas for each of the three categories. (And notice, alas, how these categories break the bands of a tidy, independent "revision stage" of our learning cycle.)

Play

Imitation. Find a really cool compound-complex sentence. It doesn't have to be long. Ask students to read the sentence out loud and then write it, word for word. Then invite them to write their own sentence using the same structure of phrases and clauses. Have them share their sentences with the class or a peer and compare strategies. *Example sentence*: Torpid conformity was a kind of sin; it was stupidity itself, the mighty stream against which Mother would never cease to struggle (from Annie Dillard's *An American Childhood*). *My imitation*: Slavish imitation is an embarrassment; it is hackery at its best, a worthless practice to which my writing instructor is adamantly opposed.

Sentence combining. You can look this up online to see how it works. List a series of independent clauses. Ask students to combine them into one sentence by using punctuation, rearranging the order of the clauses, changing nouns into adjectives, adding minor details, and so on (Strong 1994). The empirical research on sentence combining is quite clear: Somehow, it leads students to write more sophisticated sentences (Connors 2000; see also Graham and Perin 2007). *Example clauses*: There has been a recent trend. Food companies have been fortifying foods with omega-3 fatty acid supplements. There is little evidence that omega-3 reduces cancer risk. *Combined sentence* (one option among many): While there is little evidence that omega-3 fatty acid reduces cancer risk, it's trendy now for food companies to add omega-3 supplements to everything from popcorn to pizza. When my students read a few of their combined sentences out loud, we debate what constitutes the part of the sentence that deserves the emphatic end slot.

Read a variety of writing styles. Assign students to read texts written by different voices and in different styles and invite them to analyze specific strategies the writers use in their style. It is particularly important to show students that even so-called academic writing (with sources, e.g.) has a range of possible voices.

Go sentence hunting. Open up a Google Document. Ask students to find cool sentences wherever they find them and write them on the shared doc. I've been collecting sentences for several years now—I have twenty-two pages of them. I can use them for imitation exercises. Hunt for sentences in student writing that dazzle you. Collect them, and show them to your students.

Get goofy. This category is a catch-all for a variety of activities that habituate students to style. Some of them come from the *progymnasmata*, the classical prose composition method. (See the word *gym* in there?) We have "who can write the longest sentence" contests. I read out loud a tale from Aesop's fables and ask students to rewrite it in a different voice (that of a seven-year-old) or from a different perspective (the lion's, in "the mouse and the lion"). I'll give them song lyrics (from, say, rapper Cardi B) and ask students to rewrite them in complete sentences and by so doing translate them to interpret their meaning. To teach wordiness, I've given them an over-the-top sentence and assigned them to slash it down by half and talk about the strategies they used to do it. I've scrambled the order of sentences in a paragraph and had students put them in the order they think they should go, using their cohesive instincts.

Revise

Ask students to read out loud. In your revision checklist, require students to read their essays out loud to see if they can "hear" places that need revision. In *Vernacular Eloquence,* Elbow tells his own FYW students that "readers will find your writing clearer and more inviting when your language is *comfortable to say aloud*" (2012, 220, Elbow's emphasis). Spoken sentences start with main clauses and then branch to the right with modifiers, which is easier for us to process than sentences with longish dependent clauses as openers (e.g., the first sentence of the Declaration of Independence). Elbow also suggests that speaking our writing aloud kind-of "others" it by giving us some critical distance from the words as they appear on the page.

Teach syntactic exercises. Back in chapter 14 I shared a "how to teach anything" method called *notice, name, now you.* This method works wonderfully for teaching any stylistic strategy, particularly ones that involve modification with phrases and clauses. (It would be useful for you to review the different kinds of phrases and clauses in a good book such as *Rhetorical Grammar, Rhetorical Style, Sentence Composing for College, The Well-Crafted Sentence,* or *The Writer's Options.* See the references.) Introduce students to the idea that writing sentences involves writing phrases and clauses in often movable relationships. Show them several sentences that have openers, interruptors, and closers as modifiers—and show them examples that set apart phrases from clauses with dashes instead of commas. Then use notice, name, now you to teach them how to practice syntactic maturity and variation. *Example*: "Take a look at this sentence, class: 'Gina Haspel, *the first female director of the CIA*, appeared before the Senate Intelligence Committee.' What is the italicized phrase doing in this sentence? Is it an opener, interruptor, or closer? This phrase is called an appositive, a phrase used to modify a noun close by, in this case Gina Haspel. How are appositives useful to writers? Here's another example [show a different way to use appositives, such as 'renaming with a twist' (Bacon 2009, 109).] Now, revise a sentence in your own essay to include an appositive."

Rewrite. In 1512, the Dutch scholar Erasmus wrote a book called *Copia*, a Latin textbook on style. *Copia* means "abundance" in Latin, so Erasmus means an abundance of rhetorical options when you write and rewrite. At one point in the book he offers as "practical demonstration" several pages of revisions of the simple sentence "Your letter pleased me mightily," which is a sentence we each say at least eleven times a day. ("Your 2 a.m. text message pleased me mightily.") He first lists several dozen synonyms for each of the five words ("on no small scale," for "mightily"), and then dives into the rewrites with zest (Erasmus 2001, 605–9). Sometimes I ask my students to rewrite an entire paragraph twice, without looking at the old one, to see what comes of a new attempt. This simple rewrite method works quite well in conferences when I ask students to speak out loud what they're trying to say in a particularly tricky sentence. Many times, what they say out loud sounds clearer, and closer to what they were trying to say.

I've used cutting exercises for rewriting as well. I show students how to eliminate redundancy without changing the meaning of sentences. Then I share with them the more complicated strategy of changing nouns into verbs and bringing subjects and verbs together, a process made famous by Richard Lanham and Joseph Williams.

Reflect

Hold students accountable. If you teach a new syntactic strategy, tell students to highlight one to two sentences that show how they're playing with the strategy in their final draft. This method encourages them to be deliberate in their practice.

Imitation reflection. After students have read a variety of texts and/or imitated a variety of sentences, ask them to reflect on their own style—what kind of writing styles have been influential to them as writers, how they want to project a kind of ethos, what kind of relationship they want to establish with their readers through their style.

Reflection on completed drafts. When students turn in a final draft, ask them to reflect on their style decisions and justify them rhetorically for the genre, audience, and purpose.

A SEQUENCE FOR STYLE

Dear friends, I wish I could tell you where to start and where to end when it comes to style. I can't. I've never settled on a clear scaffolding for a curriculum on style; perhaps this ill-placed chapter reflects this weakness. In my classes, the first few weeks of the semester are pretty intensive with rhetoric and writing processes, though I can slip in some sentence-combining and imitation exercises to get students in a playful mood about style at the top of class. As I said, we talk informally about style when we do genre analysis. I wait until students have a complete draft to talk to them about syntax and modification, and when I do I use examples to show them how they can revise to add phrase/clause variety. After we've talked about revision in the first unit, I will show them a few strategies for separating phrases and clauses with commas or dashes to show them how punctuation works as a rhetorical tool (thanks to John Dawkins [1995] for this insight). I'll use modeling to do that—that is, example, practice, share, feedback. Later in the semester, once I feel that students have caught the vision for style, I will ask them to add metaphors or schemes or intentional fragments to their essays, showing (again!) various models for doing so.

Ultimately, I want my students to geek out about stylistic decisions as a means not only to engage with readers but to be engaged in their own writing. I want them to see style rhetorically as an opportunity to give someone—a flesh-and-blood reader! another human being! in the for-real world!—a meaningful experience reading a text.

PART V

Reflect

23
REFLECTION AS MINDFULNESS

I write to define myself—an act of self-creation—part of process of becoming—in a dialogue with myself, with writers I admire living and dead, with ideal readers.

—Susan Sontag, "On Self"

We're in the home stretch. Let me sum up what I've said so far:

> Our new understanding of learning to write puts a premium on not just the words students produce but the habits of mind (curiosity, persistence, etc.) students exercise while in a writing task, any writing task. One of the most important habits of an expert writer is the habit of *metacognition*, or the deliberate awareness of what we are doing and how we can do it to the best of our ability. I've called this habit of metacognition *mindfulness*, and mindful writers tack back and forth between assessing a writing task and regulating their activities to succeed at that task, considering the social goals for writing in the first place. Such activity is intimately intertwined with, but also cognitively distinguished from, the process a writer goes through to complete the writing itself. One way to habituate students to mindfulness is to lead them through a writing process that includes opportunities to plan, practice, revise, and reflect. This habituation may be the most important quality students take from our FYW classes to apply to new writing tasks and situations, and research in learning theory and writing studies supports this conclusion. Therefore, learning to teach this process effectively is one of the most important things writing teachers can learn how to do. Finally, while this kind of pedagogical content knowledge can fit any of the going brands of FYW (cultural studies, personal essay, academic argument), the *content* of a mindful writing course is writing itself, which includes rhetoric as a useful pragmatic theory for understanding genre, audience, and purpose in a social context in meaningful writing tasks organized with outcomes in mind. Students can develop mindfulness through informal, low-stakes interventions (e.g., writing-to-learn activities) throughout a writing task.

Again, I'm not the originator of this perspective on teaching FYW. I'm synthesizing the fantastic research of greater minds, which I hope has been clear from all the citations I've thrown in here.

DOI: 10.7330/9781607329374.c023

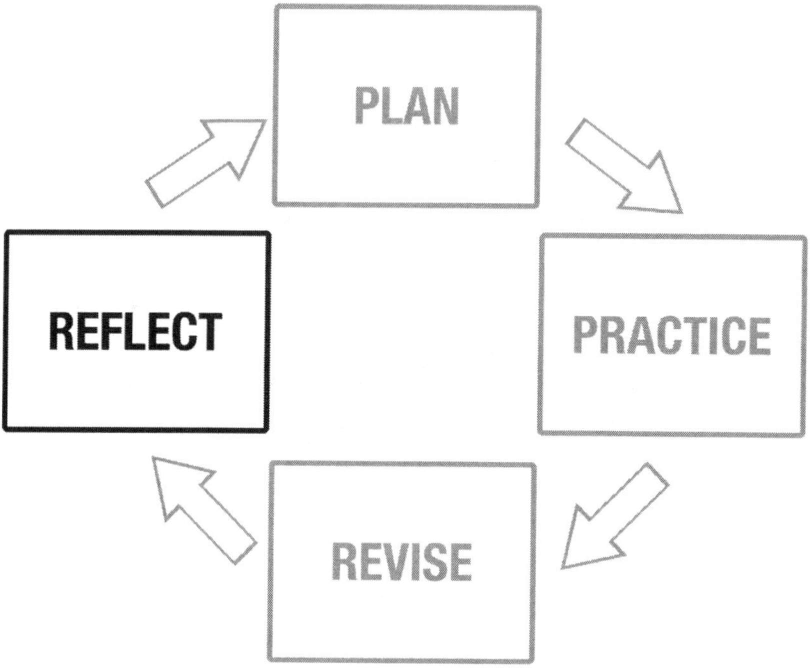

Figure 23.1. The reflection stage

In the interest of being useful, I've also spent time talking about practical concerns such as leading class discussions or responding to writing—concerns that may, or may not necessarily, immediately support mindfulness. In the process I'm quite certain I've left out some important aspects of teaching writing. As basketball phenom LeBron James taught us in the 2018 NBA Finals, there's only so much one man can do.

Now, onto the last part of our four-part learning cycle for mindful writers. I suggested in chapter 4 that though writing is an idiosyncratic, recursive, social activity that often does not lend itself to linear "steps," the teaching of writing must unfold in a sequence—what Linda Nilson calls "the temporal nature of self-regulated learning" (2013, 9). I reviewed how models of metacognition—Zimmerman's "personal feedback loop" or Ambrose's "cycle of self-directed learning"—separate mindful activity into a storyline generally with three major parts: planning a task, executing a task (with monitoring, feedback, and adjustment), and then reflecting on the task when it's over. I've suggested a four-step intervention for mindfulness in writing tasks that includes planning, practicing, revising, and reflecting. This chapter and the next one are about reflection (figure 23.1).

REFLECTION AND CORE NARRATIVES

I was never not good at math. That's my double-negative way of saying that I did OK in math but never thought of myself as a "Math Person." In sixth grade, I started falling behind. Long division and percentages did me in. Mr. Meldrum would toss a worksheet on my desk, and I'd stare at it, my gut sinking to the floor. My friend Jeremy, who sat next to me, the guy who drew pornography in the snow and once stole a syringe from the nurse's station and sprayed people at recess with toilet water, would race through his worksheet, while I sat there, frozen, my pencil hovering over the numbers, wondering why my brain had stopped working.

Mr. Meldrum noticed my slide and sent me down the hall to Ms. Dawn's fifth grade class for math. I'd been demoted. When that happened, I injected a little poison into my brain by telling myself, *I'm not good at math.*

It amazes me how utterly convincing that sentence was. It rang so true to me at the time that it took on the power of an identity: Brian Jackson—*not* a Math Person! It did not occur to me to tell myself alternative statements that might have been equally convincing, for instance, *Looks like you'll need to work a little harder,* or *I'm not getting percentages—maybe even Jeremy can explain the concept to me,* or *Math is hard for me, but I like trying hard things.*

In other words, I had no metacognitive tools to help me work through my math difficulties. I told myself one thing, believed it, and never questioned the validity of it until many years later, well after high school, when I took the Graduate Record Examination (GRE), which included math problems.

The first time I took the GRE, I scored somewhere close to the twenty-fifth percentile on the math portion. (That means 75 percent of test takers scored higher than me.) My low score didn't surprise me—after all, I was not a Math Person—and since my graduate program in English didn't care how well I did on the math part, I didn't either. However, two years later when I took it again for a new graduate program, I decided to study the math stuff out of pure vanity; I didn't want a low score again, even if the schools I applied to ignored the scores. I studied the math, and when I scored in the sixty-fifth percentile (not great, still, but better), I had a new thought jump into my brain, revising the old thought I had in sixth grade, the toxic thought that told me I wasn't good at math:

I can do math if I study. I rewrote part of my learning identity that had been part of me for fifteen years.

According to one of the threshold concepts agreed upon by writing scholars, "writing enacts and creates identities and ideologies." To Tony Scott, this means that "writers are socialized, changed, through their writing" and thereby they adopt identities and ideologies "in response to social expectations" (2015, 49). Reflection is one of the more dramatic instances of enacting identity because we're not just asking students to enact identity through writing a research paper—we're asking them to *constitute*, to create, a writer's identity *as a thing in itself*.

Our emotional and intellectual well-being depend a great deal on the stories we tell ourselves. This statement is supported in a wide array of literature on human performance, mental illness, emotional intelligence, learning theory, and student success. Harvard psychologist Howard Gardner used the term *intrapersonal intelligence* to describe "the capacity to form an accurate, veridical [i.e., truthful] model of oneself and to be able to use that model to operate effectively in life" (cited in Goleman 1995, 39). These models of the self are going to happen no matter what our attitude toward them. The point is to be self-aware enough to monitor and control (our mindful terms) this self (or selves, if you want) and its emotional ecology so we can perform better. We learners have to learn to manage our Selves by reflecting on the way we feel and think, what motivates us, what cognitive heuristics help or hurt us, what mindsets we adopt, what stereotypes we operate under, how we deal with failure, how to adjust our approach, how to persist when we want to quit, how to recognize and channel emotion, how to work with people we don't necessarily like (Bain 2012; Bandura 1977; Dweck 2006; Tough 2012).

When we write about our goals, processes, successes, and failures, we "open a conversation" with ourselves, as Ken Bain writes in *What the Best College Students Do* (2004). We learn about the "power of our own paradigms"—the mental frames of reference that shape our experience (2012, 67 and 71). As we reflect on these things, we interpret what we see in ourselves in the form of personal narratives. Psychologist Timothy Wilson calls our most important narratives "core narratives" because they influence our behavior, helping us overcome adversity and find happiness in the challenges of life (2011, 9). Our core narratives influence our writing identities, and those identities influence our writing performance, for good or ill. I have students who come to my class with damnable core narratives about their writing abilities, which most often reflect psychologist Carol Dweck's fixed mindset (either "I'm so awesome at writing, I can't learn anything from you," or "I'm so terrible at writing that I'll never get it right").

Fortunately, reflective writing can serve as "story-editing," which Wilson describes as "a set of techniques designed to redirect people's narratives about themselves and the social world in a way that leads to lasting changes in behavior" (2011, 11). Story editing happens through reflective writing. In fact—and I was amazed when I read about this—a variety of studies suggest that reflective writing is powerful enough to help sufferers of post-traumatic stress disorder, personal tragedy, anxiety, depression, racial prejudice, failure in school, struggling marriages, unhealthy pessimism, low self-esteem, and criminal tendencies (see Bolton 2004; Kost-Smith et al. 2010; Pennebaker 1997; T. Wilson 2011). Reflective writing helps people reinterpret events to their advantage. Reflective writing builds self-efficacy, and writing students with high self-efficacy work harder, persist when the going gets tough, and bounce back more quickly when they fail (Pajares and Valiante 2006). They're also more eager to write and rewrite.

REFLECTION IN FYW

Reflection is at the heart of mindful writing and has been part of the conversation on teaching writing for decades. Kathleen Yancey—the Meryl Streep of reflection and writing studies—divides the research on reflection into three generations (Yancey 2016). In the first generation, in the 1970s, scholars thought of reflection as the semiconscious activity of pausing in the middle of the writing process to scan what's on the page and plan what happens next. For the second generation of scholars, a couple of decades later, reflective writing became an artifact that could be studied either by student and teacher (as part of the learning process) or by student and institution (for program assessment). Yancey's essential work, *Reflection in the Writing Classroom,* published in 1998, helped establish the research agenda for this second generation. In that work, Yancey thought of reflection both as the "processes" of discovering what a writer has learned and "the products of those processes"—the texts students create for us in the act of reflection (1998, 6).

We are now in the third generation of scholarship on reflective writing. In the twenty-first century, scholars in and out of writing studies have rediscovered the role of metacognition in the entire cycle of the learning experience, turning students into philosophers and creators of their own learning in an individual course and beyond. This new generation of practitioner-researchers sees "the epistemological value of reflection" (Yancey 2016, 10) to help students develop habits of mind conducive to growth. Reflection has epistemic power; by reflecting, students take control of their learning. In Yancey's words, reflection—as both a projecting and reviewing activity—is "a Bakhtinian rhetorical exercise through which one engages with the cultural [learning setting], to draw from it and give back to it in an exercise of meaning making at once both individual and social" (10). Reflection helps writers become self-aware writers qua writers. I have organized this book with this kind of reflection in mind.

Remember in chapter 2 when we talked about how the content of a writing class is *writing*—specifically, rhetoric and writing processes? I suggested that key terms from rhetoric and writing studies help students understand writing in its sociocultural and sociocognitive contexts. This assumption is foundational to the writing about writing movement. (For more on this, check out Wardle and Downs's remarkable textbook *Writing about Writing*, now in its third edition.) In *Writing across Contexts* (2014), Yancey, Robertson, and Taczak describe an adjustable FYW curriculum that includes scholarly readings on reflection, such as the chapter on transfer from *How People Learn* (National Research Council 2002). Think about that for a moment. Instead of requiring students to read "Once More to the Lake" or something, we can assign students to read about reflection as a cognitive activity that will help them achieve their own goals. In later case studies, Taczak and Robertson found that students developed transferrable metacognitive habits most effectively when writing teachers make reflection itself an object of study, teaching key terms and a theory of writing (Taczak and Robertson 2016).

So, through reflective writing we compose core narratives about ourselves as writers. It helps us try on provisional identities as philosophers of writing engaged in the act of writing. Reflection develops mindfulness by inviting students to monitor and control their process from the beginning of a writing task to the end. Once developed, mindful writing helps students transfer essential practices to other settings outside our classes. As teachers, we can make reflection part of the actual content of FYW.

If reflection is both a planning and a reviewing activity, why have I used the word *plan* instead of *reflect* in the task model? One reason: because a task model labeled "reflect, reflect, reflect, reflect" would make the word *reflect* start to sound really weird, like an alien language in a sci-fi movie. I'm feeling that way right now. At some point our heads have to come back on and we have to write, not just think about writing all the time. But a real reason: because I really love the way the word *plan* orients writers forward in time in a task. The word *reflect* has that same kind of chronotopic feel but looking backward, in our case looking back at a task now complete, with a mindful orientation to the future.

REFLECTION IN YOUR CLASS

Your students have completed a draft. They've received feedback from you and their peers. You've taught them some cool revision strategies, and you've invited them to play with their language to find a new voice. Back in their apartments, they've been polishing their drafts by reading them one more time out loud to a roommate or a patient pet chinchilla. They've reviewed the revision checklist you've made for them, and they're preparing to either print out a fresh copy of their final drafts (that they will forget needs to be stapled till thirty seconds before class) or submit them online. The revision stage of the task model is complete. The drafts, though, are *due*, not done, because writing is imperfect-able. Now what?

Now it's time to evaluate their work. But before you dive in, let's first catch our breath and let the students wax philosophical about their learning. Here are a few ideas you can consider as you lead students through postwriting reflection activities.

Timing/sequence. When should you ask students to reflect? Should they turn in reflective writing (Yancey calls this "reflection-in-presentation") when they submit a final draft? Maybe. I have found that if I ask my students to give me their reflections with final drafts, they do the reflecting in the wee hours after finishing their drafts, and therefore their reflecting tends to be cursory ("I learned from my rhetorical analysis that writing can be rewarding if you put thought into it"). Therefore, I've experimented with giving students reflective writing prompts the class period (or online lesson) after they've turned in a final draft. The problem with this approach (sorry! can you see that I'm still working on this problem?) is that impromptu writing in class—usually and necessarily timed—may not bring out the best reflective thinking from the students. You want them to look over their final drafts and think about the prompts. We can help students write better reflections if we provide them with good examples from past students, create a minimal rubric for their reflective writing, and assign a portion of the paper grade to their reflective writing. We can also encourage more thorough revision in a final portfolio project at the end of the semester. In *Reflection in the Writing Classroom*, Yancey (1998) describes a variety of approaches to a final portfolio of curated work, accompanied by a reflective critical essay about what they've learned and how they've grown as writers, referring specifically to instances of growth in their texts. So, I'm trying to have shorter reflective bursts between writing tasks and a larger, more thorough reflective component at the end of the semester in a final or a portfolio.

Reflective prompts. When it came to prom night, I was a disappointing son. The second I walked in the door, if I went to prom at all, my enthusiastic mother would be at the top of the stairs barraging me with questions about who wore what and what music did they play ("Forever Young," by Alphaville) and where did we eat and did I have a good time in my ridiculous tuxedo—and I grunted monosyllabic answers that did not satisfy her curiosity. Similarly, I have to be careful that I do not ask my students "a cascade of questions" that "in no way prioritizes . . . what is valued" (Yancey 1998, 74). Between writing tasks, I want to know five things: Why did you make the rhetorical decisions you made, considering your genre, audience, and purpose? How would you change this draft if you had more time? What did you learn about yourself as a writer during this writing task? What skills or habits that you developed/used in this writing task do you imagine using in future writing tasks? What in your process needs to change in the next writing task? In the next chapter, I offer my own cascade of questions you could ask between tasks and at the end of the semester. End-of-semester reflection can, and should, be keyed to the specific outcomes of the course (Ash and Clayton 2009).

Format/genre. How should your students produce the reflections? Does it matter? Reflective writing is a genre, sure, but it's not a stable, agreed-upon genre, though it certainly fits in the personal essay supergenre (Hesse 2016; Yancey 1998). Different programs and teachers do it differently. I've tried multiparagraph brief essays. I've tried short-answer essays. In an interdisciplinary honors course I taught with a physicist, we experimented with multimodal reflections on our semester projects. Students used web design tools, audio and video programs, screencasting or slide presentation software, and we were delighted with the outcome (see Silver 2016). Generally speaking, I feel like I get more focused reflection from the students if I ask them to answer several questions in short essays. As I've said before, I use Google Drive folders that students use to curate both their drafts and their reflective work. I post the reflection questions online, and students respond in their reflection files. If they reflect in class on the day their work is due, they write by hand, and then I read their reflections as I write comments and grades.

Evaluation. Students should be held accountable for their reflective practice. If they do it poorly (because I haven't spent the time prepping them to succeed), they won't get the benefits. I treat between-task reflection as metacognitive W2L (see chapter 7), which means that I grade it less formally than I do the major writing tasks. I want students to write in their own voice, to explore and resist the course material, to try on writing selves and discover what they've learned about writing from their experiences. Like Rebecca Nowacek, I want students to convince me that they've had a mindful experience. (I'm mindful here of John Dewey's concept of "an experience" from *Art as Experience.*)

Still, as Yancey explains, we have yet to solidify exactly what we're looking for in our students' reflective work. Surely we know when it's *bad*—when, for example, reflections are too short or too abstract or lacking rhetorical understanding or "parrots the context of the class" to please the teacher (Yancey 1998, 82).

When my students use key terms we've discussed in class, and they understand those terms and repurpose them for their own learning, I feel like they are reflecting effectively. Or/and: When they deliberately inhabit a rhetorical situation; when they refer to specific moments of transformation in their learning, when what they knew got a makeover ("Before I thought . . . Now I believe . . ."); when they point to specific instances in their texts; when they see connections between what we're doing in FYW and what they're doing in other classes or what they anticipate doing in the future; when they see how their processes worked or didn't work; when they claim power for themselves as writers; when they say—imagine!—they *enjoyed* writing; when, alas but also yay, they talk specifically and sophisticatedly about how the class has somehow let them down as writers. I'm still working on how to help them make these moves. In the coming years, after I've taught FYW a few more times, I hope I will have gathered student examples and developed some kind of rubric describing what effective reflection might look like, so I can give students full or partial credit.

Our response. It's not always fun to have to grade and respond to a full draft of an essay and then also grade and respond to reflective writing (see Yancey 1998, 147, on this problem). This isn't a problem when we look at portfolios at the end of the semester, because we're assessing learning across time and not performance for a single rhetorical moment. When I respond to students on final drafts between writing tasks, I incorporate aspects of their reflective writing in my comments, especially in those sentences in which I'm orienting them to future writing tasks. I celebrate what they've learned, and I may suggest my own perspective on the relationship between their reflection and their writing performance. I don't have time to write lengthy comments on their task reflections *and* their final drafts.

ITERATIONS OF AWESOME

Reflective writing concludes the recursive learning experience of a writing task or of an entire semester of learning. It gives writers an opportunity to catch their breath and make necessary adjustments for the next iteration of writing/learning. I've tried to convince you that this kind of step-away-and-take-off-your-head mindfulness improves not only the emotional experience of the writer, but also the performance of the student in the class (see Ambrose et al. 2010; Di Stefano et al. 2016; McGuire and McGuire 2015). You will likely enjoy reading your students' deep reflections.

* * *

Sometimes teaching and learning can be like John Wisdom's Parable of the Invisible Gardener, which has been revised and expanded upon over the years. It goes something like this:

> Two explorers come to a clearing where all kinds of flowers and fauna grow in a lovely garden. "Who tends this garden?" they ask. One explorer is certain that a gardener comes and tends the plants; the other explorer doubts that any such gardener exists. They decide to hide in the bushes and wait. They see no gardener. "Well," says the first explorer, "maybe the gardener is invisible!" The second explorer thinks this is a crazy idea, but just in case the gardener is invisible, they set up cameras, tripwires, motion sensors, an electric fence, and guard dogs. Nothing trips the sensors or sends the dogs woofing, and no gardener is caught on camera. The first explorer, now defensive, says, "Surely the prodigious growth of these lovely plants attests to the tireless hands of an attentive, but invisible, gardener!" Growing impatient, the second explorer proposes that they measure the growth of the plants to see just how much of their growth can be attributed to this invisible gardener. Over several weeks (because, what the heck, they have nothing better to do), they measure all the plants in the garden. No growth is detected. Each plant is exactly the same size as it was when they first started measuring. "Aha!" shouts the first explorer, "the invisible gardener is creating *invisible effects* on these plants! Truly this is a magical gardener!"

Yes, I know this is a parable about unfalsifiability and religious belief. I'm repurposing it. Learning is a mysterious thing. Learning to write well takes time—twenty years, according to Ronald Kellogg. Trying to detect growth from student writing, particularly when we look only at a semester's worth of writing, is much like trying to measure the invisible effects of an invisible gardener.

I'm convinced, however, that the artifacts of mindful writing—for example, reflective writing between tasks—tell the tale of growth, even if it's a tale that zigs and zags. If we habituate students to metacognitive moments, and if we invite them to capture those moments in writing, they will have left behind them an archive telling the story of their transformation as writers in our community of writers. I'm not saying that we will always see a clear trajectory of improvement on some quality spectrum that likely does not exist for FYW. But we will see how our students—our fellow writers—confronted the sociocultural challenges inherent in writing and developing new capacities as a result.

24
THE REFLECTIVE COURSE

I've done my best to sell reflective writing's theory and value. Below you'll find a semester's worth of prompts for mindful writing, from the first day of class to a culminating final exam. You'll remember some of these questions from previous chapters. I've gathered these questions from a variety of sources on metacognition and reflective writing. I hope these questions help your students develop mindful writing practices. It should go without saying that you can't require them to write answers to *all* these questions. It would kill them graveyard dead.

TOPOI (I.E., CATEGORIES) FOR REFLECTIVE WRITING

Prior knowledge/experience
Writing process/strategies
Theories of writing/writers (again, I'm indebted to Yancey, Robertson, and Taczak for this)
Rhetorical situation (genres, audiences, publics, discourse communities, purposes, exigence)
Rhetorical strategies
Genre analysis
Assessing the task
Goals: final product and self-regulation
Review of draft so far
Letter to Reader
Revision plan
What was attempted and why
What was learned
Future uses

FIRST DAY(S) OF CLASS

What writing project in my past has been particularly meaningful to me?
What is my theory of writing?

DOI: 10.7330/9781607329374.c024

What does writing mean to me?
What kind of writing have I done in the past?
What kind of writing do I do outside school?
What kind of writing do I like to do?
What are my strengths as a writer? What are my weaknesses?
What do I want to learn from this class?
What do I expect to learn from this class?
What writing strategies have I used in the past that have worked well for me?
What are some of my habits that I might need to change?
What goals do I want to set for self-regulating purposes?

AFTER RECEIVING A WRITING TASK

What is this task asking me to do?
What skills, habits, or prior experience do I bring to this task?
What is the genre of this task?
What is its rhetorical situation?
What are common strategies used in this genre?
Who is the intended audience or discourse community?
What is my purpose: what do I want my audience to feel, think, believe, or do?
What will I need to know/learn/read in order to write this paper?
How is this task similar to other writing I've done? How is it different?
What technologies, modes (e.g., images), or design principles will I need to use?
How do I intend to write this paper?
What will motivate me to complete this task?
What will I do to regulate myself (e.g., write when and under what conditions)?
What challenges might arise as I write this?
What counts as successful or effective writing in this genre?
What do I want to gain/learn by writing this?
Who can help me complete this task?
How will completing this task help me in my other classes, my career, or my life?

ANY TIME DURING DRAFTING

How am I doing? What's working, what isn't?
How do I *feel*? Am I happy, confident, frustrated, bewildered, indifferent?
How am I responding to the needs of the assignment?

When have I been most productive as a writer so far?
How would I explain this writing task to a peer/friend/family member?
How am I doing on my goals? How am I regulating my distractions?
If I'm struggling, whom can I talk to, or where can I go to get help?
How can I participate in class/with peers more effectively?
What am I having trouble understanding?
How am I changing as a writer as a result of writing this?
If I met one-on-one with my instructor, what kind of help would I ask for?

PREPARING A REVIEW

What am I most confident/concerned about in this draft?
What is most weak about this draft?
Why did I use the strategies I did, considering my genre, audience, and purpose?
What do I want my reviewers to look at closely? What do I want them to ignore?

AFTER RECEIVING FEEDBACK

What did I learn about my writing from my reviewers?
What did I learn about the review process?
How would I categorize the feedback using terms from class (e.g., genre, audience, purpose)
What surprised me, what didn't?
What are common responses across reviewers?
What feedback aligns with my own impression?
What feedback do I think might not be helpful?
What do I need to do now? How and when will I do it?
Who else can help me as I complete a final draft?
How will my revisions improve the draft, considering my genre, audience, and purpose?

AFTER COMPLETING A WRITING TASK (CAN BE INCLUDED IN A PORTFOLIO)

How did completing this writing task help me achieve outcomes A, B, C for this course?
How do I feel about my final draft?
What did I do well? What would I revise if I had more time?
What did I intend to do? What did I actually do?
What did I learn about myself as a writer?

What can I see in the drafts as evidence of my learning? Where specifically in the drafts?

What do I *wish* I'd learned but didn't?

What writing strategies did I use to complete this paper? How well did they work for me?

What rhetorical strategies did I use in this writing task, and why (considering genre, audience, purpose)?

What will I need to change about my strategies in the future?

When do I think I'll write a paper like this again?

Which writing strategies will I use in future writing tasks?

Which rhetorical strategies will I use in future writing tasks?

How will completing this writing task have helped me live my everyday life?

LAST DAY OF CLASS (FINAL)

I've used variations of the following final for the last day of class. My institution requires us to have a culminating experience—a final—even if we teach a course (FYW) that doesn't lend itself that well to a three-hour examination. So, I give this prompt (or something like this) to the students a few days before the final and ask them to respond to all (or a few) of the prompts, and then we meet at our appointed hour and eat donuts and they share what they've learned from the class and read some of their responses. I know some instructors in my program require students to do TED-like presentations on their research projects or their writing growth. Perhaps you can imagine more creative ways to get students interested in sharing their reflections. One semester I had two students answer question 5 below in such creative ways: One wrote a song about claims and reasons, and another made a classic newsboy cap from scratch with style terms printed on it.

FINAL REFLECTION

This "exam" is open notes, open book, and open time. Short essays (between 300 and 500 words each). Be specific in your answers, and refer to principles and key terms you've learned in Writing 150. Quote from our textbook and class materials when appropriate. Please select a serif font and keep your essays single spaced. As always, plan your answers. Use paragraphing to organize, and to focus what you want to say.

1. *Theory of writing.* Before you took this class, you had a *theory* of writing. (Remember from class discussion that a theory is a set of assumptions, ideas, or values that help us understand something or do something.) Describe how your theory of writing has changed in at least *two* ways

since taking this class. In your answer, describe how you have changed as a writer this semester.

2. *Looking back.* Pick one of the following two tasks. [1] *Live or die.* Select *one* of the four writing tasks (opinion editorial, rhetorical analysis, conference paper, multimodal project), and write a brief argument (500 words) defending whether the assignment should "live or die," that is, continue to be required in Writing 150, or get the axe. In your response, explain what the assignment was designed to teach and whether it successfully teaches those things. If you think it should stay, suggest how it might be revised to be more effective. If you think we should eliminate it, propose a different writing task that would be more useful to future Writing 150 students. [2] *Share a hack.* Write a 500-word letter to future students of Writing 150 about *one* of the four major assignments. Explain to them what you did to prepare for the writing task, what strategies you found effective, what pitfalls to avoid, and what you learned from writing it.
3. *Looking forward.* Imagine that after taking Writing 150, you take a nutrition class to fulfill a GE requirement. In that class, the instructor gives you a writing assignment that looks like this: *Write an eight- to ten-page research paper on the US Government's new Dietary Guidelines for Americans.* Using at least three specific principles you learned from our textbook, explain how you would approach this writing task based on your understanding of rhetoric and mindful writing.
4. *Looking beyond alphabetic text.* In this class, we've written texts that are mostly "alphabetic"—made mostly of just words on page or screen. How does rhetoric work for a *multimodal* text—a text composed of images, video, audio, color, posts, links, likes, and so on? Select a multimodal text on a subject you like—an Instagram profile, a website, a series of video blog posts, a music video, a podcast, an online magazine, a photo essay, an infographic, and so forth—and answer the following questions using your skill as a rhetorical critic: (1) What can we know about the *specific* audience and purpose for this text from the rhetorical strategies of the text? (2) How is character (one of our rhetorical strategies) portrayed in this text? (3) What is something *new* we learn about rhetoric from analyzing multimodal texts?
5. *Team rhetoric for life.* "Rhetorical thinking helps us approach communication with understanding, with purpose, with mindfulness . . . Rhetorical thinking will help you live better." Explain why. Describe two rhetorical principles you've learned in this class that will help you succeed in (a) future classes, (b) your profession, and (c) your personal life. *Be specific* about which principles and how they might apply in those three areas.

PART VI

The Mindful Teacher

25
MINDFUL TEACHING

In this chapter I explore the idea that teaching, like all mindful activity, improves with a self-directed habit. As mindful teachers we monitor and control our teaching in a recursive, reflective process that never ends until we quit, retire, or die. This reflective habituation, coupled with an insatiable desire to improve, is in many ways more important than any theory or practice or lesson or YouTube video we depend on (Reid 2004).

Like any activity, teaching teaches you as you do it. On the last day of your first semester teaching, you've been transformed. Your assumptions, judgments, abilities, affects, and attitudes have been schooled in the schoolhouse of experience. Much of what you may have learned in a graduate course on teaching—history and theory, for example—melts away in the crucible of the classroom or endures alchemic transformation. To paraphrase the famous line from business management, practice eats theory for breakfast. Chances are quite good that you are a better teacher simply by having taught.

However, mindful teaching demands more of us than showing up and doing the job. In one of the most famous academic articles ever written, Swedish psychologist Anders Ericsson and his research team discovered that practice through repetition (called "massed practice" in other research) leads to a "suboptimal" plateau of human performance. Expert performance depends less on natural ability (though this point has been contested) than on years—ten years, by their calculation—of "deliberate practice": the kind attentive to the best methods for improving, the kind that receives significant feedback, the kind fueled by a mindful motivation to be fantastic (Ericsson, Krampe, Tesch-Romer 1993). Just as we want our students to think of themselves as novice writers with "more to learn" (Rose 2015; Sommers and Saltz 2004), we should think of ourselves as learner-teachers who, even after getting several semesters under our belts, have more to learn about teaching writers. The instructors I've known well who have been the most successful as teachers have this learner's disposition. My friend Debbie, who has taught as an adjunct at my school for over thirty years and has

DOI: 10.7330/9781607329374.c025

won multiple teaching awards, comes to almost every training we hold and tells us, with a contagious smile on her face, that she learned something new.

All this is going to take time. Be patient with yourself. In a journal article that doubles as a letter to you, dear teachers, Shelley Reid (2017) talks about extending "your new teacher timeline," by which she means adopting the attitude of a "pedagogy learner" for the first few years you teach, and maybe even beyond (139). You're going to experience the zig and zag of growth just as your students do.

So, practice + the learner's disposition will get you far. Getting even farther requires some cephalophoric autodecapitation—in other words, mindfulness. In the words of John Dewey, we can "direct our [teaching] activities with foresight and . . . plan according to ends-in-view" by acting "in deliberate and intentional fashion" (Dewey 1986, 125). Remember that metacognition requires a self-directed disposition to monitor and control our activity, to begin with a plan and to carry out that plan with one part of ourselves in the game and another observing and coaching on the sidelines. Andre Gide, the French novelist and Nobel laureate, said once that he "[could not] understand how a person who acts is the same as a person who is watching him act, and who wonders in astonishment and doubt how he can be actor and watcher at the same moment" (Dunlosky and Metcalfe 2009, vii). Indeed, FYW is a place of wonders.

WHAT DOES IT MEAN TO BE A MINDFUL TEACHER?

To a large extent, we've already answered this question in other chapters in this book. As a curricular architect, you will begin with outcome statements describing where you want your students to be at the end of the semester. These outcomes constitute your goals, and to some extent theirs, though they will have their own goals for learning. Your lesson plans serve as testable hypotheses that reflect certain assumptions about how students learn to write (Hillocks 1996, 31–32). Their responses in class, their drafts, and their reflective writing serve as evidence indicating whether or not your approach is working. Sometimes, after a day of teaching, even without clear student evidence, I can tell—by spooky intuition, or by the bewildered look on students' faces—that something in that lesson did not work. Sometimes I need to make adjustments to the next lesson to make up for the shortcomings of the last one.

Mindfulness is often intuitive, informal, subconscious, ever working in the background of our minds, making subtle adjustments that are lost to memory, like tears in the rain. By asking students to enact mindfulness in reflective writing, from beginning to end, we are asking them to capture all those moments and curate them in a deliberate way useful to them as learners. What if we did the same with our teaching? What if we kept a reflective journal in which we work through our own teaching as reflective practitioners? Shelley Reid encourages this; she points out that writing about our teaching experience emphasizes "inquiry into rather than mere acceptance of writing pedagogies" (2009, W204–5). She notes that such struggles in writing help us develop empathy for the novices we teach. It can also help us develop a more sophisticated teaching philosophy, a professional genre that many programs ask us to write. In a teaching philosophy, we balance our principles with our practices (e.g., "This is what I believe, and this is what I do in class because of it").

What kinds of questions might we ask ourselves as we engage in reflective teaching? Here are a few you might consider:

- What usually motivates me to learn?
- How did I learn to write? What were my most meaningful writing experiences?
- What is my theory of writing?
- How do I believe people learn to write?
- What to me makes writing "good"?
- What role does writing play at my institution?
- What do I want my students to learn in my writing class?
- What is my theory of teaching?
- Which teaching methods will lead student writers to learn?
- What are my goals as a teacher?
- How do I want to improve as a teacher? What specific methods will I use to improve?
- What metaphors inform my teaching?
- What is my plan to learn more about how people learn?
- How do/will I show students I care about them?
- How do/will I create a class environment open to all, safe for all?
- How do/will I establish credibility with students?
- How do/will I monitor whether students are learning what I want them to learn?
- How can I assess student learning *in the moment*?
- How did today's lesson go? What did the students learn? How do/will I know they learned it?
- How do/will I monitor myself as a teacher-learner?
- What kind of writer am I?
- How do/will I balance work and life?

Some of these questions can be answered once and revisited during your career at pivotal moments of reflection. Others you'd want to answer as part of the routine of daily teaching. Write answers to these questions over time to archive your reflective teaching. When I look back at the way I've answered these questions in the past, I see how I have developed as a teacher, mostly for the better.

DOMAINS OF GOOD TEACHING

Teaching is an invitation to lifelong learning. Every time I teach, I learn something new about how people learn to write, usually because an aspect of my teaching fails in a spectacular way. I have found that teaching beckons a variety of skill sets out of me, some of which need refinement still. I had a student just last semester challenge me, both emotionally and intellectually, to harmonize justice, fairness, and mercy while trying to avoid loathing the both of us. Frankly, I felt somewhat inadequate to the task, even after seventeen years of teaching.

Teaching is a multifaceted activity with multiple domains of expertise. In *College Writing and Beyond*, Anne Beaufort taught us that effective writers have advanced skills in five knowledge domains: writing process, rhetoric, subject matter, genre, and discourse community (2007, 19). What are the knowledge domains of an effective teacher?

In the movies, effective teachers inspire students to stand up on their desks and recite Walt Whitman poems in *encomium* of the teacher's ability to ignite them with vague, watered-down transcendentalism. In the real world, students appreciate teachers who are credible, responsive, personable, accessible, engaging (Brookfield 2006; Chambliss and Takacs 2014). If we want to know what the best college teachers do, we can read Ken Bain's *What the Best College Teachers Do* and learn that they

- know their content well,
- think of teaching as an intellectual activity,
- expect more from their students,
- provide authentic learning experiences,
- treat students kindly, and
- critically and systematically reflect on their teaching. (Bain 2004, 15–20)

And even this masterful list is incomplete. We also know that good teachers organize materials logically, use effective models or examples, get students to participate actively, experiment and adjust, lead effective classroom discussions, provide clear and copious feedback, believe in their students, handle disagreement and power dynamics gracefully,

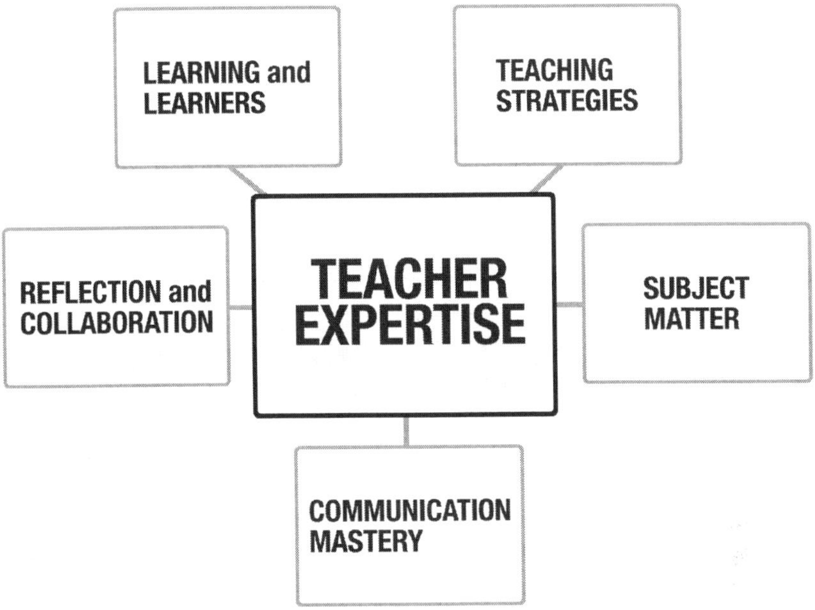

Figure 25.1. Five domains of teaching expertise

assess often and accurately, model intellectual engagement, challenge and provoke critical thinking, and make learning meaningful for the lives of their students. Essentially, good teachers walk on water.

For a rookie teacher, this list of teacher tools can be daunting. As for my own teaching, I'd say I'm pretty good (maybe not great) in six of those twelve categories I mentioned. It helps me, though, to think of my teaching the way Beaufort thinks about writing—as domains of expertise that I improve upon during my career (figure 25.1). Here I'll suggest five domains of expertise for writing teachers: learning and learners, teaching strategies, subject matter, communication mastery, and reflection and collaboration. Let me say a little something about all five.

Learning and Learners

Effective writing teachers should know something about how people learn, specifically how diverse writers learn to write. Our students are at various stages in a developmental continuum of writing expertise. How we teach is greatly influenced by our assumptions about who learns to write, how they learn and when, and why or why not. We are challenged to imagine how an enduring, generalizable curriculum of writing pedagogy can be most effectively delivered to a specific group of students in a specific sociocultural context. Does everyone learn to write in the same way, or do various cultural or developmental groups learn differently, and *better* differently? "Teaching and learning are social processes," writes Carter and Darling-Hammond, and therefore they are not "culturally neutral," even though many of our practices may be effective across cultures and contexts (2016, 594).

We've already established that writing curricula reflect cultural values, even when we think of them, mistakenly, as being culturally neutral. In addition, our students come to us fully loaded, culturally speaking. They come with their own idiosyncratic assumptions about education through their experience with it. Their racial and ethnic status, their family ties, their social groups, their cognitive and emotional range of abilities, their home language, their access to education, their twisty ladders of DNA, their mysterious neural firings, their linguistic background, their gender identification, their socioeconomic status, their self-efficacy—all these factors make a learning medley out of each of them. These factors influence what students experience in our classes. For better or worse, these factors also influence teachers' assumptions about learners, and teacher perception reflects back on student learners, disproportionately hurting various student identities, particularly nondominant ones.

Even in situations in which students and teachers share significant cultural overlap, there will be "cultural incongruence" (Carter and Darling-Hammond 2016, 603), which I observe every time I make a now-dated reference to popular culture. But that kind of incongruence is trivial when compared to potentially deeper differences in outlook when cultures meet. What is to be done in an FYW landscape that will only continue to diversify as the American educational landscape diversifies? I don't know that I have a good answer for this question. For the past ten years I've taught at a selective institution where nearly 99 percent of the students belong to the same faith tradition and 82 percent of them are white. (We boast, if that word is even remotely appropriate, a wider-than-average US geographic diversity, so there's that.) I acknowledge that my experience with diverse learners in the last decade has been limited; I have so much more to learn. From my experience at two culturally different teaching sites, and from the literature on learning, I'd suggest that a "culturally responsive pedagogy" for FYW (Carter and Darling-Hammond 2016, 604; see also Gay 2002) would include the following characteristics:

Deep concern for students. If we care for students as much as we possibly can, if we, in fact, respect them and show concern for their learning, if we have an open and accepting classroom, consistently optimistic about their performance as writers, then we will be receptive to the cultural identities students bring to the classroom. An essential component of this deep concern is cross-cultural listening. Sometimes the best thing we can do in the contact zone is to listen to others. Krista Ratcliffe (2005) defines "rhetorical listening" as a "code of cross-cultural conduct" and a "stance of openness" (17). When it comes to diverse learners, we can practice perpetual curiosity. We get into trouble when we enter the contact zone assuming we know what this or that identity is all about. Our shorthand thinking about identity—the stereotypes and prejudices we carry around with us—makes it hard for us to attend to differences *within* groups. We can ask students about their experiences and worldview and listen carefully, without critiquing or judging. We can also attune ourselves to the emotional responses of nondominant students of all kinds (e.g., LGBTQ students) to make sure they feel connected to the course. In sum, we know that positive relationships with students foster strong learning environments. Students may not remember individual class lessons, but they'll likely remember one-on-one conferences in which we can establish more intimate mentoring relationships with them. We must look for opportunities to talk to students about their lives, concerns, and interests apart from all the things we want them to get out of our writing class.

A cultural "funds" perspective. Often college educators adopt a deficit model for students. The word *woefully* makes an appearance—as in, "Our students are *woefully* unprepared to learn the blah blah blah essential thing I've spent my life studying." In *Funds of Knowledge* (2005), Norma González, Luis Moll, and Cathy Amanti conclude from an intensive ethnographic study in Tucson, Arizona that K–12 students come to schooling with a storehouse of knowledge and experience that often is overlooked in traditional academic paradigms. Although this "funds of knowledge" perspective has been slow to migrate into higher education, new work on the subject has encouraged us to think of new ways to see the knowledge students bring with them as a resource rather than an impediment (Rios-Aguilar and Kiyama 2018). In a writing class, a funds of knowledge approach would include invitations for students to see how all the writing and speaking they've done at home reflect meaningful rhetorical practices that then provide theoretical ballast for writing in academic communities.

A cultural knowledge base. We should tune into research conversations about specific student populations we teach. For example, if a large proportion of our students are second-language learners, we should be familiar with some of the extensive research tradition on English language-learners as writing students. If we teach in an institution or city with a predominant religion different from our own, we can play the role of ethnographer to understand the values, traditions, and cultural practices of the community. As we assign texts and create writing tasks, we can consult the scholarship of those who have made considerable efforts to study and support diverse learners.

A culturally plural curriculum. Educator Geneva Gay encourages teachers to study cultural characteristics and contributions of various ethnic groups through their own artifacts (2002). Recently I taught a course on narratology and film. When I had finished preparing the first half of the course, I discovered, with some discomfort, that every text I had assigned for the first two months had been written by a white American man, and—worse, but not surprising—I hadn't even noticed. I realized that in spite of my best intentions, I must continue to scrutinize my own pedagogy to avoid a parade of privilege. A culturally responsive teacher will assign theory, narrative, and argument from a diverse range of experience. However, a diverse curriculum is only half of a full culturally engaged writing class. As I've discovered in my clumsy striving, we should not shy away from addressing the uncomfortable issues of privilege, power, and oppression when we talk about how language circulates in the cultural publics we and our students belong to. I'm still learning how to teach through my and my students' discomfort with addressing racism as an enduring social problem (DiAngelo 2018).

Metacognitive practices. I'd argue that many of the metacognitive strategies I've talked about in this book will help us understand our learners better. When we ask students to formulate theories of writing or reflect on prior knowledge or talk about previous writing experiences or set goals or write literacy narratives or describe how what they're learning connects to other aspects of their lives, we're asking them to reflect from their own identity space, expressing local values to see how those values validate, expand on, revise, challenge, obscure, ignore, or reject the value system presented by our writing programs. Reading someone's mindful reflection is an act of cultural attunement. Students with neurological diversity can have insightful reflections into what it means to learn to write mindfully.

Rhetorical practices. Aristotle was a fourth century Stagirite trying to make sense of how his contemporaries used language to influence each other. His conclusions, while in many ways still useful, are culturally situated in Aristotle's own rhetorical realm. When we talk with our students about rhetorical theory, we invite conversations about writing's *situatedness* in cultures of practice. Genres, audiences, and purposes are defined by culture; communities are constructed through rhetorical practices. Additionally, if we incorporate critical rhetorical theory, we discuss with our students the way power circulates unevenly in rhetorical situations, favoring some participants and not others. Rhetoric invites conversations about acculturation and justice.

One way we can improve as teachers of FYW is to become lifelong learners of learners and learning. As a parent of four kids, I'm still learning how to be curious (instead of, say, peeved) about my children's idiosyncratic and altogether unpredictable reactions to my parenting styles. I often find that my expectations for them are just that: *my* expectations, which often clash with what they themselves want to get out of life. Last year, dismayed at the time they spent playing video games or watching YouTube videos of cats jumping into toilets, I bought a ping-pong table. Surely ping-pong would bring us together as a family. The kids haven't used it once. Last time I looked, it had been turned into a Lego landscape overlooked by big-eyed stuffed animals. I find I enjoy parenting more when I turn into an amateur anthropologist rather than a petty tyrant. Teaching isn't parenting, but learning about learners is a habit of mind conducive to both.

Teaching Strategies

Effective writing teachers know how to use teaching strategies: how to write a lesson plan, lead class discussions, explain concepts effectively, evaluate student work, and the like. Every teacher in any setting should know a variety of best practices, but there are specialized teaching strategies for each subject. In the K–12 research, this domain is called "pedagogical content knowledge," defined as "what it means to understand one's subject matter for the purpose of teaching it to others" (Grossman, Schoenfeld, and Lee 2005, 207). It goes without saying that a math teacher should understand math (doesn't it—*please*—go without saying?), but less understood is the extent to which subject matter expertise is useless to an instructor who doesn't know how to teach it. Academic graduate programs compound this problem by almost universally refusing to teach grad students how to teach their subjects, even though many of them will have significant teaching obligations in their careers.

The master writing teacher knows what strategies or approaches have been shown, through research studies or experience, to be effective for college writers. In 2006, for example, the Carnegie Corporation released a metastudy called *Writing Next,* authored by two leading researchers in the field of adolescent writers, describing eleven practices with demonstrated track records for improving student writing. At the top of the list, with a strong effect size (0.82), was teaching students specific writing strategies. Successful writing teachers know "what works in writing instruction" (Dean 2010). I hope this book has suggested a variety of research-based teaching practices. If it hasn't, find a book that does. Rely on mentors and fellow teachers who can share teaching strategies with you. Reid urges new teachers to "integrate multiple learning approaches" and "learn from multiple sources and experiences" (2017, 133–36).

Subject Matter

As Bain explained, the best teachers know their stuff, and they know it well. In the popular imagination, this domain is likely the first qualification that comes to mind for any teacher, even though, as I suggested, knowing your stuff gets you only halfway there. Knowing *too much* of your stuff can be a curse, leading to an "expert blind spot" in teachers who lack empathy for learners because it all seems so obvious (Ambrose et al. 2010, 99).

What is a writing teacher's subject? This is a tricky question to answer. We've been debating the issue for centuries. In his *Rhetoric*, Aristotle argues that his communication theory belongs to no subject but is the general method used to invent the available means of persuasion for any subject under the sun. For years, writing teachers have taught the course assuming that any ol' content can be poured in—you need something to write about, after all—so long as students learn how to write a clear sentence. Recently, as we discussed in part I, many convincing arguments have been made that both teachers and students should understand key principles from rhetorical theory and writing studies such as genre, audience, multimodality, or process *as content*, not merely as tricks to get the writing done.

An effective writing teacher—no matter what was studied in graduate school (literature, linguistics, creative writing, rhetoric)—knows something of the prevailing theories of communication, language, learning, and writing as a social and mediated activity. Additionally, the expert writing teacher understands how the subject matter serves curricular, institutional, and social goals. They understand how a first-year writing course integrates with other courses across campus (e.g., a required advanced writing course), maybe also with workplace needs. Take time each year to read a few journal articles and a book or two from the field of rhetoric and writing studies. I learn so much by reading books on learning theory published by Jossey-Bass, Stylus, and other presses. Read journal articles that approach research with methodologies with which you're not yet familiar. Learn the threshold concepts in *Naming What We Know*. They represent several decades worth of specialized research in communication. I haven't talked about it nearly enough, but learn more about how writing across the curriculum (WAC) and writing in the disciplines (WID) supports student writers throughout college. It is likely that your institution will have one or both of these programs. After taking your class, many students will have to take another advanced writing class that likely will be more discipline specific (e.g., writing in the social sciences).

Communication Mastery

As teacher, you are a communicator. You are a coach, a facilitator, a cheerleader, a lecturer, a performer, a comic, an amateur counselor, a public speaker. Whether you teach online or in a classroom, you are constantly communicating with your students. Our audience is restless; their always-with-them phones drag on their attention, whether they are on or off (Thorton et al. 2014). Often you hear that a college student's attention span lasts no more than about ten minutes. The truth is both better and worse than that (see Wilson and Korn 2007). According to one study, students alternate between attention and nonattention in cycles much shorter than ten minutes throughout a class period. And inattention periods often last no longer than one minute; students "leave," and then come back quickly, even though they pay a cognitive price (Bunce, Flens, and Neiles 2010). Master teachers know how to stand and speak, tell stories, provide concrete details, arrange a sequence of learning experiences, write clear emails or feedback, lead class discussions, give instructions, respond to dissent with grace, or repeat back comments or questions to show they can listen as well.

Through our communication with students, we construct a teacherly ethos that projects kindness and concern but also high standards. In *What the Best College Teachers Do*, Bain describes quite eloquently the way Harvard chemistry professor Dudley Herschbach and other master teachers communicated an inspiring teacher ethos: "They were fellow students—no, fellow human beings—struggling with the mysteries of the universe, human society, historical development, or whatever. They found affinity with their students in their own ignorance and curiosity, in their love of life and beauty, in their mixture of respect and fear, and in that mix they discovered more similarities than differences between themselves and the people who populated their classes. A sense of awe at the world and the human condition stood at the center of their relationships with those students" (2004, 144). Stand in front of your students. Look them in the eye, each of them, one at a time. Smile. Speak clearly, but remain vulnerable. Speak and move slowly and deliberately. Avoid histrionics; research in public speaking shows that audiences favor a natural speaking style that sounds like "the language we would use in an everyday conversation—but not exactly like it" (Crystal 2016, 120). Linguist David Crystal writes that excessive voice hesitations—our uhs and ums and yeahs and likes—can lead audiences to be impatient or doubt our credibility (131).

Express concern, curiosity, confusion, care. Other research into persuasion suggests that *likability* influences audiences—of students or jurors or voters. A halo effect descends upon people who share our interests, whom we deem complimentary, cooperative, reciprocal, agreeable, respectful, trustworthy, and caring. (Attractiveness also plays a ridiculously outsized role in persuasion, because we're dumb and life's not fair.) In other words, people we like have an unfair pre-persuasive advantage when trying to influence us (Cialdini 2009, 2016). Learners learn better when they feel they are liked, respected, believed in, identified with. We can learn deeply from people we love because the arrows of our hearts are already oriented in their direction. We can communicate agreeableness to our students without losing our rigor.

Throughout a career, we can continue to grow as communicators by paying mindful attention to the consequences of our rhetorical practices. I know there is nothing more painful, but ask someone to make a video recording of a teaching period. You'll learn more than you wanted to know about your communication trends—your endless pacing, for example. You'll be able to make adjustments that make a difference.

Reflection and Collaboration

This is what mindful teaching is all about.

There's a great scene in Tom McCarthy's movie *The Visitor* in which a washed-up economics professor prepares for a new semester by whiting out the date on an old syllabus and adding the new semester's date. If it ain't broke, don't fix it. There's a natural economy to human behavior. If we discover a way of doing things, we're loathe to change.

Resisting Newton's First Law of inertia, expert writing teachers reflect on their teaching and work with others to improve. Education researcher Lee Shulman, the originator of the idea of pedagogical content knowledge, explained that transformational teaching takes place when teachers can explain why they do what they do. That kind of awareness cannot take place without rigorous "reviewing, reconstructing, reenacting and critically analyzing one's own and the class's performance, and grounding explanations in evidence" (1987, 15). Teaching in this way requires deliberateness, a mindfulness about the vocation of teaching. It invites us to form hypotheses about teaching and learning at the beginning of the semester that we then revisit and revise at the end. Reflection, as Yancey has written, is the projecting and reviewing activity of the practitioner scrambling to improve (1998). Successful writing teachers can attribute course practices to their assumptions, values, and philosophies related to how people learn to write. This expertise is reflected in teaching portfolios, which, I've suggested, demonstrate a philosophy of teaching informed by trial and error.

One of the most important moments of reflection is also one of the most painful: reviewing student ratings. Student ratings are killers. Unless you're a high-functioning sociopath a la Sherlock Holmes and immune to what others think of you, you'll open your student ratings with a mixture of hope and dread. I've seen student ratings from a dozen or so institutions, and they all look the same. Most of them have averaged scores for trait categories such as "organized" or "prompt feedback" or "overall instructor." These scores won't mean much if too few of your students responded or if you do not know the average score for each category *and* the statistical spread of the data (meaning margin of error or confidence in the data). Generally, it is not a good idea for programs to benchmark scores for hiring and firing. According to the Center for Research on Learning and Teaching at the University of Michigan, student ratings are best used to measure "instructional delivery skills" and not "content expertise" or "instructional design skills," pedagogical dimensions best measured by experts ("Frequently Asked Questions" n.d.).

While your scores may not measure your teaching skills with exactness, they do give you a sense of the way students *perceive* your teaching, feedback, and emotional connection to them. If you are scoring lower than average in several categories consistently across semesters, visit with your program director and ask for some feedback on ways you can improve. If you feel your students have written prejudicial comments or comments related to your race, age, gender identity, sexuality, religion, or any or aspect of yourself not relevant to your performance as a teacher, take the comments to your program director to have a conversation about them.

In addition to the numerical scores, student ratings almost always give students opportunities to write open comments on your teaching. In my experience reading hundreds of student ratings, students for the most part are good natured or lethargic in writing these comments. Look for patterns; ignore outliers. It's hard not to fixate on that one student who thought the class was terrible and blasted you. It happens to me almost every semester I teach. (Here's a favorite mixed review from a course I taught a few semesters ago: "I think you genuinely care about other people and I think that that's awesome. Having said that, I hated this class.") Rather, look for repeated comments. If two to three of your students say they felt the class was unorganized, think about what that might mean. As a program director, I was particularly concerned about patterns related to organization, prompt and useful feedback, and general humanity (i.e., comments about feeling belittled or ignored, etc.).

If you detect patterns in your numerical scores and written comments, don't panic. I'm pretty sure no one's going to fire you for a single less-than-stellar semester. Ask fellow teachers or program directors for help as you prepare for the next semester. Hypothesize about the patterns, and make changes in your syllabus, schedule, or approach. Think about using your school's teaching and learning center; usually they jump at the chance to help someone in your situation. In the past I've used our Center for Teaching and Learning to give my students a midcourse evaluation, with questions related to their learning so far. Sometimes all students need to feel to change their perspective on the merits of the course is to be asked about it. That's some powerful magic. Don't be afraid to tell students you are changing your approach (to giving written comments, e.g.) based on their feedback. They'll appreciate the seriousness with which you're taking their learning.

In the next chapter, I'll spend more time talking about how we can get better as teachers through professional collaborations, which I've lumped together with reflection as a domain of teaching expertise. For now, let me conclude this chapter by saying that teaching, though surely not "perfectable," is certainly improvable. The better I get at it, the more I enjoy it. Improvement takes time. You don't need to swallow the elephant all in one gulp. But you can begin, right now, to ask yourself important questions about your teaching. You can look at these five teaching domains, or others of your choosing, and ask yourself what you can do this week to improve in that domain. You can plan to "fail forward," which is Reid's term to describe how to see our mistakes as opportunities to learn, adjust, experiment, grow (2017, 138). Recently when I stepped down from running a writing program, I discovered that what I missed the most was watching new teachers grow exponentially in their capacities to teach.

26
COMMUNITY

This last chapter is about *us*. It's about how we can depend on each other to improve our own mindful teaching. We can learn to monitor and control our own efforts to empower students by working with others in communities of practice. We don't have to go it alone. Just as we teach our students to depend on responders to awaken them to the social nature of their writing, we can depend on community to support us in our teaching. I've written this chapter particularly with contingent faculty (grad students or adjuncts) in mind.

I taught FYW for the first time while working on a master's degree in English. On the first day of our training, I sat by a guy who wanted to talk about Jimmy Hendrix. He became a close friend. I also met a woman, a brilliant and fast-talking creative writer, who had just returned from a mission for her church to Hong Kong. We became good friends. Against my better judgment, I set her up with one of my high school buddies, and they got married. Now she's an established young adult novelist working here in town, so I get to hang out with their family.

In my PhD program I taught alongside three grad students I consider lifelong friends. One ended up watching my two kids when my wife and I raced off to a family funeral in California. Another shared a room with me in Philadelphia when we were on the job market applying *for the same positions* at three different schools. His friendship was a comfort to me during one of the most difficult and anxiety-inducing experiences in my life. The last one split a room with me in Las Vegas at an academic conference a few months after his partner had passed away unexpectedly. When I'm at conferences and I see these people, and the other colleagues I met in graduate school, including all my mentors and teachers, I feel like I've come home.

Amy and I had two kids when I started and three when I defended my dissertation. Because of my home situation, I didn't go to happy hour as often as I should have; I went to karaoke night only once. (If you're wondering, I sang Bon Jovi's "Wanted Dead or Alive.") And yet I felt a strong sense of community with my colleagues, a bond that

DOI: 10.7330/9781607329374.c026

became more meaningful than the accidents and occupational goals that brought us together for a few years. We learned together, and we taught together. We shared workspace—in "carrels," a euphemism for cubicles, sqwooshed nice and cozy so that we heard every student conference held by every other teacher all day long. We swapped ideas and materials. We backed each other up in student conflicts. We watched movie trailers and documentaries on the shared computers. We nuked our leftovers in the same disgusting microwave. We debated politics. We shared whatever diseases one might get by napping on the communal couch. We also worked with incredible mentor-professors who encouraged our teaching along the way.

We teach and learn in communities of practice in which we construct a "shared repertoire" of meaning and doing (Wenger 2000, 82). Expert writing teachers know how to develop supportive relationships with teachers teaching the same course in the same program. Since teaching is so close to our personalities, we often feel like we need to hide it from the scrutiny of others to avoid looking stupid. A few years back, a colleague in my department suggested we form teacher observation groups and watch each other teach. The proposal went nowhere. It is fascinating that advanced-degree holders who project expertise and confidence in academic settings would be so insecure about their teaching. We know from K–12 teaching research that some of the most successful teachers in the world do not have such reservations about collaborating. They have strong peer learning groups they work with throughout their careers.

Over the years my teaching has been refined significantly by active collaboration with other teachers. It started in graduate school when they put us in learning communities—at one institution, they were called weekly instructor meeting (WIM) groups, at another teaching advisor (TEAD) groups. These groups met weekly for structured, and sometimes unstructured and free-ranging, in-service meetings. We were instructed by mentors, we received piles of handouts, we discussed approaches. We were observed by mentors, and we observed each other. I learned so much and so quickly from these collaborations that I can't say how much of my teaching is my own and how much is a mashup of everyone else's great ideas.

Beyond these institutionally assigned groups, I talked about teaching with peers while microwaving burritos. Sometimes I'd be talking to one person about this or that problem, and they'd say, "Hey: Chiara does something like that. You should talk to her." So I would. Scored some great ideas that way. A few times I would team up with a colleague, and we would experiment with X or Y approach and then debrief afterward. I've mentioned my three-course collaboration with two colleagues on a role play with our students. Even after becoming a professor and writing program director, I cherished meeting with grad students and part-time instructors to share ideas about teaching. This book is in large part a product of two collaborations: (a) a professional development reading group with writing instructors, in which we read *How Learning Works*, and (b) an informal research group made up of second-year grad student mentors who loved teaching. I cannot do this job alone, nor do I want to.

FIRST-YEAR WRITING AND IMPERFECT COMMUNITIES

Because of the institutional nature of FYW, teachers often have to settle for teaching conditions that are less than ideal. This is particularly true for all of you readers who are graduate students and (especially) adjuncts. Community can mitigate these challenges, to a degree.

In August 1889, when Fred Newton Scott arrived at a train station in Ann Arbor to teach FYW at the University of Michigan, his supervisor was getting on a train bound for the University of California. When Scott realized that the person who was supposed to train him was "training him"—that is, leaving on a train—Scott shouted at him, "What should I do? I've never taught before." His supervisor shouted back: "Don't let them make fun of you!" (Roen, Goggin, and Clary-Lemon 2008, 357). That's all the training he got.

It wasn't until the last few decades of the twentieth century that most college writing teachers received more prep beyond being handed a textbook and a syllabus. In that era, graduate programs in rhetoric and writing emerged, offering graduate courses focused on the teaching of writing. Textbooks such as *The Writing Teacher's Sourcebook* (Corbett, Myers, and Tate 1981) presented new instructors with theories and practices. Writing programs, now being run to a large extent by scholars with PhDs in rhetoric and writing, offer intensive seminars, in-service training, mentoring, and graduate work. Many of you graduate instructors will write theses or dissertations on topics directly related to the teaching of writing. We've come a long way.

But in some ways we're nowhere near where we should be. Consider the way that countries with high-achieving K–12 students handle teaching as a profession. Stanford professor of education Linda Darling-Hammond reports that Israel, Norway, Singapore, and other high-performing countries recognize that teacher training and support are vital to student achievement. Many of these countries pay every penny of a teacher's postsecondary education. All rookies get high-quality mentoring, including "shared planning time" together and modeling. Teachers receive "ongoing professional learning," which includes more than fifteen hours a week of mindful collaboration and several weeks a year for professional development, including research. (Teachers in the United States get less than one-tenth the annual professional development time that teachers in Singapore get.) Stand-out teachers have leadership opportunities to mentor or create curriculum (Darling-Hammond 2010, 198). Darling-Hammond describes how Japanese school teachers practice *jugyou kenkyuu,* translated as "research lessons":

> Every teacher periodically prepares a best possible lesson that demonstrates strategies to achieve a specific goal (e.g., students becoming active problem solvers or students learning more from one another) in collaboration with other colleagues. A group of teachers observes while the lesson is taught; teachers record the lesson in a number of ways, including videotapes, audiotapes, and narrative and/or checklist observations that focus on areas of interest to the instructing teacher (e.g., how many students volunteered their own ideas). Afterward, the teachers, and sometimes outside educators, discuss the lesson's strengths and weaknesses, ask questions, and make suggestions to improve the lesson. In some cases, the revised lesson is given by another teacher only a few days later and observed and discussed again. (200–201)

These programs think of teaching as lifelong mindful learning in communities of practice. The practices are informed by rigorous research based on student progress rather than the scattered intuitions of professionals who may or may not know with confidence that what they're doing is doing anything (see Green 2014). Intuition, of course, is essential but not sufficient.

Now, consider the situation with FYW. I work at a research institution that requires one course of FYW of any undergraduate student who did not take a dual-credit/concurrent enrollment course in high school or receive at least a 4 on the AP Language and Composition exam. We offer around 370 sections a year of FYW, capped at twenty students per section—that's 7,400 students, if we fill every seat (which we don't, but it's close). The writing program is housed in the English Department and run by people with PhDs in rhetoric and writing studies. These people—called writing program administrators (WPAs)—likely did not receive any training or do any formal research on teaching beyond what they did as graduate students in someone else's writing program. (Remember, the paucity of teacher training and research for PhDs across disciplines is an embarrassing scandal. I'd guess even graduate programs in rhetoric and writing studies may lack the pedagogical rigor of a good undergraduate English education major.) The WPA is appointed by the chair of the English Department to establish an FYW curriculum, train graduate student teachers, hire and professionalize part-time writing teachers (adjuncts), and perform unsavory tasks such as handle grade disputes or field phone calls from parents.

In April, at least in our program, the WPA interviews students who have been accepted to the English MA or MFA program. These students, most of them English majors, have little or no experience teaching, and, since almost all of them are English majors in a literature-heavy program, they've taken no coursework on teaching, linguistics, rhetoric, or writing studies. In August, these teachers are rounded up the week before school starts and blasted in the face with a firehose of training on how to teach. They learn about the major assignments, they norm the first paper, they learn about lesson plans, they see second-year mentors model lessons, and they write up (or cut and paste) a syllabus—for a course well over half of them never took. Then, the next week, ready or not, they teach what I think is the most important course a student takes at college.

There's more training, of course. The MA/MFA students take one graduate course on teaching writing that includes some of the essential subject matter I discussed in the last chapter. They attend weekly in-service meetings run by the WPA and a cheery group of second-year program assistants. They observe two experienced teachers teach, and they get observed twice by the WPA. A handful of them take an additional graduate course and receive mentoring to teach advanced writing. And then they leave—most of them forever. A few stay and become adjuncts. The adjuncts, though paid more per course than at comparable institutions (twice the national average), have no job security or benefits, beyond parking. We have about fifty of them, mostly women with MAs, many of whom have been teaching for us for over ten years. The program can pay them to come to course-specific training twice a year. Every other year the program pays them to perform informal research on their courses and report at a biennial academic conference. They have an annual dinner, one or two available teaching awards, opportunities to earn money through assessment or course coordination. For the most part, they are invisible to the nonrhetoric English faculty. Some of them drive in, teach, and leave; some leave to other part-time teaching gigs to cobble together a living wage, which is a reasonable response to the labor market. Others come eagerly to every professional lunch and training the program holds, even when there are no institutional rewards for doing so.

My guess is that this setup, with variations in size and organization, is typical across the United States. There are programs with better arrangements (e.g., full-time, nontenure yet renewable positions—still a rarity), and there are programs with worse. The first-year writing requirement has created a learning environment where economic priority often enough leads to contingent and transient labor. (The American Association of University Professors [n.d.] reports on the surprising fact that the growth of contingent labor coincided with "times of economic prosperity.") Well over 50 percent of all higher-ed faculty are now non-tenure-line part-time faculty; that number is higher, by as much as 20 percent, for writing courses. At my institution, almost all FYW courses are taught by contingent faculty. I'm one of the few full-time, tenure-line faculty teaching FYW regularly, a common scenario in larger research universities. As I said in the first chapter, our institutions want to teach writing badly enough to require it for incoming students, but not badly enough to offer full-time status to all those who teach it. Scholars such as Sharon Crowley, Seth Kahn, and Robert Samuels have argued forcefully against these conditions of labor, some of them arguing we should abolish FYW because of it.

I hope these arguments about labor and the course continue, even though I do not have much faith that universities on the whole will transform themselves and create more full-time, benefited slots. The economy, with the help of automation, is going in the other direction. Anyway, looking at the Big Picture makes me feel helpless. The reality is that you, dear teacher, are in a program over which you likely do not have much control. That said, you (with the help of a progressive WPA) can make your teaching experience as fulfilling as possible under these challenging conditions, and with imperfect communities.

If you are a graduate instructor or adjunct, familiarize yourself with the "CCCC Statement on Working Conditions for Non-Tenure-Track Writing Faculty," a document composed in 2016 that you can find online. The statement encourages programs to use equitable practices for hiring, compensation, access to resources and governance, and professionalism. There is much that can be done, even at colleges that make extensive use of adjuncts (see Kahn 2017).

As I've said before, it's nothing short of a miracle that rookie first-year writing teachers can be as successful as they are in the classroom. Their experience and goodwill, coupled with competently run programs founded upon solid theory and research, give hundreds of thousands of students a good experience in a class they may not have been all that enthusiastic about taking. We have so much to work with, and so much more to do to improve the conditions of our intellectual work teaching FYW.

WHEN ROOKIE TEACHERS CREATE COMMUNITY

One time I watched a teacher introduce her class to library research with kissing. No, she did not go around kissing all her students, which likely would have led to some legal excitement. She asked three students to step out into the hall with her. The rest of the students and I sat quietly. When the students came back in, they sat in the front, panel-like, and each described their philosophy of kissing, with the second and third students striking a different stance from the students' argument that preceded them. It was not a perfect analogy of writing with sources—entering the *parlor*, a term Kenneth Burke used as a metaphor for academic conversation—but it got the students energized.

A few days later, I saw the kissing panel again in another class. And then another. After observing over 300 instructors over the last ten years, I've seen other teaching trends spread, trends such as "Mount RA" (RA = rhetorical analysis), which included a rough sketch on the dry-erase board of a stick-figure hiker and a mountain with several base camps representing cognitive tasks. Or the "Backpack" lesson, in which the teacher pretends to find a backpack or purse, left by a stranger, and starts pulling out random items to teach students a lesson on critical inference. I remember one year seeing the same Benedict Cumberbatch–as–Sherlock Holmes clip in several classrooms. I think the purpose was lost on most students, but Cumberbatch is pretty cool as Holmes so nobody minded.

While serving as a WPA, I was amazed each year at the transformation that takes place in rookie teachers after a few short months of teaching. They come to us with so much to offer already; their prior knowledge is more impressive than they think it is (Reid 2017). Their teaching strategies, content knowledge, and sociocultural intelligence (i.e., learning to interact with students and colleagues) take off like a rocket ship. I watched how quickly and effectively they grafted specialized knowledge onto their everyday understanding of how learning works (Russ, Sherin, and Sherin 2016). In a miraculously short period of time, they shed common misconceptions about teaching writing and became fully functioning college teachers receiving, on average, higher student ratings than the full-time faculty. I'm convinced that rigorous training programs make a significant difference in teacher confidence and effectiveness.

But a writing program can only do so much for teachers. "Quick competence" after all may be institutional magical thinking (Estrem and Reid 2012). These viral lessons—the kissing panel, Mount RA, the backpack thing, Cumberbatch—reflect how writing teachers come to depend on each other as a community of learners growing organically outside the controlled confines of a program's protocol. New teachers teach each other (see Taggart and Lowry 2011).

I'm reminded of psychologist Alice Gopnik's competing parenting metaphors: the carpenter follows the pattern and makes the exact chair she wants, while the gardener sets the conditions of soil and sun and plants the seed and then delights in whatever ends up growing (2017). In no way do I want to compare new writing teachers to children, but there's an aspect of the analogy I like: new writing teachers take control of their own learning in their own communities in ways that suggest that teacher training programs are more like gardening than carpentering, and we should be happy with that.

In many ways, learning to tap into community as a reflective teacher is more important to a teacher than anything I might cover in a graduate seminar on teaching writing—which includes great stuff that can be easily forgotten in the crucible of the classroom. In two studies, graduate instructors reported depending on their colleagues and their own experience teaching more than on course materials, readings, or workshops for effective classroom practices (Estrem and Reid 2012; Reid, Estrem, and Belcheir 2012; my colleague Meridith Reed is in the process of publishing similar findings). Shelley Reid has concluded that "long-term learning"—learning, specifically, to think like a teacher—is more important than training "immediate competencies" (Reid 2009, 16). This makes very good sense when you consider how important *dispositional* learning is for our writing students. The same can be said of us, their teachers. An essential part of our professional habituation is learning how to participate in a community of learner-teachers, even if we end up doing it for just a short period of time on the way through a grad program.

HOW TO CREATE COMMUNITY

None of us should have to teach in isolation. Below are some ideas for how you can engage with a teaching community no matter how long you've been teaching.

Apply to work in the writing program. Whether you're a grad student or faculty, your writing program is a busy machine. Lots to be done. You may have opportunities to work in teams on projects dealing with assessment, curriculum development, outreach, editing/publishing materials, mentoring, and so on. Working for the program is a great way to learn how writing programs function, and you'll get to work with people who will teach you something new about teaching. While volunteering may be an option for contingent faculty, you should be paid for significant work you do for the program.

Share documents. In grad school I worked for a while developing teaching materials on style. We wrote lesson plans for other instructors and posted them online on a website reserved for all FYW instructors. When I became writing program director, we created a wiki through PBWorks, a free online collaboration program. After building a little architecture into the home page, we invited all instructors to post class materials, assignment sheets, lesson plans, university resources, and other ideas to the wiki. The grad students went way beyond what we'd set up. They even created what they affectionately called the "Shadow Wiki," an off-site webpage full of links to cool media. Your institution should have some cloud computing space; use it to share materials with other instructors, and invite them to upload their materials.

Attend faculty development meetings. If your program holds faculty development seminars, go to them. Sometimes programs bring in scholars from other institutions to share research. With any luck, they will give you some kind of stipend for attending. Talk to the other instructors there about your teaching challenges. If you teach one of a variety of writing courses, find the community of practice teaching that class and ask them to share ideas with you.

Join or start a reading group. One of the best experiences I had as a grad student was when one of our professors invited a handful of us into a Marxist reading group during the summer. We met at Zach's Pizza or this weird, cool tea room above a clothing store. We read Marx's foundational writings, including *Capital*, which most of us, including myself, pretended to read and understand. Even though we didn't talk much about teaching, I felt intellectually energized by our conversations. Each year for the past ten years, my new reading group has selected one book or series of articles on writing studies and one book on rhetoric. Find a few people willing to read a book on teaching writing with you—a book such as *The Meaningful Writing Project* or *Race and Writing Assessment*.

Join or start a writing group. As teachers of writing, we should think of ourselves as writers, too. Join a writing group and share work in progress. If you don't have a writing project, keep a critically reflective journal of your experience teaching. Such open, exploratory writing helps new teachers form what Reid calls a "learner-into-teacher perspective" that shapes their pedagogy (2009, W211). If it's available in your area, join The National Writing Project, an organization that has had a demonstrable effect on the quality of K–16 writing instruction. As a fellow with the Central Utah Writing Project, I learned new things about writing from all kinds of teachers, including a junior high math teacher who was working on incorporating more writing into his class. I also learned to think of myself as a writer who writes not just professionally (for the four scholars who actually read my articles) but for pleasure.

Read the journals. As a writing teacher, I feel part of a larger conversation when I read academic journal articles on rhetoric, writing, and the teaching of writing. Not everything I read is useful; in fact, I'd say around 75 percent of what I read is "gee whiz" more than "gotta use this!" I read journal articles sporadically and strategically. Some years the issues pile up on my shelf and gather dust. (I'm a hard-copy subscriber to only two journals.) Some days, when I have an hour or two, I will breeze through several volumes reading only abstracts and conclusions. The Council of Writing Program Administrators has an online list of journals in rhetoric and composition you can scan to see which ones interest you most. Find journals that publish articles in a variety of research methods.

Join national and regional organizations. We have some very good learned (pronounced, by divine decree, in a two-syllable trochee: LEARN-ed) societies in our field, organizations filled with good-natured leaders trying to get us together to produce the best stuff possible. In writing studies, we have several biggies—the National Council of Teachers of English, the Conference on College Composition and Communication, the Council of Writing Program Administrators, the Modern Language Association and its regional affiliates, and others. There are also more specialized organizations, for instance, the Association of Teachers of Technical Writing. The conferences almost always make you enlist as a member of these orgs for at least a year when you register for their conferences.

Attend and present at conferences. Your program may have money to support you as you share your work at an academic conference. I presented at a conference for the first time as a young teacher at the Spilman Symposium for Educators at the Virginia Military Institute in 2003. At the time I didn't know I would be reading my paper in front of *all* conference participants, not just a handful of folks in a concurrent panel. I was excited, and petrified; I misread the dress code of academic conferences and showed up uncomfortably casual. But wow—what a thrill to have other teacher-scholars talking with you about the things you care about! And kicking the crap outta your ideas! After that, I tried to attend at least one conference a year for many years. At conferences, I meet wonderful new people. I hear about cutting-edge scholarship. I see rock stars in the field give presentations that may or may not have been written the day before on the plane ride. I listen to invigorating conversations.

I also battle agoraphobia. Are we close enough, after all these pages, that I can disclose something a little personal? Sometimes academic conferences intimidate me. I feel lost in a sea of people. When I present, no matter my level of confidence in the material, I'm nervous. I don't want anyone to ask me questions, and most of the time the four to five people in the audience oblige. I'm a lousy networker. I'm just too timid. I end up spending hours walking the streets of the city I'm in, enjoying the sights and smells, alone, maybe even going to a movie, alone!, until it's time to get back to the hotel and (with any luck) watch some college basketball. I know how much of this phobia is in my head because I've had nothing but positive interactions with all the people I meet at conferences, including the so-called celebrity scholars entirely out of my league. In spite of my timidity, I've learned to feel a sense of community at conferences, especially when I meet up and go to lunch with old friends. I do love doing that. You feel part of something much greater than your own teaching when you go to conferences. If you see me at a conference, please come up and say hello.

Maybe better yet, attend seminars and workshops. I've felt a much stronger sense of community at seminars and workshops than I do at conferences. I feel like I'm getting more done, too, as a teacher and scholar. I highly recommend the Rhetoric Society of America Summer Institute and Workshops, the workshops before the Conference on College Composition and Communication (4Cs), and the special-interest groups at 4Cs (including workshops by ATTW). If you are interested in writing program administration, I recommend the WPA Summer Workshop. The groups are much smaller than the crowds at conferences. You can talk to colleagues extensively and form long-term collaborations.

I know these professional programs are often financially out of reach for grad students and adjuncts, which is yet another example of how we shoot ourselves in the foot professionally by undervaluing the people who teach FYW. Ask your program if they have funding for you to go, even if you're not presenting. Sometimes a conference or workshop is within driving distance. I drive up to the Rocky Mountain Modern Language Association when it comes to Salt Lake City, and then I drive home at the end of the day, saving on hotel fees.

Observe people teach and let them observe you teach. This one's free and right there at your school. Ask a friend or two, or a mentor, if you can watch them teach, or ask your program director to recommend seasoned, successful instructors to spy on. Go early and sit in the back of the room. Write down what you see happening—what the teacher does, and how the students respond. Talk to them afterward about what you saw. Write down what you want to change in your own teaching based on your observation. Let others come and watch you teach as often as possible. I know how unnerving this can be, but it is essential. Even worse/better: let them record you with a phone or digital camcorder. Together watch a segment of your teaching and ask them what they see.

Invite specialists to come to your class. You may know someone who knows something interesting about the topic you are discussing. You may know someone who understands a kind of writing software (e.g., an Adobe product) better than you. There may be student support people on campus who help students with study skills or reading strategies, or coping strategies. Maybe a representative of your writing center, career center, cultural center, or counseling center would be willing to visit your class.

Talk to everyone. I learn so much talking to various campus entities, from academic specialists for student athletes to career advisement specialists to therapists in the counseling center. When you hit a snag, call someone. If you have a question about your university's Title IX policy, as I have, call the specialists up and talk to them. Visit the writing center and other campus support programs. Commiserate with other writing instructors. (I'd advise against taking to social media with exasperated or mocking anecdotes about your students.) Go see your program director when troubles come. Many times I've met with an instructor about a minor issue but then had a deeper, sometimes more teary, conversation about difficulties they faced as a teacher. If your life starts to spiral out of your control, don't withdraw. Talk to your WPA or graduate program director. Several years ago I ended up in the emergency room with a graduate instructor who had tried to take her own life. We had no idea she was in such a dark place. She was far from home and reasonably did not want to burden her boss, whom she knew only professionally and superficially, with her problems. People in programs can take care of each other. We found subs for the instructor for a couple of weeks, and she came back with renewed confidence and taught for us for a few years after that. Stay connected. It's good for your teaching and your soul.

TO CONCLUDE AT THE BEGINNING

At the beginning of this book, I expressed the sincere hope that you will enjoy your experience teaching as much as I have enjoyed mine. There is so much energy in literacy empowerment. I'm convinced that most of our students believe already that we offer something they probably want, that we can guide them as they learn to act in all their rhetorical situations, their writing tasks and challenges. We can convince them further to be mindful writers in their tasks, planning and reflecting in new ways as they develop a philosophy for being a writer in a language-mediated world. We, too, can monitor and control our own efforts as teachers and learners in whatever community we find ourselves in.

REFERENCES

Abbott, Don Paul. 2001. "Rhetoric and Writing in the Renaissance." *A Short History of Writing Instruction*, 2nd ed., edited by James J. Murphy, 145–72. Mahwah, NJ: Lawrence Erlbaum.

Adler-Kassner, Linda, and Heidi Estrem. 2007. "Reading Practices in the Writing Classroom." *WPA: Writing Program Administration* 31 (1–2): 35–47.

Adler-Kassner, Linda, and Elizabeth Wardle, eds. 2015. *Naming What We Know*. Logan: Utah State University Press.

Ambrose, Susan A., Michael, W. Bridges, Michele DiPietro, Marsha C. Lovett, and Marie K. Norman. 2010. *How Learning Works*. San Francisco: Jossey-Bass.

American Association of University Professors. N.d. "Background Facts on Contingent Faculty." Accessed June 13, 2018. https://www.aaup.org/issues/contingency/background-facts.

Anderson, Paul, Chris M. Anson, Robert M. Gonyea, and Charles Paine. 2015. "The Contributions of Writing to Learning and Development: Results from a Large-Scale Multi-Institutional Study." *Research in the Teaching of English* 50 (2): 199–239.

Angier, Natalie. 2007. *The Canon: A Whirligig Tour of the Beautiful Basics of Science*. Boston: Mariner.

Anzaldúa, Gloria. 2001. "How to Tame a Wild Tongue." In *The Rhetorical Tradition*, 2nd ed., edited by Patricia Bizzell and Bruce Herzberg, 1585–1604. Boston: Bedford/St. Martin's.

Anson, Chris M. 1999. "Reflective Reading: Developing Thoughtful Ways to Respond to Students' Writing." In *Evaluating Writing*, edited by Charles R. Cooper and Lee Odell, 302–24. Urbana, IL: National Council of Teachers of English.

Anson, Chris M. 2014. "Process Pedagogy and Its Legacy." In *A Guide to Composition Pedagogies*, 2nd ed., edited by Gary Tate, Amy Rupiper Taggart, Kurt Schick, and H. Brooke Hessler, 212–30. New York: Oxford University Press.

Anson, Chris M., Deanna P. Dannels, Johanne I. Laboy, and Larissa Carneiro. 2016. "Students' Perceptions of Oral Screencast Responses to Their Writing." *Journal of Business and Technical Communication* 30 (3): 378–411.

Anson, Chris M. and Jessie L. Moore, eds. 2017. *Critical Transitions: Writing and the Question of Transfer*. Fort Collins, CO: The WAC Clearinghouse.

Aristotle. 1947. *Nicomachean Ethics*. Translated by Richard McKeon. New York: Modern Library.

Aristotle. 2007. *On Rhetoric*. Translated by George A. Kennedy. 2nd ed. New York: Oxford.

Aronson, Eliot. 2012. *The Social Animal*. 11th ed. New York: Worth.

Artemeva, Natasha, and Janna Fox. 2010. "Awareness versus Production: Probing Students' Antecedent Genre Knowledge." *Journal of Business and Technical Communication* 24 (October): 476–515.

Ash, Sarah L., and Patti H. Clayton. 2009. "Generating, Deepening, and Documenting Learning: The Power of Critical Reflection in Applied Learning." *Journal of Applied Learning in Higher Education* 1 (Fall): 25–48.

Atkinson, Dwight, and Ulla Connor. 2008. "Multilingual Writing Development." In *Handbook of Research on Writing*, edited by Charles Bazerman, 515–32. New York: Lawrence Erlbaum.

DOI: 10.7330/9781607329374.c027

Bacon, Nora. 2009. *The Well-Crafted Sentence: A Writer's Guide to Style.* Boston: Bedford/St. Martin's.

Bain, Ken. 2004. *What the Best College Teachers Do.* Cambridge, MA: Harvard University Press.

Bain, Ken. 2012. *What the Best College Students Do.* Cambridge: Belknap.

Bandura, Albert. 1977. "Self-Efficacy: Toward a Unifying Theory of Behavioral Change." *Psychological Review* 84 (2): 191–215.

Barkley, Elizabeth F., K. Patricia Cross, and Claire Howell Major. 2005. *Collaborative Learning Techniques.* San Francisco: Jossey-Bass.

Barry, Dave. 1996. *Dave Barry's Complete Guide to Guys.* New York: Ballantine Books.

Bawarshi, Anis, and Mary Jo Reiff. 2010. *Genre: An Introduction to History, Theory, Research, and Pedagogy.* West Lafayette, Indiana: Parlor Press. https://wac.colostate.edu/docs/books/bawarshi_reiff/front.pdf.

Bazerman, Charles. 2016. "What Do Sociocultural Studies of Writing Tell Us about Learning to Write?" In *Handbook of Writing Research,* 2nd ed., edited by Charles A. MacArthur, Steve Graham, and Jill Fitzgerald, 11–23. New York: Guilford.

Bazerman, Charles, Joseph Little, Lisa Bethel, Teri Chavkin, Danielle Fouquette, and Janet Garufis. 2005. *Reference Guide to Writing across the Curriculum.* West Lafayette, IN: Parlor.

Bazerman, Charles, and Howard Tinberg. 2015. "Text Is an Object Outside of Oneself That Can Be Improved and Developed." In *Naming What We Know,* edited by Linda Adler-Kassner and Elizabeth Wardle, 61–62. Logan: Utah State University Press.

Beach, Richard. 1989. "Showing Students How to Assess: Demonstrating Techniques for Response in the Writing Conference." In *Writing and Response: Theory, Practice, and Research,* edited by Chris M. Anson, 127–48. Urbana, IL: National Council of Teachers of English.

Beach, Richard, and Tom Friedrich. 2006. "Response to Writing." In *The Handbook of Writing Research,* edited by Charles A. MacArthur, Steve Graham, and Jill Fitzgerald, 222–34. New York: Guilford.

Beach, Richard, George E. Newell, and Jennifer VanDerHeide. 2016. "A Sociocultural Perspective on Writing Development." In *Handbook of Writing Research,* 2nd ed., edited by Charles A. MacArthur, Steve Graham, and Jill Fitzgerald, 88–101. New York: Guilford.

Bean, John C. 2011. *Engaging Ideas.* 2nd ed. San Francisco: Jossey-Bass.

Bean, John, Virginia A. Chappell, and Alice M. Gillam. 2014. *Reading Rhetorically.* 4th ed. Boston: Pearson.

Beaufort, Anne. 2007. *College Writing and Beyond.* Logan: Utah State University Press.

Beaufort, Anne. 2016. "Reflection: The Metacognitive Move towards Transfer of Learning." In *A Rhetoric of Reflection,* edited by Kathleen Blake Yancey, 23–41. Logan: Utah State University Press.

Beck, Aaron. 1979. *Cognitive Therapy and the Emotional Disorders.* New York: Plume.

Behm, Nicholas, Sherry Rankins-Robertson, and Duane Roen, eds. 2017. *The Framework for Success in Postsecondary Writing.* Anderson, SC: Parlor.

Belanoff, Pat, and Marcia Dickson, eds. 1991. *Portfolios: Process and Product.* Heinemann: Boynton/Cook.

Bereiter, Carl, and Marlene Scardamalia. 1987. *The Psychology of Written Composition.* Hillsdale, NJ: LEA.

Berlin, James A. 1982. "Contemporary Composition: The Major Pedagogical Theories." *College English* 44 (8): 765–77.

Berthoff, Ann E. 1981. *The Making of Meaning.* Upper Montclair, NJ: Boynton/Cook.

Bishop, Wendy. 2014. "Helping Peer Writing Groups Succeed." *St. Martin's Guide to Teaching Writing,* 7th ed., edited by Cheryl Glenn and Melissa A. Goldthwaite, 309–17. Boston: Bedford/St. Martin's.

Bolton, Gillie, ed. 2004. *Writing Cures: An Introductory Handbook of Writing in Counseling and Therapy.* London: Routledge.

Bondy, Elizabeth, and Dorene D. Ross. 2008. "The Teacher as Warm Demander." *Educational Leadership* 66 (1): 54–58.

Boscolo, Pietro, and Carmen Gelati. 2013. "Best Practices in Promoting Motivation in Writing." In *Best Practices in Writing Instruction*, 2nd ed., edited by Steve Graham, Charles A. MacArthur, and Jill Fitzgerald, 284–308. New York: Guilford.

Bowden, Mark. 2009. "The Hardest Job in Football." *Atlantic*. Accessed March 3, 2017. https://www.theatlantic.com/magazine/archive/2009/01/the-hardest-job-in-football/307212/.

Brame, Cynthia, and Rachel Biel. 2015. "Group Work: Using Cooperative Learning Groups Effectively." Vanderbilt University Center for Teaching. Accessed April 23, 2018. https://cft.vanderbilt.edu/guides-sub-pages/setting-up-and-facilitating-group-work-using-cooperative-learning-groups-effectively/.

Brandt, Deborah. 2009. *Literacy and Learning*. San Francisco: Jossey-Bass.

Brandt, Deborah. 2015. *The Rise of Writing*. Cambridge University Press.

Breidenbach, Cathleen. 2006. "Practical Guidelines for Writers and Teachers." In *Revision: History, Theory, and Practice*, edited by Alice Horning and Anne Becker, 197–219. West Lafayette, IN: Parlor.

Brereton, John C., ed. 1995. *The Origins of Composition Studies in the American College: A Documentary History, 1875–1925*. Pittsburgh: University of Pittsburgh Press.

Broad, Bob. 2003. *What We Really Value*. Logan: Utah State University Press.

Bronson, Po, and Ashley Merryman. 2009. *Nurture Shock*. New York: Twelve.

Brooke, Collin, and Allison Carr. 2015. "Failure Can Be an Important Part of Writing Development." In *Naming What We Know*, edited by Linda Adler-Kassner and Elizabeth Wardle, 62–64. Logan: Utah State University Press.

Brooke, Collin, and Jeffrey T. Grabill. 2015. "Writing Is a Technology through Which Writers Create and Recreate Meaning." In *Naming What We Know: Threshold Concepts of Writing Studies*, edited by Linda Adler-Kassner and Elizabeth Wardle, 32–33. Logan: Utah State University Press.

Brookfield, Stephen D. 2006. *The Skillful Teacher*. 2nd ed. San Francisco: Jossey-Bass.

Brown, Peter C., Henry L. Roediger III, and Mark A. McDaniel. 2014. *Make It Stick: The Science of Successful Learning*. Cambridge, MA: Belknap.

Bruffee, Kenneth A. 1999. *Collaborative Learning*. 2nd ed. Baltimore: Johns Hopkins University Press.

Bruning, Roger H., and Douglas F. Kauffman. 2016. "Self-Efficacy Beliefs and Motivation in Writing Development." In *Handbook on Writing Research*, 2nd ed., edited by Charles A. MacArthur, Steve Graham, and Jill Fitzgerald, 160–73. New York: Guilford.

Bunce, Diane M., Elizabeth A. Flens, and Kelly Y. Neiles. 2010. "How Long Can Students Pay Attention in Class?" *Journal of Chemical Education* 87 (12): 1438–43.

Burke, Kenneth. 1973. *The Philosophy of Literary Form*. 3rd ed. Berkeley: University of California Press.

Burke, Kenneth. 1984. *Attitudes toward History*, 3rd ed. Berkeley: University of California Press.

Butler, Paul. 2008. *Out of Style: Reanimating Stylistic Study in Composition and Rhetoric*. Logan: Utah State University Press.

Capella, Elise, J. Lawrence Aber, and Ha Yeon Kim. 2016. "Teaching beyond Achievement Tests: Perspectives from Developmental and Education Science." In *Handbook of Research on Teaching*, 5th ed., edited by Drew H. Gitomer and Courtney A. Bell, 249–347. Washington, DC: American Educational Research Association.

Carey, Benedict. 2014. *How We Learn*. New York: Random House.

Carillo, Ellen C. 2015. *Securing a Place for Reading in Composition*. Logan: Utah State University Press.

Carroll, Lee Ann. 2002. *Rehearsing New Roles: How College Students Develop as Writers*. Carbondale: Southern Illinois University Press.

Carter, Prudence L., and Linda Darling-Hammond. 2016. "Teaching Diverse Learners." *Handbook of Research on Teaching*, 5th ed., edited by Drew H. Gitomer and Courtney A. Bell, 593–637. Washington, DC: American Educational Research Association.

"CCCC Statement on Second-Language Writing and Writers." 2011. In *Second-Language Writing in the Composition Classroom: A Critical Sourcebook*, edited by Paul Kei Matsuda, Michelle Cox, Jay Jordan, and Christina Ortmeier-Hooper, 10–19. Boston: Bedford/St. Martin's.

"CCCC Statement on Working Conditions for Non-Tenure-Track Writing Faculty." 2016. Conference on College Composition and Communication. Accessed March 21, 2018. https://cccc.ncte.org/cccc/resources/positions/working-conditions-ntt.

Carnes, Mark C. 2014. *Minds on Fire: How Role-Immersion Games Can Transform College*. Cambridge: Harvard University Press.

Chambliss, Daniel F., and Christopher G. Takacs. 2014. *How College Works*. Cambridge, MA: Harvard University Press.

Christensen, Francis. 1963. "A Generative Rhetoric of the Sentence." *CCC* 14 (3): 155–61.

Christiansen, M. Sidury, and Joel Bloch. 2016. "Papers Are Never Finished, Just Abandoned: The Role of Written Teacher Comments in the Revision Process." *Journal of Response to Writing* 2 (1): 6–42.

Chua, Amy. 2011. "Why Chinese Mothers Are Superior." *Wall Street Journal*. Accessed January 13, 2020. https://www.wsj.com/articles/SB10001424052748704111504576059713528698754.

Cialdini, Robert. 2009. *Influence: Science and Practice*. 5th ed. Boston: Pearson.

Cialdini, Robert. 2016. *Pre-suasion*. New York: Simon and Schuster.

Cicero, Marcus Tullius. 2001. *On the Ideal Orator*. Translated by James M. May and Jakob Wisse. Oxford: Oxford University Press.

Clark, Irene L. 2012. *Concepts in Composition: Theory and Practice in the Teaching of Writing*. 2nd ed. New York: Routledge.

Comer, Amber R. 2016. "The Syllabus as a Contract." *Chronicle of Higher Education*. Accessed Jan 31, 2018. https://www.chronicle.com/article/The-Syllabus-as-a-Contract/237251.

Conley, Thomas, M. 1990. *Rhetoric in the European Tradition*. Chicago: University of Chicago Press.

Connors, Robert J. 2000. "The Erasure of the Sentence." *CCC* 52 (1): 95–128.

Cope, Bill, and Mary Kalantzis, eds. 1993. *The Powers of Literacy: A Genre Approach to Teaching Writing*. New York: Routledge.

Corbett, Edward P. J., Nancy Myers, and Gary Tate, eds. 1981. *The Writing Teacher's Sourcebook*. Oxford: Oxford University Press.

Corbett, Edward P. J., and Robert J. Connors. 1998. *Classical Rhetoric for Modern Students*. 4th ed. Oxford: Oxford University Press.

Coyle, Daniel. 2018. *The Culture Code*. New York: Bantam.

Crowley, Sharon. 1998. *Composition in the University: Historical and Polemical Essays*. Pittsburgh, PA: University of Pittsburgh Press.

Crowley, Sharon, and Debra Hawhee. 2011. *Ancient Rhetorics for Contemporary Students*. 5th ed. New York: Pearson.

Crystal, David. 2016. *The Gift of the Gab*. New Haven, CT: Yale University Press.

Cumming, Alister, ed. 2006. *Goals for Academic Writing: ESL Students and Their Instructors*. Amsterdam: John Benjamins.

Daiker, Donald A. 1989. "Learning to Praise." In *Writing and Response: Theory, Practice, and Research*, edited by Chris M. Anson, 103–13. Urbana, IL: National Council of Teachers of English.

Dallimore, Elise J., Julie H. Hertenstein, and Marjorie B. Platt. 2017. "How Do Students Learn from Participation in Class Discussion?" *Faculty Focus*. Accessed April 13, 2018. https://www.facultyfocus.com/articles/effective-teaching-strategies/students-learn-participation-class-discussion/.

Danielewicz, Jane, and Peter Elbow. 2009. "A Unilateral Grading Contract to Improve Learning and Teaching." *CCC* 61 (2): 244–68.

Dannels, Deanna P. 2015. *Eight Essential Questions Teachers Ask.* Oxford: Oxford University Press.

Darling-Hammond, Linda. 2010. *The Flat World of Education.* New York: Teachers College Press.

Davis, Barbara Gross. 2009. *Tools for Teaching.* San Francisco: Jossey-Bass.

Davis, Lauren Cassani. 2015. "When Mindfulness Meets the Classroom." *Atlantic.* Accessed January 16, 2018. https://www.theatlantic.com/education/archive/2015/08/mindfulness-education-schools-meditation/402469/.

Dawkins, John. 1995. "Punctuation as a Rhetorical Tool." *CCC* 46 (4): 533–48.

Dean, Deborah. 2010. *What Works in Writing Instruction.* Urbana, IL: National Council of Teachers of English.

Dehaene, Stanislas. 2009. *Reading in the Brain.* New York: Viking.

Devitt, Amy. 2004. *Writing Genres.* Carbondale: Southern Illinois University Press.

Devitt, Amy J. 2014. "Genre Pedagogies." In *A Guide to Composition Pedagogies,* 2nd ed., edited by Gary Tate, Amy Rupiper Taggart, Kurt Schick, and H. Brooke Hessler, 146–62. New York: Oxford University Press.

Devitt, Amy, Mary Jo Reiff, and Anis Bawarshi. 2004. *Scenes of Writing: Strategies for Composing with Genres.* New York: Pearson.

Dewey, John. 1972a. "Ethical Principles Underlying Education." Vol. 5 of *John Dewey: The Early Works, 1882–1898,* edited by Jo Ann Boydston, 54–83. Carbondale: Southern Illinois University Press.

Dewey, John. 1972b. "My Pedagogic Creed." Vol. 5 of *John Dewey: The Early Works, 1882–1898,* edited by Jo Ann Boydston, 84–95. Carbondale: Southern Illinois University Press.

Dewey, John. 1985. *The Middle Works of John Dewey, 1899–1924.* Vol. 9, edited by Jo Ann Boydston. Carbondale: Southern Illinois University Press.

Dewey, John. 1986. *How We Think.* Vol. 8 of *John Dewey: The Later Works, 1925–1953,* edited by Jo Ann Boydston, 105–352. Carbondale: Southern Illinois University Press.

Dewey, John. 2008. *The Child and the Curriculum. John Dewey: The Middle Works, 1899–1924.* Vol. 2, edited by Jo Ann Boydston, 271–91. Carbondale: Southern Illinois University Press.

DiAngelo, Robin. 2018. *White Fragility.* Boston: Beacon.

Dillard, Annie. 2000. *Pilgrim at Tinker Creek.* New York: Harper Perennial.

DiPardo, Anne, and Sarah Warshauer Freedman. 1988. "Peer Response Groups in the Writing Classroom: Theoretic Foundations and New Directions." *Review of Educational Research* 58 (2): 119–49.

Di Stefano, Giada, Francesca Gino, Gary Pisano, and Bradley Staats. 2016. "Making Experience Count: The Role of Reflection in Individual Learning." Working Paper. Harvard Business School. Accessed July 9, 2018. https://www.hbs.edu/faculty/Publication%20Files/14-093_defe8327-eeb6-40c3-aafe-26194181cfd2.pdf.

Dochy, F., M. Segers, and D. Sluijsmans. 1999. "The Use of Self-, Peer and Co-Assessment in Higher Education: A Review." *Studies in Higher Education* 24 (3): 331–50.

Downs, Doug, and Elizabeth Wardle. 2012. "Reimagining the Nature of FYC: Trends in Writing-about-Writing Pedagogies." In *Exploring Composition Studies: Sites, Issues, and Perspectives,* edited by Kelly Ritter and Paul Kei Matsuda, 123–44. Logan: Utah State University Press.

Doyle, Terry, and Todd Zakrajsek. 2013. *The New Science of Learning.* Sterling, VA: Stylus.

Driscoll, Dana Lynn, and Jennifer Wells. 2012. "Beyond Knowledge and Skills: Writing Transfer and the Role of Dispositions." *Composition Forum* 26. http://compositionforum.com/issue/26/beyond-knowledge-skills.php.

Dryer, Dylan B. 2015. "Writing Is Not Natural." In *Naming What We Know*, edited by Linda Adler-Kassner and Elizabeth Wardle, 27–29. Logan: Utah State University Press.

Dryer, Dylan B., and David R. Russell. 2017. "Attending to Phenomenology: Rethinking Cognition and Reflection in North American Writing Studies." In *Contemporary Perspectives on Cognition and Writing*, edited by Patricia Portanova, Michael Rifenburg, and Duane Roen, 57–76. Fort Collins: WAC Clearinghouse.

Dunlosky, John, and Janet Metcalfe. 2009. *Metacognition*. Los Angeles: Sage.

Dweck, Carol. 2006. *Mindset: The New Psychology of Success*. New York: Ballantine.

Dynarski, Susan. 2017. "Laptops Are Great. But Not during a Lecture or Meeting." *New York Times*. Accessed April 26, 2018. https://www.nytimes.com/2017/11/22/business/laptops-not-during-lecture-or-meeting.html.

Eberly, Rosa. 1999. "From Writers, Audiences, and Communities to Publics: Writing Classrooms as Protopublic Spaces." *Rhetoric Review* 18 (1): 165–78.

Elbow, Peter. 1981. *Writing with Power*. New York: Oxford.

Elbow, Peter. 1987. "Closing My Eyes as I Speak: An Argument for Ignoring Audience." *College English* 49 (1): 50–69.

Elbow, Peter. 2012. *Vernacular Eloquence: What Speech Can Bring to Writing*. Oxford: Oxford University Press.

Enkvist, Nils Erik. 1969. "From 'On Defining Style.'" In *Contemporary Essays on Style*, edited by Glen A. Love and Michael Payne, 120–32. Glenview, IL: Scott, Foresman.

Enos, Richard Leo. 2001. "Ancient Greek Writing Instruction." In *A Short History of Writing Instruction*, 2nd ed., edited by James J. Murphy. 9–34. Mahwah, NJ: Lawrence Erlbaum.

Eodice, Michele, Anne Ellen Geller, and Neal Lerner. 2016. *The Meaningful Writing Project*. Logan: Utah State University Press.

Erasmus, Desiderius. 2001. "From *Copia: Foundations of the Abundant Style*." In *The Rhetorical Tradition*, edited by Patricia Bizzell and Bruce Herzberg, 597–627. Boston: Bedford/St. Martin's.

Ericsson, K. Anders, Ralf Th. Krampe, and Clemens Tesch-Romer. 1993. "The Role of Deliberate Practice in the Acquisition of Expert Performance." *Psychological Review* 100 (3): 363–406.

Estrem, Heidi, and E. Shelley Reid. 2012. "What New Writing Teachers Talk about When They Talk about Teaching." *Pedagogy* 12 (3): 449–80.

Fahnestock, Jeanne. 2001. "Modern Arrangement." In *Encyclopedia of Rhetoric*, edited by Thomas O. Sloane, 44–50. Oxford: Oxford University Press.

Fahnestock, Jeanne. 2011. *Rhetorical Style: The Uses of Language in Persuasion*. Oxford: Oxford University Press.

Faigley, Lester, Roger D. Cherry, David A. Jolliffe, and Anna M. Skinner. 1985. *Assessing Writers' Knowledge and Processes of Composing*. Norwood, NJ: Ablex.

"Fast Facts: Back to School Statistics." 2018. National Center for Education Statistics. Accessed January 11, 2018. https://nces.ed.gov/fastfacts/display.asp?id=372.

Felski, Rita. 2015. *The Limits of Critique*. Chicago: University of Chicago Press.

Ferris, Dana R., and John S. Hedgcock. 2014. *Teaching L2 Composition*. 3rd ed. New York: Routledge.

Fink, L. Dee. 2003. *Creating Significant Learning Experiences*. San Francisco: Jossey-Bass.

Fitzgerald, Jill. 1987. "Research on Revision in Writing." *Review of Educational Research* 57 (4): 481–506.

Flavell, John H. 1979. "Metacognition and Cognitive Monitoring." *American Psychologist* 34 (10): 906–11.

Flower, Linda S., and John R. Hayes. 1980. "The Dynamics of Composing: Making Plans and Juggling Constraints." *Cognitive Processing and Writing*, edited by L. W. Gregg and E. R. Steinberg, 31–50. Hillsdale, NJ: Erlbaum.

Foer, Jonathan Safran. 2009. *Eating Animals*. New York: Back Bay.

"Framework for Success in Postsecondary Writing." 2011. Council of Writing Program Administrators, National Council of Teachers of English, and the National Writing Project. Accessed January 8, 2018. http://wpacouncil.org/files/framework-for-success-postsecondary-writing.pdf.

"Frequently Asked Questions about Student Ratings." N.d. Center for Research on Learning and Teaching. University of Michigan. Accessed August 3, 2018. http://www.crlt.umich.edu/tstrategies/studentratingfaq.

Friedman, Thomas. 2017. *Thank You for Being Late.* New York: Picador.

Fulkerson, Richard. 2005. "Composition at the Turn of the Twenty-First Century." *CCC* 56 (4): 654–87.

Galbraith, David, and Mark Torrance. 2004. "Revision in the Context of Different Drafting Strategies." In *Revision: Cognitive and Instructional Processes,* edited by Linda Allal, Lucile Chanquoy, and Pierre Largy, 63–85. Boston: Kluwer Academic.

Gallagher, Chris W. 2002. *Radical Departures.* Urbana, IL: National Council of Teachers of English.

Gallagher, Kelly. 2004. *Deeper Reading.* Portland, ME: Stenhouse.

Gallagher, Kelly. 2011. *Write like This: Teaching Real-World Writing through Modeling and Mentor Texts.* Portland, ME: Stenhouse.

Gay, Geneva. 2002. "Preparing for Culturally Responsive Teaching." *Journal of Teacher Education* 53 (2): 106–16.

Geary, James. 2011. *I Is an Other.* New York: Harper.

Gee, James Paul. 2012. *Social Linguistics and Literacies.* 4th ed. New York: Routledge.

George, Ann. 2014. "Critical Pedagogies: Dreaming of Democracy." In *A Guide to Composition Pedagogies,* 2nd ed., edited by Gary Tate, Amy Rupiper Taggart, Kurt Schick, and H. Brooke Hessler, 77–93. New York: Oxford University Press.

Gladwell, Malcolm. 2008. *Outliers: The Story of Success.* New York: Little, Brown and Company.

Glenn, Cheryl, and Melissa A. Goldthwaite. 2014. *The St. Martin's Guide to Teaching Writing.* 7th ed. Boston: Bedford/St. Martin's.

Goleman, Daniel. 1995. *Emotional Intelligence.* New York: Bantam.

González, Norma, Luis C. Moll, and Cathy Amanti. 2005. *Funds of Knowledge.* Mahwah, NJ: Lawrence Erlbaum.

Gopnik, Alison. 2017. *The Gardener and the Carpenter.* New York: Picador.

Graff, Gerald. 2003. *Clueless in Academe.* New Haven, CT: Yale University Press.

Graff, Gerald, and Cathy Birkenstein. 2018. *They Say/I Say.* 4th ed. New York: Norton.

Graham, Steve, and Delores Perin. 2007. *Writing Next.* Carnegie Corporation of New York. Accessed April 3, 2018. https://www.carnegie.org/media/filer_public/3c/f5/3cf58727-34f4-4140-a014-723a00ac56f7/ccny_report_2007_writing.pdf.

Graham, Steve, Karen R. Harris, and Amber B. Chambers. 2016. "Evidence-Based Practice and Writing Instruction." *Handbook of Writing Research,* edited by Charles A. MacArthur, Steve Graham, and Jill Fitzgerald, 211–26. New York: Guilford.

Green, Elizabeth. 2014. *Building a Better Teacher.* New York: Norton.

Gregory, Marshall. 2001. "Curriculum, Pedagogy, and Teacherly Ethos." *Pedagogy* 1 (1): 69–89.

Grigoryan, Anna. 2017. "Audiovisual Commentary as a Way to Reduce Transactional Distance and Increase Presence in Online Writing Instruction." *Journal of Response to Writing* 3 (1): 83–128.

Grossman, Pamela, Alan Schoenfeld, and Carol Lee. 2005. "Teaching Subject Matter." In *Preparing Teachers for a Changing World,* edited by Linda Darling-Hammond and John Bransford, 201–31. San Francisco: Jossey-Bass.

Hansen, Mogens Herman. 1999. *The Athenian Democracy in the Age of Demosthenes.* Translated by J. A. Crook. Norman: University of Oklahoma Press.

Harr, Catherine. 2006. "Definitions and Distinctions." *Revision: History, Theory, and Practice,* edited by Alice Horning and Anne Becker, 10–24. West Lafayette, IN: Parlor.

Harris, Joseph. 2006. *Rewriting: How to Do Things with Texts.* Logan: Utah State University Press.

Harris, Karen R., Tanya Santangelo, and Steve Graham. 2010. "Metacognition and Strategies Instruction in Writing." In *Metacognition, Strategy, Use, and Instruction,* edited by Harriet Salatas Waters and Wolfgang Schneider, 226–56. New York: Guilford.

Harris, Muriel. 1992. "Collaboration Is Not Collaboration Is Not Collaboration: Writing Center Tutorials vs. Peer-Response Groups." *College Composition and Communication* 43 (3): 369–83.

Harris, Muriel. 1995. "Talking in the Middle: Why Writers Need Writing Tutors." *College English* 57 (1): 27–42.

Harris, Muriel. 2010. "Assignments from Hell: The View from the Writing Center." In *What is "College-Level" Writing?* Vol. 2, edited by Patrick Sullivan, Howard Tinberg, and Sheridan Blau, 183–206. Urbana, IL: National Council of Teachers of English.

Haswell, Richard. 1983. "Minimal Marking." *College English* 45 (6): 600–604.

Haswell, Richard. 1991. *Gaining Ground in College Writing.* Dallas: Southern Methodist University Press.

Haswell, Richard H. 2008. "Teaching of Writing in Higher Education." In *Handbook of Research on Writing,* ed. Charles Bazerman, 331–46. New York: Lawrence Erlbaum.

Hattie, John. 2012. *Visible Learning for Teachers.* New York: Routledge.

Hattie, John, and Gregory Yates. 2014. *Visible Learning and the Science of How We Learn.* New York: Routledge.

Hayes, John. 1996. "A New Framework for Understanding Cognition and Affect in Writing." In *The Science of Writing,* edited by C. Michael Levy and Sarah Ransdell, 1–13. Mahwah, NJ: Lawrence Erbaum.

Hayes, John R. 2006. "New Directions in Writing Theory." In *Handbook of Writing Research,* edited by Charles A. MacArthur, Steve Graham, and Jill Fitzgerald, 28–40. New York: Guilford.

Hayes, John R. 2012. "Modeling and Remodeling Writing." *Written Communication* 29 (3): 369–88.

Heckman, James J., and Tim Kautz. 2014. "Achievement Tests and the Role of Character in American Life." In *The Myth of Achievement Tests,* edited by James J. Heckman, John Eric Humphries, and Tim Kautz, 3–54. Chicago: University of Chicago Press.

Herrera, Tim. "Hide Your Phone When You're Trying to Work. Seriously." 2018. *New York Times.* Accessed December 22, 2018. https://www.nytimes.com/2018/12/02/smarter-living/be-more-productive-hide-your-phone.html.

Hesse, Doug. 2014. "Occasions, Sources, and Strategies." In *First-Year Composition: From Theory to Practice,* edited by Deborah Coxwell-Teague and Ronald F. Lunsford, 49–70. Anderson, SC: Parlor.

Hesse, Doug. 2016. "Reflection and the Essay." In *Rhetoric of Reflection,* edited by Kathleen Blake Yancey, 288–99. Logan: Utah State University Press.

Hesse, Doug. 2017. "We Know What Works in Teaching Composition." *The Chronicle of Higher Education.* Accessed March 15, 2018. https://www.chronicle.com/article/We-Know-What-Works-in-Teaching/238792.

Hidi, Suzanne, and Pietro Boscolo. 2006. "Motivation and Writing." In *Handbook of Writing Research,* edited by Charles A. MacArthur, Steve Graham, and Jill Fitzgerald, 144–57. New York: Guilford.

Hillocks, George. 1986. *Research on Written Composition.* Urbana, IL: ERIC Clearinghouse and the National Conference on Research in English.

Hillocks, George. 1996. *Teaching Writing as Reflective Practice.* New York: Teachers College Press.

Holcomb, Chris, and M. Jimmie Killingsworth. 2010. *Performing Prose: The Study and Practice of Style in Composition.* Carbondale: Southern Illinois University Press.

Hoogeveen, Mariëtte, and Amos van Gelderen. 2013. "What Works in Writing with Peer Response? A Review of Intervention Studies with Children and Adolescents." *Educational Psychology Review* 25 (4): 473–502.

Horning, Alice. 2006. "Professional Writers and Revision." In *Revision: History, Theory, and Practice,* edited by Alice Horning and Anne Becker, 117–41. West Lafayette, IN: Parlor.

Horning, Alice. 2011. "Where to Put the Manicules: A Theory of Expert Reading." *Across the Disciplines* 8 (2): 1–18.

Horning, Alice, 2017. "Enhancing the *Framework for Success:* Adding Experiences in Critical Reading." In *The Framework for Success in Postsecondary Writing,* edited by Behm, Nicholas, Sherry Rankins-Robertson, and Duane Roen, 54–68. Anderson, SC: Parlor.

Howard, Rebecca Moore. 2005. "Contextualist Stylistics: Breaking Down the Binaries in Sentence-level Pedagogy." In *Refiguring Prose Style,* edited by T. R. Johnson and Tom Pace, 42–56. Logan: Utah State University Press.

Hunter, Madeline. September 1989. "Madeline Hunter in the English Classroom." *English Journal* 78 (5): 16–18.

Huot, Brian. 2002. *(Re)Articulating Writing Assessment for Teaching and Learning.* Logan: Utah State University Press.

Huston, Therese. 2009. *Teaching What You Don't Know.* Cambridge: Belknap.

Inoue, Asao B. 2014. "A Grade-Less Writing Course that Focuses on Labor and Assessing." In *First-Year Composition: From Theory to Practice,* edited by Deborah Coxwell-Teague and Ronald F. Lunsford, 71–110. Anderson, SC: Parlor.

Inoue, Asao B. 2015. *Antiracist Writing Assessment Ecologies.* Fort Collins, CO: WAC Clearinghouse.

Jabr, Ferris. 2013. "The Reading Brain in the Digital Age." *Scientific American.* Accessed May 7, 2018. https://www.scientificamerican.com/article/reading-paper-screens/.

Jackson, Brian. 2009. "Role-Playing in Comp—Fake It Till You Make It?" *Writing on the Edge* 20 (1): 99–107.

James, Karin H., R. Joanne Jao, and Virginia Beringer. 2017. "The Development of Multileveled Writing Systems in the Brain." In *Handbook of Writing Research,* 2nd ed., edited by Charles A. MacArthur, Steve Graham, and Jill Fitzgerald, 116–29. New York: Guilford.

James, William. 1984. *Writings: 1878–1899.* New York: Library of America.

Jamieson, Sandra. 2013. "Reading and Engaging Sources: What Students' Use of Sources Reveals about Advanced Reading Skills." *Across the Disciplines* 10 (4): 1–20.

Jarratt, Susan. 2007. "Rhetoric." In *Introduction to Scholarship in Modern Languages and Literatures,* 3rd ed., edited by David G. Nicholls, 73–102. New York: MLA.

Jaschik, Scott. 2008. "The Adjunctification of English." *Inside Higher Ed.* Accessed March 21, 2018. https://www.insidehighered.com/news/2008/12/11/adjunctification-english.

Johnson, Sara, Robert W. Blum, and Jay N. Giedd. 2009. "Adolescent Maturity and the Brain: The Promise and Pitfalls of Neuroscience Research in Adolescent Health Policy," *Journal of Adolescent Health* 45 (3): 216–21.

Jolliffe, David A. 2017. "'Learning to Read as Continuing Education' Revisited." In *Deep Reading: Teaching Reading in the Writing Classroom,* edited by Patrick Sullivan, Howard Tinberg, and Sheridan Blau, 3–22. Urbana, IL: National Council of Teachers of English.

Kahn, Seth. 2017. "Bad Idea about Writing: Anybody Can Teach It." *Inside Higher Ed.* Accessed June 13, 2018. https://www.insidehighered.com/views/2017/08/07/colleges-should-hire-writing-instructors-right-experience-and-expertise-and-give.

Kahneman, Daniel. 2012. *Thinking, Fast and Slow.* New York: Penguin.

Kates, Susan. 2001. *Activist Rhetorics and American Higher Education.* Carbondale: Southern Illinois University Press.

Keim, Brandon. 2014. "Why the Smart Reading Device of the Future May Be . . . Paper." *Wired.* Accessed May 7, 2018. https://www.wired.com/2014/05/reading-on-screen-versus-paper/.

Keller, Daniel. 2014. *Chasing Literacy: Reading and Writing in an Age of Acceleration.* Logan: Utah State University Press.

Kellogg, Ronald T. 2008. "Training Writing Skills: A Cognitive Developmental Perspective." *Journal of Writing Research* 1 (1): 1–26.

Kellogg, Ronald T., and Alison P. Whiteford. 2009. "Training Advanced Writing Skills: The Case for Deliberate Practice." *Educational Psychologist* 44 (4): 250–66.

Kerouac, Jack. "Essentials of Spontaneous Prose." 1995. In *The Portable Beat Reader,* edited by Ann Charters, 57–58. New York: Penguin.

Killgallon, Don. 1998. *Sentence Composing for College.* Portsmouth, NH: Heinemann.

Kinneavy, James L. 1971. *A Theory of Discourse.* New York: Norton.

Klein, Perry D., and Amy Meichi Yu. 2013. "Best Practices in Writing to Learn." In *Best Practices in Writing Instruction,* 2nd ed., edited by Steve Graham, Charles A. MacArthur, and Jill Fitzgerald, 166–89. New York: Guilford.

Knoblauch, Cy, and Lil Brannon. 2006. "Introduction: The Emperor (Still) Has No Clothes—REvisiting the Myth of Improvement." In *Key Works on Teacher Response,* edited by Richard Straub, 1–16. Portsmouth, NH: Boynton/Cook.

Kolln, Martha, and Robert Funk. 2009. *Understanding English Grammar.* 8th ed. New York: Longman.

Kolln, Martha, and Loretta Gray. 2010. *Rhetorical Grammar.* 6th ed. Boston: Longman.

Kost-Smith, Lauren E., et al. 2010. "Gender Differences in Physics I: The Impact of Self-Affirmation Intervention." *AIP Proceedings* 197 (2010). Accessed March 10, 2015. https://dx.doi.org/10.1063/1.3515197.

Kuh, George. 2008. "High-Impact Educational Practices: A Brief Overview." Association of American Colleges and Universities. Accessed April 18, 2018. https://www.aacu.org/leap/hips.

Kwangsu, Cho, and Charles MacArthur. 2011. "Learning by Reviewing." *Journal of Educational Psychology* 103 (1): 73–84.

Lamott, Anne. 1995. *Bird by Bird.* New York: Anchor.

Lanham, Richard A. 1991. *A Handlist of Rhetorical Terms.* 2nd ed. Berkeley: University of California Press.

Lanham, Richard A. 2007. *Style: An Anti-Textbook.* 2nd ed. Philadelphia: Paul Dry Books.

Lang, James M. 2016. *Small Teaching.* San Francisco: Jossey-Bass.

Langer, Ellen J. 1989. *Mindfulness.* Reading, MA: Addison-Wesley.

Lauer, Janice. 2004. *Invention in Rhetoric and Composition.* West Lafayette, IN: Parlor Press.

Lemov, Doug. 2010. *Teach like a Champion.* San Francisco: Jossey-Bass.

Light, Richard. 2001. *Making the Most of College.* Cambridge, MA: Harvard University Press.

Lindemann, Erika. 2001. *A Rhetoric for Writing Teachers.* 4th ed. New York: Oxford University Press.

Lunsford, Andrea. 2015. "Writing Addresses, Invokes, and/or Creates Audiences." In *Naming What We Know,* edited by Linda Adler-Kassner and Elizabeth Wardle, 20–21. Logan: Utah State University Press.

Lunsford, Andrea A., and Lisa Ede. 2012. *Writing Together: Collaboration in Theory and Practice.* Boston: Bedford/St. Martin's.

Lunsford, Andrea A., and Karen J. Lunsford. 2008. "Mistakes Are a Fact of Life: A National Comparative Study." *CCC* 59 (4): 781–806.

MacArthur, Charles A. 2013. "Best Practices in Teaching Evaluation and Revision." In *Best Practices in Writing Instruction,* 2nd ed., edited by Steve Graham, Charles A. MacArthur, and Jill Fitzgerald, 215–37. New York: Guilford.

MacArthur, Charles A., and Steve Graham. 2016. "Writing Research from a Cognitive Perspective." In *Handbook on Writing Research*, 2nd ed., edited by Charles A. MacArthur, Steve Graham, and Jill Fitzgerald, 24–40. New York: Guilford.

MacDonald, Susan Peck. 2007. "The Erasure of Language." *CCC* 58 (4): 585–625.

Mackiewicz, Jo, and Isabelle Kramer Thompson. 2015. *Talk about Writing: The Tutoring Strategies of Experienced Writing Center Tutors.* New York: Routledge.

"The Madeline Hunter Model of Mastery Learning." 2018. Indiana Department of Education. Accessed March 7, 2018. https://www.doe.in.gov/sites/default/files/turnaround-principles/8-steps-effective-lesson-plan-design-madeline-hunter.pdf.

Manjoo, Farhad. 2018. "Welcome to the Post-Text Future." *New York Times.* Accessed March 15, 2018. https://www.nytimes.com/interactive/2018/02/09/technology/the-rise-of-a-visual-internet.html.

Marchetti, Allison, and Rebekah O'Dell. 2015. *Writing with Mentors.* Portsmouth, NH: Heinemann.

Matsuda, Paul Kei, Michelle Cox, Jay Jordan, and Christina Ortmeier-Hooper, eds. 2010. *Second-Language Writing in the Composition Classroom: A Critical Sourcebook.* Boston: Bedford/St. Martin's.

Matsuda, Paul Kei, and Matthew J. Hammill. 2014. "Second Language Writing Pedagogy." In *A Guide to Composition Pedagogies*, 2nd ed., edited by Gary Tate, Amy Rupiper Taggart, Kurt Schick, and H. Brooke Hessler, 266–82. New York: Oxford University Press.

McCormick, Christine B., Carey Dimmitt, and Florence R. Sullivan. 2013. "Metacognition, Learning, and Instruction." In *Handbook of Psychology*, 2nd ed., edited by Irving B. Weiner, 69–97. Hoboken, NJ: John Wiley.

McCutchen, Deborah, Paul Teske, and Catherine Bankston. 2008. "Writing and Cognition: Implications of the Cognitive Architecture for Learning to Write and Writing to Learn." In *Handbook of Research on Writing*, edited by Charles Bazerman, 451–70. New York: Lawrence Erlbaum.

McGonigal, Jane. 2011. *Reality Is Broken: Why Games Make Us Better and How They Can Change the World.* New York: Penguin.

McGuire, Saundra Yancy, with Stephanie McGuire. 2015. *Teach Students How to Learn.* Sterling, VA: Stylus.

Melzer, Dan. 2014. *Assignments across the Curriculum.* Logan: Utah State University Press.

Milic, Louis T. 1971. "Rhetorical Choice and Stylistic Option: The Conscious and Unconscious Poles." In *Literary Style: A Symposium*, edited by Seymour Chatman and Samuel R. Levin, 77–88. London: Oxford University Press.

Miller, Carolyn. 1984. "Genre as Social Action." *Quarterly Journal of Speech* 70 (2): 151–67.

Miller, Susan, ed. 2009. *The Norton Book of Composition Studies.* New York: Norton.

Miller, Thomas P. 2011. *The Evolution of College English.* Pittsburgh, PA: University of Pittsburgh Press.

Moe, Peter Wayne. 2018. "Something about the Written Delivery of the Line." *Rhetoric Society Quarterly* 48 (1): 71–87.

Moore, Jessie L. 2017. "Five Essential Principles about Writing Transfer." In *Understanding Writing Transfer*, edited by Jessie L. Moore and Randall Bass, 1–12. Sterling, VA: Stylus.

Moore, Jessie L., and Randall Bass, eds. 2017. *Understanding Writing Transfer.* Sterling, VA: Stylus.

Morenberg, Max. 2010. *Doing Grammar.* 4th ed. New York: Oxford University Press.

Morenberg, Max, and Jeff Sommers. 1999. *The Writer's Options.* 6th ed. New York: Longman.

"Multitasking: Switching Costs." American Psychological Association. Accessed Nov 2014. https://www.apa.org/research/action/multitask.aspx.

Murphy, James J., ed. 2001. "The Key Role of Habit in Roman Writing Instruction." In *A Short History of Writing Instruction.* 2nd ed., 35–78. Mahwah, NJ: Lawrence Erlbaum.

Murray, Donald. 2001. *The Craft of Revision.* 4th ed. Fort Worth, TX: Harcourt.

Murray, Donald M. 2003. "Teach Writing as a Process Not Product." In *Cross-Talk in Comp Theory*, 2nd ed., edited by Victor Villanueva, 3–6. Urbana, IL: National Council of Teachers of English.

National Census of Writing. 2013. Accessed March 21, 2018. https://writingcensus.swarthmore.edu/.

National Research Council. *How People Learn*. 2002. Expanded ed. Washington, DC: National Academy Press.

Nelson, Nancy. 2007. "The Reading-Writing Nexus in Discourse Research." In *Handbook of Research on Writing*, edited by Charles Bazerman, 435–50. New York: Routledge.

Nelson, Thomas O., Arie W. Kruglanski, and John T. Jost. 1998. "Knowing Thyself and Others: Progress in Metacognitive Social Psychology." In *Metacognition: Cognitive and Social Dimensions*, edited by Vincent Y. Yzerbyt, Guy Lories, and Benoit Dardenne, 69–89. London: Sage.

Newkirk, Thomas. 1984. "Direction and Misdirection in Peer Response." *College Composition and Communication* 35 (3): 301–11.

Nhat Hanh, Thich. 1973. *The Heart of the Buddha's Teaching*. New York: Broadway Books.

Nilson, Linda B. 2013. *Creating Self-Regulated Learners*. Sterling, VA: Stylus.

North, Stephen M. 1987. *The Making of Knowledge in Composition*. Portsmouth, NH: Boynton/Cook.

Nowacek, Rebecca S. 2011. *Agents of Integration: Understanding Transfer as a Rhetorical Act*. Carbondale: Southern Illinois University Press.

Nowacek, Rebecca S., and Bradley Hughes. 2015. "Threshold Concepts in the Writing Center." *Naming What We Know*, edited by Linda Adler-Kassner and Elizabeth Wardle, 171–85. Logan: Utah State University Press.

Nystrand, Martin, and Deborah Brandt. 1989. "Response to Writing as a Context for Learning to Write." In *Writing and Response: Theory, Practice, and Research*, edited by Chris M. Anson, 209–30. Urbana, IL: National Council of Teachers of English.

O'Malley, Sharon. 2017. "There's No Easy Answer." *Inside Higher Ed*. Accessed May 7, 2018. https://www.insidehighered.com/digital-learning/article/2017/08/16/which-better-reading-print-or-screen.

Pajares, Frank, and Gio Valiante. 2006. "Self-Efficacy Beliefs and Motivation in Writing Development." In *Handbook of Writing Research*, edited by Charles A. MacArthur, Steven Graham, and Jill Fitzgerald, 158–70. New York: Guilford.

Paton, Fiona. 2002. "Approaches to Productive Peer Review." In *Strategies for Teaching First-Year Composition*, edited by Duane Roen, Veronica Pantoja, Lauren Yena, Susan K. Miller, and Eric Waggoner, 290–301. Urbana, IL: National Council of Teachers of English.

Pennebaker, J. W. 1997. *Writing to Heal: A Guided Journal for Recovering from Trauma and Emotional Upheaval*. Oakland, CA: New Harbinger.

Perl, Sondra. 1979. "The Composing Process of Unskilled College Writers." *Research in the Teaching of English* 13 (4): 317–36.

Perrin, Andrew. 2016. "Book Reading 2016." The Pew Research Center. Accessed May 1, 2018. http://www.pewinternet.org/2016/09/01/book-reading-2016/.

Phelps, Louise Wetherbee. 1989. "Images of Student Writing: The Deep Structure of Teacher Response." In *Writing and Response: Theory, Practice, and Research*, edited by Chris M. Anson, 37–67. Urbana, IL: National Council of Teachers of English.

Phelps, Louise Weatherbee. 1996. "Composition Studies." In *Encyclopedia of Rhetoric and Composition*, edited by Theresa Enos, 123–34. New York: Garland.

Pink, Daniel H. 2009. *Drive*. New York: Riverhead.

Pinker, Steven. 1994. *The Language Instinct*. New York: Harper Perennial.

Pinker, Steven. 2014. *The Sense of Style*. New York: Viking.

Portanova, Patricia, Michael Rifenburg, and Duane Roen, eds. 2017. *Contemporary Perspectives on Cognition and Writing*. Fort Collins, CO: WAC Clearinghouse.

Proust, Joelle. 2013. *The Philosophy of Metacognition*. New York: Oxford.

Proust, Joelle, and Martin Fortier. 2018. *Metacognitive Diversity: An Interdisciplinary Approach*. Oxford: Oxford University Press.

Pulfrey, Caroline, Celine Buchs, and Fabrizio Butera. 2011. "Why Grades Engender Performance-Avoidance Goals: The Mediating Role of Autonomous Motivation." *Journal of Educational Psychology* 103 (3): 683–700.

Quintilian. 1987. *On the Teaching of Speaking and Writing*. Translated and edited by James J. Murphy. Carbondale: Southern Illinois University Press.

Ratcliffe, Krista. 2005. *Rhetorical Listening: Identification, Gender, Whiteness*. Carbondale: Southern Illinois University Press.

Ravizza, Sarah M., Mitchell Uitvlugt, and Kimberly M. Fenn. 2017. "Logged In and Zoned Out: How Laptop Internet Use Relates to Classroom Learning." *Psychological Science* 28 (2): 171–80.

Ray, Brian. 2015. *Style: An Introduction to History, Theory, Research, and Pedagogy*. Anderson, SC: Parlor.

Ray, Katie Wood. 1999. *Wondrous Words*. Urbana, IL: National Council of Teachers of English.

"Reading Performance." 2017. National Center for Education Statistics. Accessed May 1, 2018. https://nces.ed.gov/programs/coe/indicator_cnb.asp.

Reid, E. Shelley. 2004. "Uncoverage in Composition Pedagogy." *Composition Studies* 32 (1): 15–34.

Reid, E. Shelley. 2008. "Shelley's (Quick) Guides for Writing Teachers: Full-Circle Peer Review." Accessed May 21, 2018. http://mason.gmu.edu/~ereid1/teachers/tchguide peerrev.htm.

Reid, E. Shelley. 2009. "Teaching Writing Teachers Writing: Difficulty, Exploration, and Critical Reflection." *CCC* 61 (2): W197–221.

Reid, E. Shelley. 2017. "On Learning to Teach: Letter to a New TA." *WPA: Writing Program Administration* 40 (2): 129–45.

Reid, E. Shelley, Heidi Estrem, and Marcia Belcheir. 2012. "The Effects of Writing Pedagogy Education on Graduate Teaching Assistants' Approaches to Teaching Composition." *WPA: Writing Program Administration* 36 (1): 32–73.

Reiff, Mary Jo, and Anis Bawarshi. 2011. "Tracing Discursive Resources: How Students Use Prior Genre Knowledge to Negotiate New Writing Contexts in First-Year Composition." *Written Communication* 28 (3): 312–37.

Richardson, Robert D. 2009. *First We Read, Then We Write*. Iowa City: University of Iowa Press.

Rickert, Thomas. 2013. *Ambient Rhetoric*. Pittsburgh, PA: University of Pittsburgh Press.

Rios-Aguilar, Cecilia, and Judy Marquez Kiyama, eds. 2018. *Funds of Knowledge in Higher Education*. New York: Routledge.

Ritter, Kelly, and Paul Kei Matsuda, eds. 2012. *Exploring Composition Studies: Sites, Issues, and Perspectives*. Logan: Utah State University Press.

Robinson, Andrew. 2009. *Writing and Script: A Very Short Introduction*. Oxford: Oxford University Press.

Roen, Duane, Maureen Daly Goggin, and Jennifer Clary-Lemon. 2008. "Teaching of Writing and Writing Teachers through the Ages." In *Handbook of Research on Writing*, edited by Charles Bazerman, 347–64. New York: Lawrence Erlbaum.

Rogers, Carl R. 1961. *On Becoming a Person*. Boston: Houghton Mifflin.

Roozen, Kevin. 2015. "Texts Get Their Meaning from Other Texts." In *Naming What We Know*, edited by Linda Adler-Kassner and Elizabeth Wardle, 44–47. Logan: Utah State University Press.

Rose, Shirley. 2015. "All Writers Have More to Learn." *Naming What We Know*, edited by Linda Adler-Kassner and Elizabeth Wardle, 59–61. Logan: Utah State University Press.

Rowe, Deborah Wells. 2008. "The Development of Writing Abilities in Childhood." In *Handbook of Research on Writing*, edited by Charles Bazerman, 401–19. New York: Lawrence Erlbaum.

Rule, Hannah J. 2017. "Sensing the Sentence: An Embodied Simulation Approach to Rhetorical Grammar." *Composition Studies* 45 (1): 19–38.

Russ, Rosemary S., Bruce L. Sherin, and Miriam Gamoran Sherin. 2016. "What Constitutes Teacher Learning?" In *Handbook of Research on Teaching*, edited by Drew H. Gitomer and Courtney A. Bell, 391–438. Washington, DC: American Educational Research Association.

Russell, David R. 2002. *Writing in the Academic Disciplines*. 2nd ed. Carbondale: Southern Illinois University Press.

Santangelo, Tanya, Karen R. Harris, and Steve Graham. 2016. "Self-Regulation and Writing." In *Handbook of Writing Research*, 2nd ed., edited by Charles A. Macarthur, Steve Graham, and Jill Fitzgerald, 174–93. New York: Guilford.

Schaub, Michael. 2016. "92% of College Students Prefer Print Books to e-Books, Study Finds." *Los Angeles Times*. Accessed May 7, 2018. https://www.latimes.com/books/jacketcopy/la-et-jc-92-percent-college-students-prefer-paper-over-pixels-20160208-story.html.

Schiappa, Edward. 1999. *The Beginnings of Rhetorical Theory in Classical Greece*. New Haven, CT: Yale University Press.

Schilb, John. 2007. *Rhetorical Refusals*. Carbondale: Southern Illinois University Press.

Schuster, Edgar H. 2003. *Breaking the Rules*. Portsmouth, NH: Heinemann.

Schwartz, N. H., B. M. Scott, and D. Holzberger. 2013. "Metacognition: A Closed-Loop Model of Biased Competition–Evidence from Neuroscience, Cognition, and Instructional Research." In *International Handbook of Metacognition and Learning Technologies*, edited by Roger Azevedo and Vincent Aleven, 79–94. New York: Springer.

Scott, Tony. 2015. "Writing Enacts and Creates Identities and Ideologies." In *Naming What We Know*, edited by Linda Adler-Kassner and Elizabeth Wardle, 48–50. Logan: Utah State University Press.

Shaughnessy, Mina P. 1977. *Errors and Expectations*. New York: Oxford University Press.

Shulman, Lee. 1987. "Knowledge and Teaching: Foundations of the New Reform." *Harvard Educational Review* 57 (1): 1–22.

Shvidko, Elena. 2015. "Beyond 'Giver-Receiver' Relationships: Facilitating an Interactive Revision Process." *Journal of Response to Writing* 1 (2): 55–74.

Silver, Naomi. 2016. "Reflection in Digital Spaces: Publication, Conversation, Collaboration." In *Rhetoric of Reflection*, edited by Kathleen Blake Yancey, 166–200. Logan: Utah State University Press.

Smitherman, Geneva. 2015. "'Students' Right to Their Own Language': A Retrospective." *Students' Right to Their Own Language: A Critical Sourcebook*, edited by Staci Perryman-Clark, David E. Kirkland, and Austin Jackson, 140–49. Boston: Bedford/St. Martin's.

Sommers, Jeff. 2011. "Reflection Revisited: The Class Collage." *Journal of Basic Writing* 30 (1): 99–129.

Sommers, Jeff. 2012. "Response Rethought . . . Again: Exploring Recorded Comments and the Teacher-Student Bond." *The Journal of Writing Assessment* 5 (1). Accessed May 15, 2018. http://journalofwritingassessment.org/article.php?article=59.

Sommers, Jeff. 2016. "Problematizing Reflection." In *A Rhetoric of Reflection*, edited by Kathleen Blake Yancey, 271–87. Logan: Utah State University Press.

Sommers, Nancy. 1980. "Revision Strategies of Student Writers and Experienced Adult Writers." *CCC* 31 (4): 378–88.

Sommers, Nancy. 2013. *Responding to Student Writers*. Boston: Bedford/St. Martin's.

Sommers, Nancy, and Laura Saltz. 2004. "The Novice as Expert: Writing the Freshman Year." *CCC* 56 (1): 124–49.

Sontag, Susan. 2006. "On Self." *New York Times Magazine*. Accessed July 5, 2018. https://www.nytimes.com/2006/09/10/magazine/10sontag.html.

Stangor, Charles. 2017. "Group Processes." *Oxford Research Encyclopedia of Psychology*, edited by Oliver Braddick. Accessed April 18, 2018. http://oxfordre.com/psychology/view/10.1093/acrefore/9780190236557.001.0001/acrefore-9780190236557-e-255.

Strong, William. 1994. *Sentence Combining*. 3rd ed. New York: McGraw-Hill.

"Students' Right to Their Own Language." *Students' Right to Their Own Language: A Critical Sourcebook*, edited by Staci Perryman-Clark, David E. Kirkland, and Austin Jackson, 19–57. Boston: Bedford/St. Martin's.

Subrahmanyam, Kaveri, et al. 2013. "Learning from Paper, Learning from Screens." *International Journal of Cyberbehavior, Psychology, and Learning* 3 (4): 1–27.

Suskie, Linda. 2009. *Assessing Student Learning: A Common Sense Guide*. San Francisco: Jossey-Bass.

Taczak, Kara, and Liane Robertson. 2016. "Reiterative Reflection in the Twenty-First Century Writing Classroom." In *A Rhetoric of Reflection*, edited by Kathleen Blake Yancey, 42–63. Logan: Utah State University Press.

Taggart, Amy Rupiper, and Margaret Lowry. 2011. "Cohorts, Grading, and Ethos: Listening to TAs Enhances Teacher Preparation." *WPA: Writing Program Administration* 34 (2): 89–114.

Tarricone, Pina. 2011. *The Taxonomy of Metacognition*. New York: Psychology.

Tate, Gary, Amy Rupiper Taggart, Kurt Schick, and H. Brooke Hessler, eds. 2014. *A Guide to Composition Pedagogies*. 2nd ed. New York: Oxford University Press.

Tate, Marcia L. 2010. *Worksheets Don't Grow Dendrites: 20 Instructional Strategies that Engage the Brain*. 2nd ed. Thousand Oaks, CA: Corwin.

Thelin, John R. 2004. *A History of American Higher Education*. Baltimore: Johns Hopkins University Press.

Thorton, Bill, Maija Robbins, Alyson Faires, and Eric Rollins. 2014. "The Mere Presence of a Cell Phone May Be Distracting: Implications for Attention and Task Performance." *Social Psychology* 45 (6): 479–88.

Tinberg, Howard. 2015. "Metacognition Is Not Cognition." In *Naming What We Know: Threshold Concepts of Writing Studies*, edited by Linda Adler-Kassner and Elizabeth Wardle, 75–76. Logan: Utah State University Press.

Tolchinsky, Liliana. 2016. "From Text to Language and Back." In *Handbook of Writing Instruction*, 2nd ed., edited by Charles A. MacArthur, Steve Graham, and Jill Fitzgerald, 144–59. New York: Guilford.

Torrence, Mark. 2016. "Understanding Planning in Text Production." In *Handbook on Writing Research*, 2nd ed., edited by Charles A. MacArthur, Steve Graham, and Jill Fitzgerald, 72–87. New York: Guilford.

Toth, Christie, Patrick Sullivan, and Carolyn Calhoon-Dillahunt. 2019. "Two-Year College Teacher-Scholar-Activism: Reconstructing the Disciplinary Matrix of Writing Studies." *College Composition and Communication* 71 (1): 86–116.

Tough, Paul. 2012. *How Children Succeed*. Boston: Mariner.

Troia, Gary A. 2013. "Writing Instruction within a Response-to-Intervention Framework." In *Best Practices in Writing Instruction*, 2nd ed., edited by Steve Graham, Charles A. MacArthur, and Jill Fitzgerald, 403–27. New York: Guilford.

Tufte, Virginia. 2006. *Artful Sentences: Syntax as Style*. Cheshire, CN: Graphics.

Turkle, Sherry. 2015. *Reclaiming Conversation: The Power of Talk in a Digital Age*. New York: Penguin.

"TYCA Guidelines for Preparing Teachers of English in the Two-Year College." 2016. Task Force of the Two-Year College English Association of the National Council of Teachers of English. https://secure.ncte.org/library/NCTEFiles/Groups/TYCA/GuidelinesPrep2YCEngFac_REVISED.pdf.

Venkatraman, Vijaysree. 2010. "Conventions of Scientific Authorship." *Science*. Accessed April 18, 2018. https://www.sciencemag.org/careers/2010/04/conventions-scientific-authorship.

Villanueva, Victor, and Kristin L. Arola, eds. 2011. *Cross-Talk in Comp Theory*. Urbana, IL: National Council of Teachers of English.

Vygotsky, L. S. 1978. *Mind in Society*, edited by Michael Cole, Vera John-Steiner, Sylvia Scribner, and Ellen Souberman. Cambridge, MA: Harvard University Press.

Walker, Jeffrey. 2011. *The Genuine Teachers of This Art: Rhetorical Education in Antiquity*. Columbia, SC: University of South Carolina Press.

Wall, Susan V., and Glynda A. Hull. 1989. "The Semantics of Error." In *Writing and Response: Theory, Practice, and Research*, edited by Chris M. Anson, 261–92. Urbana, IL: National Council of Teachers of English.

Walvoord, Barbara E., and Virginia Johnson Anderson. 2010. *Effective Grading*. 2nd ed. San Francisco: Jossey-Bass.

Wanzer-Serrano, Darrel. 2018. "Decolonial Rhetoric and a Future Yet-to-Become." *Advances in the History of Rhetoric* 21 (3): 326–30.

Wardle, Elizabeth. 2009. "'Mutt Genres' and the Goal of FYC: Can We Help Students Write the Genres of the University?" *College Composition and Communication* 60 (4): 765–89.

Wardle, Elizabeth, and Doug Downs. 2017. *Writing about Writing*. 3rd ed. Boston: Bedford/St. Martin's.

Weaver, Constance, ed. 1998. *Lessons to Share: On Teaching Grammar in Context*. Portsmouth, NH: Boynton/Cook.

Wenger, Etienne. 2000. *Communities of Practice*. Cambridge: Cambridge University Press.

White, Edward M., and Cassie A. Wright. 2016. *Assigning, Responding, Evaluating*. 5th ed. Boston: Bedford/St. Martin's.

Wiggins, Grant, and Jay McTighe. 2005. *Understanding by Design*. Expanded 2nd ed. Alexandria, VA: Association for Supervision and Curriculum Development.

Williams, Joseph. 1981. "The Phenomenology of Error." *College Composition and Communication* 32 (2): 152–68.

Williams, Joseph. 2010. "Defining Complexity." In *Style in Rhetoric and Composition: A Critical Sourcebook*, edited by Paul Butler, 186–201. Boston: Bedford/St. Martin's.

Willingham, Daniel T. 2009. *Why Don't Students like School?* San Francisco: Jossey-Bass.

Wilmer, Henry H., Lauren E. Sherman, and Jason M. Chein. 2017. "Smartphones and Cognition: A Review of Research Exploring the Links between Mobile Technology Habits and Cognitive Functioning." *Frontiers in Psychology* 8. Accessed May 7, 2018. https://www.ncbi.nlm.nih.gov/pmc/articles/PMC5403814/.

Wilson, Karen, and James H. Korn. 2007. "Attention during Lectures: Beyond Ten Minutes." *Teaching of Psychology* 34 (2): 85–89.

Wilson, Timothy D. 2011. *Redirect*. New York: Back Bay.

"WPA Outcomes Statement for First-Year Composition." 2014. Version 3.0. Council of Writing Program Administrators. Accessed March 22, 2018. http://wpacouncil.org/positions/outcomes.html.

Wolf, Maryanne. 2016. *Tales of Literacy for the 21st Century*. Oxford: Oxford University Press.

Wolfe, Joanna. 2010. *Team Writing: A Guide to Working in Groups*. Boston: Bedford/St. Martin's.

Yagoda, Ben. 2004. *The Sound on the Page*. New York: HarperCollins.

Yancey, Kathleen Blake. 1998. *Reflection in the Writing Classroom*. Logan: Utah State University Press.

Yancey, Kathleen Blake. 2016. "Contextualizing Reflection." In *A Rhetoric of Reflection*, edited by Kathleen Blake Yancey, 3–20. Logan: Utah State University Press.

Yancey, Kathleen Blake. 2017. "Mapping the Prior: A Beginning Typology and Its Impact on Writing." In *Contemporary Perspectives on Cognition and Writing*, edited by Patricia Portanova, Michael Rifenburg, and Duane Roen, 313–30. Boulder: University Press of Colorado.

Yancey, Kathleen Blake, Liane Robertson, and Kara Taczak. 2014. *Writing across Contexts*. Logan: Utah State University Press.

Young, Vershawn Ashanti. 2009. "'Nah, We Straight': An Argument against Code Switching." *Jac* 29 (1/2): 49–76.

Yule, George. 1996. *The Study of Language.* 2nd ed. Cambridge: Cambridge University Press.

Zhang, Fuhui, Christian Schunn, and Alok Baikadi. 2017. "Charting the Routes to Revision: An Interplay of Writing Goals, Peer Comments, and Self-Reflections from Peer Review." *Instructional Science: An International Journal of the Learning Sciences* 45 (5): 679–707.

Zimmerman, Barry J. 2009. "Self-Regulation." In *Handbook of Metacognition in Education,* edited by Douglas J. Hacker, John Dunlosky, and Arthur C. Graesser, 299–315. New York: Routledge.

Zimmerman, Barry J., and Adam R. Myolan. 2009. "Self-Regulation." In *Handbook of Metacognition in Education,* edited by Douglas J. Hacker, John Dunlosky, and Arthur C. Graesser, 154–172. New York: Routledge.

ABOUT THE AUTHOR

Like you, **Brian Jackson** teaches first-year writing. It's his favorite class to teach. He received a PhD in Rhetoric, Composition, and the Teaching of English from the University of Arizona in 2007. Since then, he's been an English professor at Brigham Young University, where he worked in the University Writing program for ten years, training graduate students to teach writing, which was the best thing ever. He teaches rhetoric and writing courses to undergrads and grad students. He and his wife, Amy, have four kids. They live in Provo, Utah, near the Wasatch Mountains.

INDEX